Citizen Groups in Local Politics

Citizen Groups in Local Politics
A Bibliographic Review

John D. Hutcheson, Jr., and Jann Shevin

Clio Books
Santa Barbara, California   •   Oxford, England

Z7165
U5
H87

© 1976 by John D. Hutcheson, Jr., and Jann Shevin

Library of Congress Cataloging in Publication Data

Hutcheson, John D
  Citizen groups in local politics.

  Includes index.
    1. Citizens associations—United States—Bibliography.
  2. Political participation—United States—Bibliography.
  3. Local government—United States—Bibliography.
  I. Shevin, Jann, joint author.   II. Title.
  Z7165.U5H87   [JS303.5]   016.3224'3'06273   76-23441
  ISBN 0-87436-231-8

American Bibliographical Center—Clio Press, Inc.
2040 Alameda Padre Serra
Santa Barbara, California

European Bibliographical Center—Clio Press
Woodside House, Hinksey Hill
Oxford OX1 5BE, England

Contents

Acknowledgments

Some of the citations in this bibliography were compiled during a 1969–1970 study of citizen participation sponsored by the Atlanta Urban Observatory. We are indebted to a number of individuals involved in that study. Frank X. Steggert, Fred R. Crawford, Jenann Olsen, Mildred Shaw, Merle Lefkoff, and John Haydock participated in the urban observatory project and helped with the initial collection of pertinent literature. William W. Nash, Donald S. Bradley, and Edward B. Lewis reviewed a draft of the manuscript and offered helpful comments and suggestions. Barbara Larson, Brenda Hicks, Jane Moorer, and Jackie Williams bore most of the responsibility for typing the manuscript. Frank P. Young reviewed the final manuscript and helped in the preparation of the author index. We appreciate the efforts of all these individuals and acknowledge the support of the School of Urban Life, Georgia State University, as well as the efforts of the staff of the Georgia State University library. Without this help and support, this review would not have been possible. The authors, however, are responsible for any omissions or errors in interpretation.

Introduction

Even though citizen participation is a subject that has long been prominent in the work of political and social scientists, interest in the topic, both popular and academic, seemed to accelerate in the mid-1960s and early 1970s. The terms "citizen participation," "consumer involvement," "community control," "participatory democracy," and many similar phrases have been widely used but seldom defined. This bibliographic study focuses upon a particular type of citizen participation—the attempts of groups of citizens to influence local politics and decision making. Thus, the subject of this work may be defined as the interaction of citizen groups with governmental decision makers in political or administrative processes and the factors which influence this interaction.

Reflecting the breadth of the topic, the literature relevant to citizen group participation in governmental decision making takes many different forms—numerous professional journals and periodicals, government documents, books, monographs, and professional papers. This book compiles references to the most important literature on this subject and organizes the material in a manner which will permit, for example, a researcher interested in citizen participation in health care delivery systems to identify literature on that topic. Similarly, citizen group leaders, attempting to learn from the experiences of other citizen groups, can find references to materials describing and analyzing the activities and strategies of groups in situations comparable to their own. Public officials seeking methods of involving citizen groups in public decision making can find references to materials explaining useful models. Brief introductions to each of the chapters outline the material included and attempt to identify directions for future research. An introductory essay provides an overview of the literature.

References to a major portion of the material dealing with citizen group participation in governmental decision making can be found in the following chapters. This interaction, and the factors influencing it, comprises a broad topic; several guidelines were therefore necessary to limit the scope of the bibliography. For the most part, works written before 1950 have been excluded; the vast majority of the materials included were produced in the fifteen years preceding 1975. Only works on local politics and decision making in communities in the United States are included. Materials available only in languages other than English are excluded.

Most of the research on this subject involved urban communities. Although there are several mutually influential interactions in those communities, the emphasis here is on works dealing directly with citizen group participation and its relationships to other forms of participation, and to political and power structures. Therefore, many of the major works on political participation (especially individual participation), on local politics and government, and on community power structures are absent from this bibliography. Further, an effort has been made to limit the scope of the bibliography to materials concerning community or community-issue-based organizations. Literature focusing on national or regional organizations or on occupational or professional interest groups is excluded.

In sum, this bibliography focuses on the organization, activities, strategies, and impacts of citizen groups attempting to influence local governmental decision-making processes in the United States. In some cases, the citizen groups may be attempting to influence the administration of federally sponsored programs at the local level. Some citizen groups described here function within the structures of federal or local programs. In other instances, voluntary or self-initiated groups are the subjects of the cited works.

More than 90 percent of the entries are annotated. When the materials cited are largely narrative or impressionistic, the authors' major arguments are briefly summarized. When the material is based on empirical research, the annotation includes an identification of the locale and a summary of objectives, methods, and findings. The introduction and, in some cases, the prefatory remarks in each chapter, however, evaluate the contributions of the materials cited and indicate some valid directions for future work.

Where books and monographs have been reviewed in scholarly journals and other publications, listings of some reviews follow the citations of the works to which they refer. References to materials available through the Educational Resources Information Center (ERIC) include ERIC identification numbers. Relevant doctoral dissertations are listed at the end of appropriate chapters. Most of the cited dissertations were identified by consulting *Dissertation Abstracts*. Because abstracts are available in this publication, the dissertations are not annotated. In addition, there is an author index.

Chapter 1 provides an overview of the literature on citizen group participation in local politics. This brief essay is followed by references to bibliographies related to the topic. The literature in Chapter 2, although not representative of a cohesive theory or of generally applicable models, does reflect efforts to generalize beyond specific situations and to develop a general theory of citizen group participation. Chapter 3, "Citizen Groups in Planning and Community Development," lists and describes works on citizen involvement in planning and in community development efforts such as urban renewal, juvenile delinquency, community action, and model cities. "Citizen Involvement in Service Delivery Systems," Chapter 4, identifies a substantial body of literature on different types of service delivery systems or different policy-issue areas. Section titles are:

1. Criminal Justice
2. Education
3. Environment and Natural Resources
4. Health
5. Housing
6. Social Welfare
7. Transportation

Chapter 5 treats some of the major works about voluntary associations, or self-initiating citizen groups, and their political activities, strategies, and impacts. Local governments, in some cases, have responded to increasing demands for citizen access to public decision-making processes by creating various opportunities for citizen participation. In Chapter 6, literature focusing on and assessing those opportunities is identified and summarized. Chapter 7 includes guides and handbooks useful to members and leaders of citizen groups.

1

Citizen Groups in Local Politics:
An Overview of the Literature

Citizen group participation is not new in American political life, but it has received an increasing amount of attention in the past decade. In the late 1940s, Saul Alinsky urged that the urban poor organize and aggressively seek remedies for the many problems that beset them.[1] This tactic was adopted, to some degree, by civil rights and reform organizations in the late fifties but did not begin to become widely recognized until the early sixties. Federally sponsored, locally administered programs like the agricultural extension services had utilized citizen advisory boards for many years, but citizen advisory boards had not been used extensively in urban areas until adopted by the Urban Renewal Program in the fifties and suggested in the Ford Foundation's Gray Areas Program in the early sixties. From the Ford Foundation's experience, the Office of Economic Opportunity's Community Action Program developed, incorporating the concept of "maximum feasible participation" of the poor. Even though it was the subject of much controversy the idea of citizen participation in the formation of programs and policies began to be incorporated into other federal programs and was adopted by a number of state and local agencies.[2]

As government agencies have continued to establish and modify citizen participation mechanisms, voluntary associations or self-initiating citizen groups have become more aggressive in demanding access to governmental decision making. The result has been a sharp increase in citizen group activity in federally and locally sponsored government

1. For a detailed description of Alinsky's approach to community organization, see Saul D. Alinsky, *Reveille for Radicals* (Chicago: University of Chicago Press, 1946). For a comprehensive analysis of the "Alinsky approach," see Robert Bailey, Jr., *Radicals in Urban Politics: The Alinsky Approach* (Chicago: University of Chicago Press, 1974).
2. Howard W. Hallman, "Federally Financed Citizen Participation," *Public Administration Review* 32, special issue (September 1972):421–27, provides a more detailed account of the historical development of citizen participation in federal programs.

programs and in local political decision making in general.[3] Citizen group activity has expanded so rapidly in the past ten years that the authors of a 1969 article speculated that it "may be true—that there is more participation than ever before in American society, particularly in the large urban centers such as New York, and more opportunity for the active and interested person to express his political and social concerns."[4] Whether or not this statement is in fact true, it is clear that citizen group participation has become an increasingly important political force in local politics, and this fact is reflected by the volume of literature on the topic that has appeared in the past ten years. The subject has aroused the interest of writers in a number of professions and academic disciplines.

A large portion of the literature on citizen group participation is devoted to arguments for and against citizen participation in different situations and to descriptions of citizen participation in specific cases. If there is, however, a consensus among those who have recently written on the topic, it is on the desirability of increasing citizen access to public decision making. The question, it seems, is no longer whether citizens should participate but how and to what degree citizens should influence governmental decision making. There is, of course, less agreement with regard to answering the latter questions.

One of the difficulties in answering the questions "how?" and "to what degree?" is that citizen participation itself is a rather nebulous term. It has been defined as merely attending public hearings; others have argued that participation does not occur unless citizens actually influence a decision—something occurs that would not have occurred in their absence, or without their efforts. Both Edmund Burke[5] and Sherry Arnstein[6] have pointed out that the term citizen participation has been used in reference to situations ranging from virtual nonparticipation to citizen control. Arnstein's "ladder" is among the most widely used typologies attempting to identify degrees of participation. Arnstein illustrates how citizens can be manipu-

3. This trend has been documented in several cities. The third volume of *Citizen Participation in Denver* (Denver: Denver Urban Observatory, 1972) traces the growth and activities of citizen groups in Denver since 1965. A study, in progress at the time of this writing, directed by Donald S. Bradley (Department of Sociology, Georgia State University), indicates that the activities of citizen groups in Atlanta have become increasingly more "political" (1963–1973). Groups in Atlanta, during this period, seem to have become more actively involved in attempting to influence public policy decisions.

4. Daniel Bell and Virginia Held, "The Community Revolution," *The Public Interest* 16 (Summer 1969):142.

5. Edmund M. Burke, "Citizen Participation Strategies," *Journal of the American Institute of Planners* 34:5 (September 1968):287–94.

6. Sherry R. Arnstein, "A Ladder of Citizen Participation," *Journal of the American Institute of Planners* 29:4 (July 1969):216–24.

lated and "treated," in a therapeutic sense, under the guise of citizen participation. She identifies "degrees of tokenism" which require some recognition of citizen demands but seldom facilitate influence. Finally, "degrees of citizen power" are defined in terms of the extent of influence which may be exerted by citizen participants.[7]

Another difficulty that has inhibited the formulation of a generally applicable definition of how and to what degree citizen groups should influence governmental decision making has been the number of different types of groups that have demanded some form of access to governmental decision making. A number of attempts to develop typologies have been reported in the literature. One of the objectives of the national network of urban observatories' first national agenda project was to develop at least a general typology of citizen groups; and several of the participating observatories suggested categories of variables which should be considered in such a typology. The typology suggested by the Kansas City (Kansas) report is the most comprehensive. The authors suggest nine categories of variables, or dimensions, for consideration: (1) the membership characteristics of the group; (2) the group's organizational structure; (3) the resources available to the group; (4) the "target conditions," or that "set of conditions in which the group wishes and attempts to effect change" (the conditions which dictate, for example, educational policy); (5) the "target instrumentality," or the institution or agency which the group must influence in order to accomplish its objectives; (6) the relationship between the group and the target instrumentality, whether the group and the target agree or disagree; (7) the strategy or "mode of action" employed by the group in efforts to influence the target; (8) the groups' relationships with other groups concerned with the same target; and (9) the beneficiaries of the groups' actions.[8]

It is obvious that possible variations along these dimensions are innumerable. Yet, in order to explain the impact, or the success or failure of citizen groups' efforts, it would be necessary to examine a number of groups exhibiting observable differences along at least the nine dimensions described above. The complexity and sheer magnitude of such an effort perhaps helps account for the preponderance of impressionistic and case study material found in the literature on citizen group participation. Yet, in order to suggest how and to what degree groups should influence governmental decision making (given different desired outcomes), it is necessary to explain the impacts of alternative group actions within different contexts

7. Arnstein, "Ladder of Citizen Participation."
8. Kansas City Urban Observatory, *Citizen Participation Groups: A Report to the National Urban Observatory* (Lawrence: Urban Studies Group, University of Kansas, n. d.), pp. 2–12.

and the program and policy implications of different degrees of group influence.

Some writers, in attempts to explain the impacts and effects of group actions, have found it useful to develop general analytic frameworks or models which attempt to conceptualize some of the possible relationships between and interaction of the above variables. Such analytic frameworks or models have been used in the development of hypotheses relating to the determinants of the impacts and effects of citizen group efforts.

In an extensive analysis of one neighborhood council, Harold H. Weissman used an exchange process model.[9] Later, David R. Godschalk based his "collaborative planning" paradigm on exchange theory and employed this paradigm in several comparative case studies of citizen participation in community planning.[10] In systematizing the case study process—analyzing the collaborative efforts of planners, their clients, and community residents—Godschalk's study illustrates the utility of such analytic frameworks in facilitating comparative analysis that offer some promise of yielding generally applicable findings. Similarly, in an analysis of citizen participation in community action agencies in five cities, J. David Greenstone and Paul E. Peterson have used an approach referred to as "role interest" analysis which is employed to "explain the intercity differences in community participation."[11]

While the exchange and role-interest approaches have served to conceptualize the processes through which citizens participate in specific decision-making contexts (planning and community action), the systems approach has been used in efforts to conceptualize citizen group participation in governmental decision making in general.[12] In their first national agenda project each observatory in the national network of urban observatories conducted a series of case studies of citizen groups. Several of the observatories used the systems framework, suggested by the Atlanta observatory, as a guide in conceptualizing and conducting these case studies.[13] The use of a general framework, such as the systems model, permits attempts to facilitate comparability of citizen participation cases

9. Harold H. Weissman, *Community Councils and Community Control: The Workings of Democratic Mythology* (Pittsburgh: University of Pittsburgh Press, 1970).

10. David R. Godschalk, *Participation, Planning, and Exchange in Old and New Communities: A Collaborative Paradigm* (Chapel Hill: Center for Urban and Regional Studies, University of North Carolina, 1972).

11. J. David Greenstone and Paul E. Peterson, *Race and Authority in Urban Politics: Community Participation and the War on Poverty* (New York: Russell Sage Foundation, 1973), p. 52.

12. John D. Hutcheson, Jr., and Frank X. Steggart, *Organized Citizen Participation in Urban Areas* (Atlanta: Center for Research in Social Change, Emory University, 1970).

13. See, for example, Miriam G. Palay, *Citizen Participation: Issues and Groups, Milwaukee, 1969* (Milwaukee: Milwaukee Urban Observatory, 1972).

involving participation in different types of decision-making structures and in different locales. In doing so, the feasibility of generally applicable findings is enhanced, and the possibility of identifying some reasonably satisfactory answers to the questions "how?" and "to what degree?" citizens groups should participate in governmental decision making becomes less remote.

Because, however, citizen group participation is often a means or a process rather than an end in itself, the questions "how?" and "to what degree?" must be answered within the context of various, perhaps at times conflicting, objectives. Edgar and Jean Cahn have noted that the objectives or the "values" of citizen participation fall into three rather broad classifications: a means of mobilizing unutilized resources—a source of productivity and labor not otherwise tapped; a source of knowledge—both corrective and creative—a means of securing feedback regarding policy and programs, and also a source of new, inventive, and innovative approaches; and an end in itself—an affirmation of democracy and the elimination of alienation and withdrawal of destructiveness, hostility, and lack of faith in relying on the people.[14]

Underlying the citizens participation efforts of a number of federally sponsored programs was the idea that social ills stemmed, at least in part, from social disorganization, the loss or lack of "community." Programs such as the Mobilization for Youth and the Community Action Program, therefore, encouraged the mobilization of communities with various organizational efforts. While some authors[15] report successful mobilization efforts sponsored by such programs, others report dismal failures. Gove and Costner, for example, document the failure of a community action agency's attempts to encourage the development of neighborhood self-improvement associations.[16]

The early governmental efforts to encourage citizen participation as well as many, more recent similar efforts of federal categorical programs were predicated on the assumption that program implementation or the quality of service delivery could be improved by the involvement of citizens affected by the activities of such programs. Again the literature is inconclusive. Some argue that citizen participation has only created additional obstacles to program implementation and has had detrimental effects upon

14. Edgar S. Cahn and Jean Camper Cahn, "Maximum Feasible Participation: A General Overview," in Edgar S. Cahn and Barry A. Passett, eds., *Citizen Participation: Effecting Community Change* (New York: Praeger, 1971), p. 16.
15. Several successful efforts are described in Cahn and Cahn.
16. Walter Gove and Herbert Costner, "Organizing the Poor: An Evaluation of a Strategy," *Social Science Quarterly* 50:3 (December 1969):643–56.

program objectives.[17] On the other hand, Richard Cole, from an analysis of twenty-six programs, concludes that involvement, at least in the participants' judgments, achieved more favorable allocations of goods and services;[18] and Marcia Guttentag reports favorable educational impacts in a community controlled school in New York City.[19] While the policy implications of research focusing on the impacts of citizen participation upon program implementation and outcomes are obvious, far too few studies have emphasized such impacts. There is, however, some evidence that researchers are beginning to direct their efforts toward policy-relevant questions. A review of the Smithsonian Science Information Exchange's listings and abstracts reveals that a number of current and ongoing research efforts are attempting to clarify the program-related impacts of citizen group participation.[20]

Closely related to the mobilization objective of citizen participation is the objective of enhancing involvement in democratic processes. Cole's study illustrates that citizen participation is likely to improve the participative skills of those involved and increase political efficacy.[21] On an aggregate level (cities), however, Robert Yin and William Lucas found no evidence to support the theory that decentralization and subsequent increases in participative opportunities reduce political alienation.[22]

Whether or not citizen group participation accomplishes intended objectives obviously depends upon the conditions within which such participation occurs and which objectives are paramount in any given situation. General assessments of citizen group participation, in terms of the broadly defined objectives noted above, are hazardous. It seems more desirable, at this time, to seek to define the circumstances within which different forms of citizen group activity may have differing effects. In doing so, researchers will contribute to providing answers to the questions "how?" and "to what degree?" citizens should influence governmental decision making if the possibility of desired outcomes is to be enhanced. However, the current literature, and consequently this bibliography, are replete with

17. Several examples are cited in John P. Hall, "The Case Against Citizen Participation: A Suggested Retreat" (Paper presented at the Southwestern Political Science Association meeting, Dallas, Texas, March 23, 1973), mimeograph.

18. Richard L. Cole, *Citizen Participation and the Urban Policy Process* (Lexington, Massachusetts: D. C. Heath, 1974).

19. Marcia Guttentag, "Children in Harlem's Community Controlled Schools," *Journal of Social Issues* 28:4 (1972):1–20.

20. Smithsonian Science Information Exchange, Inc., "Citizen Participation," Information Package CN02C. Available from Smithsonian Science Information Exchange, Inc., 1730 M Street, N.W., Washington, D.C. 20036.

21. Cole, *Citizen Participation.*

22. Robert K. Yin and William A. Lucas, "Decentralization and Alienation," *Policy Sciences* 4:3 (September 1973):327–36.

descriptive case studies, analyses of citizen group participation within the context of a single agency, issue, or political unit. Some of these cases seem to have little relevance beyond the case described; others have more generally applicable implications. Such case studies may provide the bases for more extensive and more meaningful comparative analysis. Several conceptual approaches promise to help guide much comparative effort. The use of such approaches, analytic frameworks, or models in broadly defined comparative studies offers the best available means of providing a fuller understanding of the impacts of citizen participation and more generally applicable answers to the questions "how?" and "to what degree?". If this bibliography helps facilitate, in even a small way, the accomplishing of these ends, it will have served its purpose.

Related Bibliographies

Bestor, George C., and Holway R. Jones. *City Planning Bibliography*. 3d ed. New York: American Society of Civil Engineers, 1972, pp. 251–55, 288–90.

The brief "Citizen Participation" section of this bibliography (Sec. 3, Chap. 1, Part 2) emphasizes citizens' guides to participation in city planning processes. For the most part, the entries in this bibliography represent efforts to introduce the layman to urban planning. The section on citizen participation in "Housing and Urban Renewal" (Sec. 3, Chap. 1, Part 3h) includes references to several guides to participation in housing programs as well as to several related case studies. A few other items related to community group participation in planning are scattered throughout the bibliography. Most of the items are annotated.

Bolton, Charles K., and Kenneth E. Corey. *A Selected Bibliography for the Training of Citizen-Agents of Planned Community Change*. Exchange Bibliography no. 286. Monticello, Illinois: Council of Planning Librarians, 1971.

Originating in an effort by a University of Cincinnati project team to help inner city and suburban residents "become effective participants in the public policy and planned development decisions of their community," this bibliography is divided into four major sections:

    1. Functions of the Community—Education, Community Health Services and Environmental Health, Social and Community

Organization, Political Organization, The Economy, and Physical Environment
2. Community Interrelationships—Urban Ecology and Locational and Territorial Change
3. Selected Community Change Processes—Planned Change, Citizen Participation and Advocacy Planning, and Black Community Change
4. Philosophical Roots of Planned Community Change

The first three sections are divided into "primary" and "advanced" bibliographies. The items are not annotated.

Boothe, William; Mary Alice Beetham; and Marvin Strauss. *Consumer Participation in Comprehensive Health Planning*. Exchange Bibliography no. 72. Monticello, Illinois: Council of Planning Librarians, 1969.

This bibliography was prepared for a workshop in February 1969. It contains about seventy-five items; they are not annotated. Most of the references pertain to community organization and power in general; a few focus upon citizen participation in health care delivery systems and in health planning.

Brown, Ruth E. *Community Action Programs: An Annotated Bibliography*. Exchange Bibliography no. 277. Monticello, Illinois; Council of Planning Librarians, 1972.

This annotated bibliography includes a number of items which pertain to citizen participation in community action agencies.

Contant, Florence. *Community Development Corporations: An Annotated Bibliography*. Exchange Bibliography no. 293. Monticello, Illinois: Council of Planning Librarians, 1972. A revision of this bibliography was published by the Center for Community Economic Development, Cambridge, Massachusetts, 1973.

Costikyan, Edward N., and Maxwell Lehman. *Re-structuring the Government of New York City: Report of the Scott Commission Task Force on Jurisdiction and Structure*. New York: Praeger, 1972, pp. 113–28.

The section "Re-structure and Citizen Involvement" includes a number of items which focus on citizen participation in general. Other sections include items pertaining to city government in New York and items referring to documents concerning the reorganization of New York City government. The items are not annotated.

"Curriculum Essays on Citizens, Politics, and Administration in Urban Neighborhoods." *Public Administration Review* 32, special issue (October 1972).

The purpose of this special issue (edited by H. George Frederickson) is to "help shorten the time lag on dissemination of knowledge about administrative decentralization and citizen participation." Each of the ten essays included is essentially a review of recent literature with, in most cases, extensive documentation. The authors and titles of the essays are:

1. Henry J. Schmandt, "Municipal Decentralization: An Overview"
2. James V. Cunningham, "Citizen Participation in Public Affairs"
3. David K. Hart, "Theories of Government Related to Decentralization and Citizen Participation"
4. Adam W. Herbert, "Management Under Conditions of Decentralization and Citizen Participation"
5. Charles V. Hamilton, "Racial, Ethnic, and Social Class Politics and Administration," Grace Olivarez, "Spanish-Speaking Americans," Richard Krickus, "White Ethnic Groups"
6. John H. Strange, "Citizen Participation in Community Action and Model Cities Programs"
7. Marilyn Gittell, "Decentralization and Citizen Participation in Education"
8. Martin Rein, "Decentralization and Citizen Participation in Social Services"
9. Lawrence C. Howard, "Decentralization and Citizen Participation in Health Services"
10. Richard A. Myren, "Decentralization and Citizen Participation in Criminal Justice Systems"

Davies, Don. *Citizen Participation in Education: Annotated Bibliography.* New Haven, Connecticut: Center for the Study of Education, Institution for Social and Policy Studies, Yale University, 1973.

Duisin, Xenia W. *Decentralization in Urban Government: An Annotated Bibliography.* Exchange Bibliography no. 347. Monticello, Illinois: Council of Planning Librarians, 1972.

The purpose of this annotated bibliography "is to gather together a number of relevant references to the recent literature on urban decentralization where some local decision-making and control over resources is involved." Seventy-six annotated items are divided into sections entitled:

1. On Decentralization
2. On Urban Decentralization
    A. Citizen Participation and Community Control Issues
    B. Neighborhood Government
3. New York City Government Decentralization

Educational Resources Information Center. *A Collection of ERIC Document Resumes on Citizen Involvement in the Control of Schools.* Washington, D.C.: National Center for Educational Research and Development, 1970, ERIC, ED044–832.

This compilation is a result of a search of *Research in Education* indexes (1966–1970) using the following key terms: citizen participation, decentralization, parent participation, parent-school relationship, school-community relationship, and school district autonomy. Forty-one annotated items and a subject index are included.

Fish, John Hall. *Black Power, White Control: The Struggle of the Woodlawn Organization in Chicago.* Princeton, New Jersey: Princeton University Press, 1973, pp. 333–48.

A rather extensive bibliography is included in this book. It is divided into three sections: "General References in Urban Problems and Issues"; "Community Organization: Strategies and Perspectives"; and "Woodlawn and the Woodlawn Organization." The second of these sections includes a number of items (not annotated) which are relevant to community group participation. The emphasis of the referenced material is on voluntary community groups and the "Alinsky approach" to community organization.

Hutcheson, John D., Jr., and Frank X. Steggert. *Organized Citizen Participation in Urban Areas.* Atlanta: Center for Research in Social Change, Emory University, 1970, pp. 139–72.

The bibliography provided in this publication includes journal articles, books, monographs, government reports, and dissertations which appeared between 1955 and 1969. The items are not annotated. Sections are entitled:

1. Organized Citizen Participation in Perspective
2. Types of Organized Citizen Participation
3. General Studies Pertaining to Organized Citizen Participation

4. Case Studies of Organized Participation
5. Comparative Case Studies of Organized Citizen Participation
6. General Bibliographic References

Sections are divided into subsections on voluntary citizens organizations, citizens organizations which are sponsored by the federal government, and citizens organizations which are sponsored by local governments. The focus of the bibliography is upon the structures, strategies, and impacts of citizens organizations involved in city politics.

Kansas City Urban Observatory. *Citizen Participation Groups: A Report to the National Urban Observatory.* Lawrence: Urban Studies Group, University of Kansas, n. d., pp. 89–130.

This report includes an indexed bibliography of 317 items. The entries are not annotated, but the indexing system helps clarify the content of some of the items: "The items in the index were systematically collected during the search of the literature and reflect the authors, names of citizen participation groups, geographical location(s) of the groups, target conditions and target instrumentality to which the participation groups seek to relate." Most of the items cited focus upon community politics and leadership and citizen groups; some of the items refer to case studies of one or more citizens organizations. Materials published through 1969 are included.

Kessler, Mary Z. *Ombudsman: A Selected Bibliography.* Exchange Bibliography no. 186. Monticello, Illinois: Council of Planning Librarians, 1971.

This is a rather extensive bibliography (about 350 items), "designed to give an overview of the ombudsman profession, its development and function." A number of the items could offer some insight into how ombudsmen can be used to facilitate citizen group access to governmental decision-making processes. The items are not annotated.

Ledyard, Julia. *Citizen Participation in Planning.* Exchange Bibliography no. 76. Monticello, Illinois: Council of Planning Librarians, 1969.

Materials included in this bibliography were published between 1962 and 1969. The items are not annotated. It is divided into three sections: "Planning"; "Citizen Involvement"; and "Related Readings." Most of the works cited in the first section focus upon city planning; a few relate to citizen participation in city planning. The majority of the items in Section

Two deal with citizen participation in general; some deal with citizen participation in planning. Section Three focuses on community affairs.

Marshall, Dale Rogers. "Who Participates in What? A Bibliographic Essay on Individual Participation in Urban Areas." *Urban Affairs Quarterly* 4:2 (December 1968): 201–23.

This extensively documented essay focuses on individual participation in mass society. There is an emphasis on voluntary associations and blue-collar participation along with a general discussion of the social and demographic correlates of participation. The author cites a number of studies involving voluntary associations.

Mathews, Vincent. *Citizen Participation: An Analytical Study of the Literature.* Washington, D.C.: Community Relations Service, U.S. Department of Justice, 1968.

Focusing on both individual and group participation, this work is divided into two parts, each of which has a corresponding bibliography. The items in the bibliography are not annotated, but they are often analyzed in the accompanying essays. Part One focuses on why and how citizens participate. The corresponding bibliography cites major works dealing with the determinants and forms of participation. Part Two considers "four basic models of participation: community development, political, program, and social protest," and the corresponding bibliography includes citations to literature pertaining to these models.

May, Judith V. *Citizen Participation: A Review of the Literature.* Exchange Bibliography no. 210–11. Monticello, Illinois: Council of Planning Librarians, 1971. Published later in the same year by the Institute of Governmental Affairs, University of California, Davis.

This work is a review essay with an extensive bibliography. The items are not annotated, but, in most cases, they are well integrated into the essay. The essay attempts "to identify the political resources and structural conditions that determine the effectiveness of citizen participation." Thus, the essay and the accompanying bibliography focus upon some of the "sociopsychological, strategic, and structural determinants of the rate at which citizens participate and the effectiveness of that participation." Participation in politics and in administration is discussed. For the most part, theoretical and generally applicable works are included, while case studies and analyses of citizen participation in specific instances are avoided.

Mazziotti, Donald F. *Advocacy Planning: A Selected Bibliography.* Exchange Bibliography no. 323. Monticello, Illinois: Council of Planning Librarians, 1972.

Mazziotti, Donald F. *Advocacy Planning—Toward the Development of Theory and Strategy.* Exchange Bibliography no. 241. Monticello, Illinois: Council of Planning Librarians, 1971.

This bibliography contains about eighty items which are not annotated. As is evident from the title, its primary focus is upon advocacy planning, but many of the items refer to general works on citizen participation. The preceding citation is, essentially, an updated version.

Melrood, Margot. *A Bibliography on Decentralization.* Milwaukee: Institute of Governmental Affairs, University of Wisconsin-Milwaukee, 1970.

Mendes, Richard H. P. *Bibliography on Community Organization for Citizen Participation in Voluntary Democratic Associations.* Prepared for the President's Committee on Juvenile Delinquency and Youth Crime. Washington, D.C.: U.S. Government Printing Office, 1965.

The materials cited in this bibliography constitute an "introduction to community organization for social welfare." It contains 750 items which are not annotated. The bibliography is divided into three parts: "Community Organization as Technique"; "Theoretical and Empirical Foundations"; and "On Citizen Participation in Voluntary Democratic Associations." Each part and section is preceded by a brief introductory essay.

Meyers, William R., and Robert A. Dorwart. *Citizen Participation in Mental Health: A Bibliography.* Exchange Bibliography no. 559. Monticello, Illinois: Council of Planning Librarians, 1974.

This bibliography includes about 175 items which are not annotated. It has no subdivisions and the foci of the materials listed range from bureaucracy and citizen participation in general to citizen participation within the context of mental health programs.

National League of Cities and United States Conference of Mayors, Library and Information Services. *Little City Halls: Selected Readings and References.* Washington, D.C.: National League of Cities and United States Conference of Mayors, 1973, pp. 10–21.

The annotated bibliography in this publication includes items on the decentralization of city governments, citizen participation, neighborhood facilities and services, and neighborhood city halls.

Parkum, Virginia C. *Citizen Participation: A Bibliography of Theory and Practice, with Special Emphasis on Comprehensive Health Planning.* Harrisburg: Pennsylvania Department of Health, n. d.

Pike, Mary L. *Citizen Participation in Community Development: A Selected Bibliography.* Washington, D.C.: National Association of Housing Redevelopment Officials, 1975.

This bibliography contains 329 items which are not annotated.

Shalala, Donna E. *Neighborhood Governance: Issues and Proposals.* New York: American Jewish Committee, 1971, pp. 40–48.

The bibliography in this publication includes references to books, pamphlets, articles, and government publications. The majority of these publications were published in the late 1960s. The citations are not annotated. The focus of the bibliography is decentralization of urban governments, community control, community corporations, and neighborhood government.

Smith, Constance, and Anne Freedman. *Voluntary Associations: Perspectives on the Literature.* Cambridge, Massachusetts: Harvard University Press, 1972.

This is a comprehensive, well-documented review of the literature on voluntary associations. It includes eight sections:

1. A Theoretical Overview
2. The Pluralist Thesis
3. Pluralism: Attack and Defense
4. Voluntary Associations and the Political System: Data
5. Surveys of Participation
6. Sociological Studies of Participation
7. The Organizations
8. Pointing to the Future

Covering both theoretical foundations and empirical studies, this is the most comprehensive analysis of the literature on voluntary associations currently available.

Spergel, Irving A., ed. *Community Organization: Studies in Constraint.* Beverly Hills, California: Sage Publications, 1972, pp. 263–73.

This book contains a rather extensive bibliography which includes items focusing on citizen participation, community organizations, and community power. The items are not annotated.

United States Department of Housing and Urban Development. *Citizen and Business Participation in Urban Affairs: A Bibliography.* Washington, D.C.: U.S. Government Printing Office, 1970.

Including 605 briefly annotated items, this bibliography covers the following topics:

1. Community Organization and Development
2. The Citizen Volunteer
3. Planning, Renewal and the Citizen
4. Case Studies in Citizen Participation
5. Model Cities
6. Business and the Urban Challenge
7. Business Participation in Housing
8. Business Participation in Employment and Civil Rights
9. Non-profit Housing
10. Institutional Participation

A list of selected films, publishers' address, and geographic and author indexes are appended.

Washington, State Library of. *Community Organization and Redevelopment: A Selective Bibliography—A Revised Edition with a Special Section on Citizen Participation.* Olympia, Washington, 1970.

Yin, Robert K.; William A. Lucas; Peter L. Szanton; and J. Andrew Spindler. *Citizen Organizations: Increasing Client Control Over Services.* Santa Monica, California: The Rand Corporation, 1973, pp. 113–95.

Originally prepared as a report for the Department of Health, Education and Welfare, this publication focuses on client participation in HEW service delivery systems. The bibliography is divided into two parts. Part One annotates "twenty prominent works." Part Two includes ten sections; the items in Part Two are not annotated. The sections in Part Two are entitled:

1. Citizen Participation and Health
2. Citizen Participation and Education

3. Citizen Participation and Social Services
4. Citizen Participation and Planning
5. Citizen Participation in Relation to Poverty and Urban Development
6. Volunteers and Voluntary Organizations
7. Community and Neighborhood Participation—General
8. Citizen Participation: General, Theoretical, and Other Works
9. Works Closely Associated with Citizen Participation
10. Selected Bibliographies

The citations are, the authors suggest, a "representative sampling of both published and unpublished writing on the subject."

Yukubousky, Richard. *Citizen Participation in Transportation Planning—A Selected Bibliography.* Albany: Research and Applied Systems Section, New York State Department of Transportation, 1973.

2

Toward a General Theory of
Citizen Group Participation in Local Politics

The literature cited in this bibliographic review reflects the many different aspects of local political life that have been influenced by the recent emphasis on citizen group participation. The works cited in this chapter focus on several different forms of group participation (governmentally sponsored groups as well as self-initiating citizen groups), a number of different strategies that have been or might be employed by citizens' organizations, and numerous agencies, programs, or levels of government that have been or might be the targets of citizen group efforts to influence public decision making. Even though the specific focus of each work may be different, each of the items included in this chapter attempts to draw general conclusions about the nature or extent of citizen group participation. A careful examination of the cited materials, however, will reveal no generally accepted models, no general theories. Undoubtedly this is due, in part, to the many different forms of political activity that have come to be referred to collectively as citizen participation. Subsequent chapters focus on literature relating to specific types of groups or relating to groups attempting to influence specific programs or policies. Due, in part, to the lack of general theory and the lack of generally accepted models, the literature in subsequent chapters is quite diverse and the many studies cited are often difficult to compare. Yet, these studies, often case studies of specific groups in specific locales, must serve as the empirical building blocks for a general theory. Further, readers interested in citizen group participation in specific programs or interested in particular types of citizen groups will find a great deal of useful information in the following chapters. In essence, then, the materials in the present chapter represent efforts to generalize beyond more focused studies like many of those cited in subsequent chapters.

Albuquerque Urban Observatory. *Organized Citizen Participation in Albuquerque.* Albuquerque: Albuquerque Urban Observatory, 1970.

17

The primary objectives in this study were to describe how citizen groups in Albuquerque influenced or attempted to influence public officials and how, in turn, public officials responded to the efforts of citizen organizations. Three issues were selected as the foci of three case studies. Interviews were conducted with actors (group leaders and members and government and private officials) in each of the case studies.

From an analysis of the case studies, the report concludes that: (1) effective communication between citizen groups and officials is best accomplished through cooperation rather than conflict; (2) cooperation is more likely when the citizen group has some economic and political power base; (3) cooperation is enhanced by a previous history of successful negotiations; and (4) communication between low income citizens and local government is most in need of improvement. The report notes "that both the local political leadership and organizational leadership should assess their present positions with regard to making cooperative endeavors more possible," and it presents a series of suggestions that could serve as a "guide which may directly affect Albuquerque's approach to (the) citizen-government relationship."

Almond, Gabriel A., and Sidney Verba. *The Civic Culture*. Boston: Little, Brown, 1965, pp. 244–65.

Chapter 10, "Organizational Membership and Civic Competence," of this book describes the extent of voluntary association membership in the United States, Great Britain, Germany, Italy, and Mexico. The authors then assess the effects of organizational membership on political attitudes and political "competence." The authors' findings are based on survey data collected in 1959 and 1960.

Altshuler, Alan A. *Community Control: The Black Demand for Participation in Large American Cities*. New York: Pegasus, 1970.

Reviews:
Dimond, P. R. *Harvard Educational Review* 41 (August 1971): 386.
Sawyer, S. G. *Library Journal* 95 (July 1970): 2443.

The arguments for and against community control are presented, in detail, in this book. Community control is seen as a strategy for the distribution of power to black communities in urban areas. In the concluding chapter, the author states his own position in the arguments discussed earlier and presents the rationale for his position.

Appleby, Thomas. "Citizen Participation in the 70's: The Need to Turn to Politics." *City* 5:3 (May/June 1971): 52–55.

The author believes that government decision making has been improved by citizen participation. He makes several suggestions for citizen participation in the 1970s including: (1) citizens should work within established political parties; (2) ultimate decisions on public programs must rest with those officials who are accountable to the public; (3) citizen participation can be effective only if the programs themselves are workable; (4) effective citizen participation must have adequate funding; and (5) the emphasis of federal requirements should be shifted from coordination to competition.

Arnold, John E. "People Involvement: Participation to Restore Confidence." *Public Management* 53:9 (September 1971): 11.

The author of this article asserts that urban problems are caused by a lack of citizen confidence in government rather than by a lack of money. He feels that the current challenge is to find new methods of involving citizens.

Arnstein, Sherry R. "A Ladder of Citizen Participation." *Journal of the American Institute of Planners* 29:4 (July 1969): 216–24.

This article presents a typology of citizen participation arranged "in a ladder pattern with each rung corresponding to the extent of citizens' power in determining" outcomes. Illustrations from urban renewal, anti-poverty, and model cities programs are used to describe the rungs on the ladder.

The author discusses two types of "nonparticipation": manipulation and therapy. These, the author believes, are contrived as substitutes for participation. There are three "degrees of tokenism": informing, consulting, and placating. Informing and consulting ensure that the citizen will hear and be heard, but these do not ensure that citizens' views will be heeded. Placating demands that something be given to the citizen, but the powerholders continue to decide *what* will be given.

The author defines three "degrees of citizen power": partnership, delegated power, and citizen control. Partnership requires that powerholders bargain or negotiate with citizens *in response to* citizen demands. Delegated power *requires* negotiation, but it *also requires* that, in certain situations, the powerholders *initiate* the bargaining process. Citizen control means that those affected by the program or decision govern the program or the outcome.

Aronowitz, Stanley. "The Dialectics of Community Control." *Social Policy* 1:1 (May/June 1970): 47–51.

The author argues against "Black capitalism," describes the movement for community control in the New York City schools and in health service delivery systems, and concludes that community control will not succeed unless it "becomes a broader struggle for popular, democratic control of all public institutions and the economy."

Bailis, Lawrence Neil. "Organizing the Poor: Some Lessons of the 1960s." *Policy Studies Journal* 2:3 (Spring 1974): 210–14.

Bailis reviews "the most incisive" recent analyses relating to the dynamics of community organizing and the impact of lower income groups' protest activities. After discussing different organizational motives and strategies and their relationships, the author describes how different public policies influence organizational tactics and how, in turn, these policies affect organizations' impacts.

Beck, Bertram. "Community Control: A Distraction, Not an Answer." *Social Work* 14:4 (October 1969): 14–20.

The author argues that community control will have all of the shortcomings of local government and will not enhance responsiveness. It will not solve the major problems of bureaucratic organization. He believes that professionals can become more responsive to clients, without lessening professionalism, by using market mechanisms. Several examples of how this could be accomplished are discussed.

Bell, Daniel, and Virginia Held. "The Community Revolution." *The Public Interest* 16 (Summer 1969): 142–77.

This article argues that "there is more participation than ever before in American society, particularly in the large urban centers such as New York, and more opportunity for the active and interested person to express his political and social concerns." But the authors also point out that increased participation often leads to an increase in perceived powerlessness and frustration. Different organizations through which individuals may participate in public affairs are discussed and examples of such organizations in New York are described. The authors conclude, however, that even though there has been a "community revolution" in terms of opportunity to participate, there has not been a concomitant increase in citizen influence— that participating citizens do not perceive an increase in their power. Cities and communities become fractionalized and individuals and groups do not get results, or do not perceive the results of their efforts. The "community revolution" increased the "politicalization" of society and the authors feel that this is one of the most important reasons why "in the last twenty years New York has been deemed to be 'ungovernable'."

Berkman, Herman G., and David Z. Robinson. *Citizen Involvement in Urban Affairs: HUD/NYU Summer Study*. Springfield, Virginia: National Technical Information Service, 1969.

This is a report on the HUD/NYU Summer Study on Citizen Participation that occurred in September 1968. The conference participants included academics, professionals, and community leaders whose efforts focused on the question "How can we get more meaningful citizen participation in all functional areas of urban service?" Discussions centered on the purposes of citizen participation, present citizen participation practices, and problems of implementation. The participants also identified a number of research objectives which they felt should be pursued.

Bodine, John W. "The Indispensable One-hundredth of 1 Percent." *Taming Megalopolis*. Vol. 2. Edited by H. Wentworth Eldredge. Garden City, New York: Anchor Books, 1967, pp. 956–71.

Bodine argues, using Philadelphia for illustrative purposes, that "massive citizen efforts" have two distinct stages. The first stage involves the efforts of people who are not elites but are active in a given effort—these people, the author argues, are the "indispensable one-hundredth of 1 percent." These are usually active members of community organizations and citizen boards and commissions whose efforts then spark the activity of elite actors who exercise influence. The author describes how this process occurred in the city of Philadelphia and discusses how it might occur (and the impediments to its occurrence) in a large metropolitan region.

Bollens, John C., and Henry J. Schmandt. *The Metropolis: Its People, Politics, and Economic Life*. New York: Harper and Row, 1965.

Reviews:
Holleb, D. B. *Journal of Political Economy* 74 (June 1966)
McKeown, J. E. *American Journal of Sociology* 71 (May 1966)
In reviewing the many dimensions of the metropolis, this book emphasizes process and behavior as well as form and structure. In Chapter 8, "The Metropolitan Citizenry as Civic Participants," citizen participation

is analyzed in terms of four aspects: (1) degree of citizen commitment or identification with the community; (2) voting in local elections; (3) membership in voluntary associations; and (4) informal group activity.

Brager, George A., and Valerie Jorrin. "Bargaining: A Method in Community Change." *Social Work* 14:4 (October 1969): 73–83.

The authors discuss bargaining as it relates to change-oriented community organizations with impoverished clienteles. Three factors that determine the outcome of a bargaining process are presented: the power resources of the bargainers, the formulation of issues, and skill in the use of strategy. The roles of social workers and community groups in the process are discussed. The authors conclude that effective involvement of the poor in community decision making will mean that bargaining mechanisms will have to be institutionalized, as in labor negotiations.

Burke, Edmund M. "Citizen Participation Strategies." *Journal of the American Institute of Planners* 34:5 (September 1968): 287–94.

Burke points out that there are basic conflicts between "participatory democracy and professional expertise." Some of this conflict, however, can be resolved by adopting citizen participation strategies appropriate to a specific organization's role and resources. The author suggests five alternative strategies: (1) education-therapy, in which clients are the objects of some treatment and that treatment becomes an end in itself; (2) behavior change (similar to education-therapy) which attempts to influence individual behavior through group reinforcement; (3) staff supplement, essentially recruiting citizens to carry out tasks for the organization; (4) cooptation, involving citizens in an organization to prevent anticipated obstructionism; and (5) community power which involves citizens' exercising power over institutions or individuals who are not residents of the community. The author concludes that agencies must be precise about how citizens are to participate, how citizens will be organized, and how they will be supported.

Cahn, Edgar S., and Barry A. Passett, eds. *Citizen Participation: Effecting Community Change.* New York: Praeger, 1971.

Review:
Eisinger, Peter K. *Journal of Politics* 34 (February 1972): 284–85.

Developed under a contract with the Office of Economic Opportunity, this book's purpose is to serve as "a casebook for trainers on the experience of citizen participation." Part One of the book is devoted to a discussion of the purposes and costs and benefits of citizen participation (especially within the context of federally sponsored programs in low income communities). In Part Two, Sherry R. Arnstein discusses degrees of participation ranging from nonparticipation to citizen control; Irving Lazar describes "Which Citizens to Participate in What?"; Wendy Goepel Brooks discusses participation of the poor in health care delivery systems; and Daniel M. Fox reviews "Federal Standards and Regulations for Participation."

Part Three focuses on "Specific Issues in Resident Participation." Economic development is discussed by Stanley Zimmerman using, as an example, an organization of black farmers in Alabama. A "block organization" program sponsored by a community action agency is described by David Borden. A Brandeis University report describes patterns of community participation in twenty community action agencies across the country. Ivan C. Elmer derives some suggestions for community organizers from the manner in which chambers of commerce have operated; Gail Saliterman describes participation in the "Model School Division" of the District of Columbia School System. Jerome Bernstein describes how the Woodlawn Organization used an OEO-funded manpower program to reduce juvenile delinquency; Ginger Rosenberg reviews the experience of residents in Dayton, Ohio, who had been active in the antipoverty structure, in attempting to influence the planning of their city's model cities program. The last section, by Patricia A. Wood, describes how citizens in the New York/New Jersey metropolitan area participated in the planning and programming of a series of television programs.

Carrell, Jeptha J. "Citizen Participation and Decentralization." *Midwest Review of Public Administration* 3:1 (February 1969): 3–12.

The author defines two kinds of citizen participation, active and passive, and two kinds of decentralization, decentralization involving certain categories of decision making and decentralization involving degrees of power. Standards for citizen participation are presented: (1) assurance of majority rule; (2) protection for minority opinion; (3) access to expert opinion and help; (4) opportunity for ego-involvement; (5) assurance of reasonably fast decisions; (6) protection against too much haste in decision making; and (7) encouragement of the development of skills for democratic participation. Standards for decentralization are also presented: (1) appropriate nature of delegated powers for the geographical area and the population; (2) provisions for increased citizen participation with ego-involvement; (3) assurance that wider community interests will prevail over narrow subdistrict interests; (4) access to expert opinion and help; (5) assurance against putting dangerous powers in the hands of submarginally skilled people; and (6) opportunity for decision makers in subdistricts to live with their mistakes as well as their successes. A brief sketch of planning-programming-budgeting systems as a tool for laymen is presented.

The author proposes an arrangement for decentralization of federal agencies: (1) regional offices of agencies to be clustered in the same city and to have the same regional boundaries; (2) regional citizens committees; (3) "general managers" of regional offices with real power; (4) regional lump-sum fund allocations; (5) regional citizens committees along with general managers and agency chiefs to determine specific allocations; and (6) decision making within regions to be within federal legislation limits but might involve different emphases. Barriers to decentralization are seen as: not enough skilled people working on alternatives; the assumption that the present system has enough citizen participation; and the fear of power sharing among many administrators and political leaders.

Cnudde, Charles F., and Peter K. Eisinger. "Group Activity and Public Policy: A Model of Impact Effectiveness." Appendix B to *Citizen Participation: Issues and Groups, Milwaukee, 1969*, by Miriam G. Palay. Milwaukee: Milwaukee Urban Observatory, 1972, pp. 134–50.

The authors develop, from existing literature, a heuristic model of impact effectiveness. Using the three case studies in the Milwaukee Urban Observatory study (see Palay, Miriam G., *Citizen Participation*, below), the authors conclude that "talking with city officials is a much more effective way to gain impacts on local policy than demonstrating," and that "political activity by the group has an impact on the policy outcome while the expected policy outcome and the group's preference or position have impacts on group activity."

Cole, Richard L. "Consequences of Citizen Participation: An Examination of Participant Characteristics, Trust, and Satisfaction." Paper prepared for the Southwestern Political Science Association meeting, Dallas, Texas, March 29, 1974. Mimeograph. Presented in more detail in Cole, Richard L. *Citizen Participation and the Urban Policy Process*. Lexington, Massachusetts: D. C. Heath, 1974.

Using data collected in 1972 and 1973 from 396 individuals participating in twenty-six neighborhood programs in six metropolitan areas, Cole examines the "degrees to which citizens' involvement programs are able to involve participants representative of the neighborhood as a whole, increase the political trust and confidence of those who participate, and improve the delivery of municipal goods and services to neighborhoods." The programs included in this study were selected in a manner which ensured adequate representation of programs with high and low levels of participation and narrow and broad definitions of the scope of program activities. Each program was rated on a five-point scale ranging from "least intensive involvement and most narrowly focused" to "most intensive involvement and broadest program coverage." A measure of how well the participants represented their "constituencies" was constructed by comparing the demographic characteristics of respondents to those of the residents of the areas which they purported to represent. The analysis includes measures of different organizational characteristics—cohesiveness, goals, and visibility— and measures of the program's effects upon neighborhood political awareness and trust. Also examined are measures of participants' program satisfaction and political trust.

Analyses of these data show that "programs of neighborhood involvement are likely to: (1) increase the participant's confidence and trust in local officials; (2) achieve, at least in the participant's own judgment, a more favorable allocation of goods and services (material rewards); and (3) improve the participant's political efficacy, competency and skills." These conclusions, which are obviously supportive of citizen participation, are tempered, however, by the following: only a small portion of neighborhood residents are actually "involved" in most programs; it is not clear "whether the balance of the benefits of citizen participation do in fact flow in the direction of the neighborhood" (rather than toward the program administration or politicians); and emphasis on neighborhood development can "neglect contacts between neighborhoods." The author concludes that citizen participation has both advantages and disadvantages but that "the merits of neighborhood participation—at least on the limited scale practiced in most American cities—far outnumber its potential demerits."

Cox, Fred M.; John L. Erlich; Jack Rothman; and John E. Tropman, eds. *Strategies of Community Organization.* Itasca, Illinois: F. E. Peacock Publishers, 1970.

This collection of writings is designed to acquaint the reader with different approaches to community organization, the nature of relationships between community organizations and other actors in the community, and to describe the roles and strategies of community organizers. Most of the works included were published previously. A bibliography of selected works relating to each chapter is appended. The items are not annotated.

Crain, Robert L.; Elihu Katz; and Donald B. Rosenthal. *The Politics of Community Conflict: The Fluoridation Decision.* New York: Bobbs-Merrill, 1969.

> Reviews:
> *Choice* 6 (February 1970): 1833.
> Corwin, R. C. *American Journal of Sociology* 76 (July 1970): 182.
> Eyestone, Robert. *American Political Science Review* 64 (March 1970): 215.
> Wehr, Paul. *American Sociological Review* 35 (August 1970): 775.

Using mailed questionnaires distributed to "informants" in 1,098 American cities, the authors describe the politics involved in fluoridation controversies. The activities of different citizen groups and how they affected referenda and fluoridation decisions are described.

Crenson, Matthew. *Citizen Participation.* Baltimore: Baltimore Urban Observatory, 1971.

The citizen organizations which are examined in this study are organizations in Baltimore which intervene, or attempt to intervene, "in the operations of administrative agencies—participation in the bureaucratic process of delivering public goods and services to the public." Seven groups, some government-sponsored and some self-initiating, were selected as case studies. Observations, examinations of records, and interviews with citizen participants and public officials were conducted during the case studies. In addition, a survey of approximately one hundred organization members and twenty organization staff members was conducted.

Sketches of four community groups which "represent most of the major variations in styles of citizen participation" are included in the report. The author concludes that "the most troublesome deficiency" for community groups is the lack of agenda items. This seems to be related to intragroup conflict and is most evident in government-sponsored groups. The lack of agenda in government-sponsored groups is attributed, in part, to the "rather ill-defined goals which had been articulated by federal administrators and legislators" and to the structure of federal programs like community action and model cities. In one case study, however, a government-sponsored group was able to establish an agenda by calling a public meeting and soliciting suggestions from its constituents; another group established an issue-oriented committee structure to define the group's courses of action. Using these conclusions and an analysis of different types of full-time group staff members, the author makes several recommendations designed to enhance the effectiveness of community organizations in Baltimore.

Crenson, Matthew. "Organizational Factors in Citizen Participation." *Journal of Politics* 36:2 (May 1974): 356–78.

This article, using the Baltimore Urban Observatory data, examines the relationships between the organizational characteristics of community groups and group effectiveness (see Crenson, Matthew, *Citizen Participation*, above).

Denver Urban Observatory. *Citizen Participation in Denver*. Vols. 1–4. Denver: Denver Urban Observatory, 1972.

The first of these volumes focuses upon the Denver Model Cities Program and concludes that, even though there were numerous struggles within and around the citizen participation mechanisms in the Denver Model Cities Program, there were some tangible accomplishments that could be attributed to citizen participation in the program. The second volume, by Jay Crowe and T. Michael Smith, is a case study of voluntary citizen participation in the planning of a higher education center in downtown Denver. The authors of the third volume, William Winter and James Adams, document the growth of citizen groups in Denver since 1965 and describe and compare the characteristics of citizen groups in that city. Volume 4 attempts to assess the degree of influence citizen groups exert in different local decision-making areas; little influence seemed to be exerted during the planning phases of the various decision-making processes, but some participation was evident after basic policy decisions had been made.

Ditz, Gerhard W. *Organized Citizen Participation in Kansas City, Missouri*. Kansas City: Mid-America Urban Observatory, University of Missouri at Kansas City, 1971.

Following the format prescribed by the first urban observatory national agenda project, this study established and analyzed a taxonomic inventory of citizen groups based on three major categories: federally initiated groups, groups organized or assisted by local governments, and voluntary organizations. Some 1,200 groups in Kansas City were identified and 150 were selected for further study. In most cases, officers of such groups were interviewed.

Several more precise classificatory schemes are presented and some generalizations about such groups are suggested. Typically, federally sponsored groups are found in lower socioeconomic areas; there normally is conflict between participants and officials; and their minimal functions are to vent the frustrations of the poor, institutionalize grievance procedures, and bring into conference government officials and inner city leaders. Locally sponsored groups are more stable and more conservative and characterized by rank and file apathy. Voluntary associations, usually middle class, are becoming more politically active and are often the "most conservative" or the "most radical" groups in the city. They are also the most effective and viable of the types of groups identified.

Eisinger, Peter K. "Control-Sharing in the City: Some Thoughts on Decentralization and Client Representation." *American Behavioral Scientist* 15:1 (September/October 1971): 36–51.

The author defines and distinguishes two types of control-sharing arrangements. Decentralization is defined as control sharing through transfer of some policy-making authority to neighborhood residents. Client representation is defined as control sharing through institutionalized representation of clients on policy-making boards. In comparing the impacts of the two types of control sharing, the author concludes that decentralization will cause greater and more lasting conflicts than will client representation. He also sees more conflict involved in setting of standards under decentralization. In terms of access to bureaucracy, he believes that decentralization has the advantage of bringing institutions physically closer to the people. In terms of control, the author maintains that clients will have more influence on policy-making boards than under decentralization.

Eisinger, Peter K. "Support for Urban Control-Sharing at the Mass Level." *American Journal of Political Science* 17:4 (November 1973): 669–94.

This study attempted to determine the degree to which blacks and whites understand the idea of control sharing, the extent of mass demand and support for control sharing and the nature of the focus of that support, and the degree of variation in these dimensions along racial lines. In 1970, interviews were conducted with a sample of Milwaukee residents—331 whites and 246 blacks. It was found that mass support for control sharing did not exist and that blacks were as indifferent as whites. The author concluded that control sharing seems to be an elite idea without mass support.

Eisinger, Peter K. "The Urban Crisis as a Failure of Community: Some Data." Paper presented at the American Political Science Association meeting, New Orleans, Louisiana, September 5, 1973. Mimeograph.

Eisinger attempts to determine if urban dwellers seek control sharing or community control. Data from a 1970 survey in Milwaukee show that Milwaukee residents are more concerned with personal problems than with communal problems and that "people neither understand nor seek control-sharing arrangements." (See Eisinger, Peter K., "Support for Urban Control-Sharing at the Mass Level," above.)

Esser, George H. "Involving the Citizen in Decision-Making." *Nation's Cities* 6:5 (May 1968): 11–14.

The author explores some effects of the reform movement in urban government which, he feels, decreased citizen participation: (1) the reformers denied the reality of politics and government involvement became limited to the educated and the well off; (2) the reformers believed in professionalism as a panacea; (3) nonpartisan elections give citizens no real choice; (4) citizens are not adequately represented under city manager forms of government; and (5) all of this excluded the poor from participating. He goes on to suggest five ways to strengthen democratic participation without harming administration, research, and planning: (1) reinstate human freedom, dignity, and justice as societal goals; (2) increase the representativeness of policy-making bodies; (3) adopt advocacy planning for the poor; (4) encourage the development of strong neighborhood groups; and (5) stimulate the advocacy of meaningful policy choices.

Fainstein, Norman I., and Susan S. Fainstein. *Urban Political Movements: The Search for Power by Minority Groups in American Cities.* Englewood Cliffs, New Jersey: Prentice-Hall, 1974.

The authors of this book define urban political movements as "non-institutionalized attempts by inner city residents to gain power over public service bureaucracies on a neighborhood basis." The movements referred to here can also be characterized as "local" and "nonwhite."

The book first discusses the historical context from which urban political movements have arisen. Next the character of such groups is examined. Then three case studies are presented: the Joan of Arc Planning/Governing Board (a community school board in New York City), which was a failure; the movement at P.S. 84 (another New York City school), which was a success; and Northside Forces (a community group based in Paterson, New Jersey), which was neither a success nor a failure. The remainder of the book discusses the nature of individual involvement in urban political movements, the relationships of the internal structure of these movements to their ability to attain external goals, and the larger significance of the movements.

Falkson, Joseph L. *An Evaluation of Alternative Models of Citizen Participation in Urban Bureaucracy.* Ann Arbor: Program in Health Planning, School of Public Health, University of Michigan, 1971.

Falkson examines various citizen organizations among the urban poor in an attempt to analyze two variants of citizen participation in urban service contexts: administrative participation observed in various neighborhood health centers and political participation examined within the context of constituent action in neighborhood schools. Four hundred seventy-one respondents in six programs in Detroit were interviewed in 1968. Health programs were classified using three models: Type I, traditional, with centralized decision making, showed the least participation; Type II, liberal, with moderately centralized decision making; and Type III, radical, with locally controlled decision making showed more participation in equal amounts. Of the two school constituency organizations, one was an elitist, more militant organization which increased dissatisfaction and alienation with the school and yet made some changes in the educational program. The other was a PTA group which was more representative and which improved school-community communications but made no substantial educational changes. The study found that citizen participation had only marginal impacts in either shaping health and educational policy making or in affecting the attitudinal and behavioral orientation of the participants.

Gerber, Eleanor; Joyce Joseph; Peter Black; and Frank Barnett. *Citizen Participation Groups in San Diego.* San Diego: San Diego Urban Observatory, 1971.

This report develops a six-dimension typology of citizen organizations which focuses on the internal structure and activities of the groups as well as on the groups' external relationships. Using this typology, six issue-oriented case studies are analyzed. Data were gathered from newspapers, documents, and some twenty-five to thirty interviews. The report concludes that city officials expect community groups to keep them informed of "community opinion," but that officials tend to work closely with only one group in a community, often excluding other interests. The groups most often consulted by officials tended to have leaders with "above-average incomes" for their communities and previous ties with city government.

Grossman, Howard J., and Robert A. Cox. "Coordination: Teamwork in a Small Community." *Public Administration Review* 23:1 (March 1963): 35–39.

This is a case study of how the small community of Royersford Borough, Pennsylvania, was able to coordinate the efforts of all levels of government and of voluntary groups to solve community problems. A chronological account is given beginning with the appointment of a local planning commission and a renewal committee. The author then describes their attempts to establish cooperation with first the county, and then with state and federal agencies.

Hall, John P. "The Case Against Citizen Participation: A Suggested Retreat." Paper presented at the Southwestern Political Science Association meeting, Dallas, Texas, March 23, 1973. Mimeograph.

The author of this paper argues that public administrators in the urban environment have been successful in delivering services at the local level without citizen participation. He sees the proper focus of citizen participation as the *political* process rather than the *administrative* process; and he cites examples of agencies' failures in attempting to involve citizens in administrative processes. Thus, the author recommends a "retreat from citizen participation" and a renewed reliance upon the "humanitarian interests" and creativity of professional urban administrators.

Hallman, Howard W. "Federally Financed Citizen Participation." Paper prepared for the National Academy of Public Administration Conference on Crisis, Conflict, and Creativity, Airlie House, Warrenton, Virginia, April 23–25, 1970. Mimeograph. Also appears in *Public Administration Review* 32, special issue (September 1972): 421–27.

Hallman examines the issue of whether federal funds should be used to support citizen participation and if so, how. He discusses the issue by describing participation in four programs: Urban Renewal, the Juvenile Delinquency and Gray Areas Program, the Community Action Program, and Model Cities. He points out that early critics of federal support for citizen participation doubted that community organizers would have enough freedom of action, but he feels that the Community Action Program has done well. He then discusses the conflict between resident participation and coordination which requires different structural arrangements and suggests that two separate organizations may be needed.

Hart, David K. "Theories of Government Related to Decentralization and Citizen Participation." *Public Administration Review* 32, special issue (October 1972): 603–21.

This article reviews literature articulating arguments for and against participatory democracy as a radical alternative to representative democracy. Representative authors and arguments are described. The focus of the article is the question of why people should participate.

Henderson, Hazel. "Information and the New Movement for Citizen Participation." *Annals of the American Academy of Political and Social Science* 412 (March 1974): 34–43.

The author argues that the primary strategy employed by citizen movements has been "to manipulate information and, in turn, to change prevailing views of what is rational." Citizen movements are seen as "social feedback mechanisms" that generate and disseminate information which modifies institutions and values. Additionally, the author discusses the tendency for citizen organizations to seek to maintain their own research capabilities in order to ensure access to information thought to be relevant to the organization.

Hutcheson, John D., Jr. *Citizen Participation in Federally-Sponsored Programs: Perspectives from the Literature.* Washington, D.C.: National Association for Community Development, 1972.

This work discusses the innovations which have encouraged citizen participation in federally sponsored programs. The development of citizen participation in the 1960s is discussed in terms of specific programs: the Delinquency Demonstration Program, the Community Action Program, Model Cities, Urban Renewal, Public Health, and Welfare. The author concludes that the missing ingredients needed for effective citizen participation are a clear and workable legislative mandate for citizen control, concrete guidelines, and definitions of appropriate participants.

Hutcheson, John D., Jr., and Frank X. Steggert. *Organized Citizen Participation in Urban Areas.* Atlanta: Center for Research in Social Change, Emory University, 1970.

Reviews:
Godschalk, David R. *Social Forces* 51 (September 1972): 120.
Jarrett, William H. *Contemporary Sociology* (September 1972): 456–60.

The study reported in this volume was conducted in conjunction with the national network of urban observatories' first national agenda project, the purpose of which was to "clarify and evaluate organized citizen participation in urban areas." The first two chapters are devoted to a review of the literature relevant to an examination of citizen groups and their political activities (a bibliography is included) and to the construction of a conceptual framework to be used in analyses of citizens' organizations and their impacts upon public decision making. Using this systemic framework, several federally sponsored groups (Community Action, Model Cities, and HUD-sponsored housing programs) and three voluntary (self-initiated) groups are examined. The data were gathered through participant-observation, examination of organizational documents, and through extensive interviews (the survey instruments are appended) with organizational leaders, rank-and-file members, and public officials (the "targets" of the organizations' activities).

The data provide little evidence that federally sponsored groups in Atlanta had encouraged community mobilization or that participants in these programs attempted to directly influence city decision making. The analysis of the voluntary or self-initiating groups indicates that the membership characteristics of voluntary groups influence the strategies employed by those groups in attempting to gain access to public decision making and that strategy is an important factor in assessing potential impact. In Atlanta, obtaining the support of an influential "third party" or a "quasi-governmental" agency was found to be a relatively successful strategy.

Kansas City Urban Observatory. *Citizen Participation Groups: A Report to the National Urban Observatory.* Lawrence: Urban Studies Group, University of Kansas, n. d.

A design for the classification of citizen groups, a test of the utility of the design, four case studies of citizen groups, and a cross-indexed bibliography are included in this work. Nine dimensions along which the authors feel citizen organizations may be placed are: membership characteristics, organizational structure, resources, target conditions, target instrumentality, the attitudinal relationship between the group and the instrumentality, the group's mode of action, its relations with other groups, and the beneficiaries of the group's activities. From an analysis of survey data, the authors conclude that membership characteristics (income and education) are "the variables most useful for classifying citizen groups."

Four "successful" citizen groups with differing characteristics are described as "case examples." The success of these groups is attributed to three characteristics which they shared: each had a "dedicated" cadre of active participants; the leaders of the groups made efforts to learn how "the system" works; and the groups' most frequent mode of action was to communicate directly with decision makers.

Kramer, Ralph M., and Harry Specht, eds. *Readings in Community Organization Practice*. Englewood Cliffs, New Jersey: Prentice-Hall, 1969.

This reader contains thirty-five selections focusing on community organization for social change. The readings in Part One describe the context of community organization activities including community analysis and organizational analysis. Part Two describes some of the different processes involved in directed community change including community problem solving, the roles of the professional change agent, the management of conflict, and social planning.

Krefetz, Sharon Perlman, and Allan E. Goodman. "Participation for What or for Whom?" *Journal of Comparative Administration* 5:3 (November 1973): 367–80.

The authors of this article argue that most studies of citizen participation in administrative systems focus either upon the processes as viewed by the participants or analyze the process from the perspective of program administrators. They contend that such studies ignore the interrelationships among participants, programs, and administrators and fail to fully explain the "consequences" of participation.

Landsberger, Henry A. "Maximum Feasible Participation: Working Class and Peasant Movements as a Theoretical Model for the Analysis of Poverty and Race." Paper prepared for the National Academy of Public Administration Conference on Participation of the Poor and Public Administration, Holly Knoll Conference Center, Williamsburg, Virginia, May 21–23, 1970. Mimeograph.

Landsberger describes a number of parallels between the labor movement and the present movement of poor racial and ethnic groups. Some of the parallels identified are: (1) participation of upwardly mobile individuals and apathy on the part of others; (2) leader corruption; (3) leader radicalism; (4) the pattern of relationships with rival and complementary organizations, e.g., factionalism and infighting; and (5) the relationships with established powers.

Lane, Robert E. *Political Life: Why People Get Involved in Politics*. Glencoe, Illinois: Free Press, 1959.

Reviews:
Campbell, A. *Annals of the American Academy of Political and Social Science* 325 (September 1959): 161.

Davies, J. C. *American Political Science Review* 53 (December 1959): 1123.

Kornhauser, W. *American Sociological Review* 24 (December 1959): 913.

Matthews, D. R. *Social Forces* 38 (March 1960): 270.

Schattschneider, E. E. *Political Science Quarterly* 75 (March 1960): 121.

Lane examines data from a number of studies on participation and nonparticipation in politics. Included are analyses of political participation, small groups, community life, content and influence of the media, ethnicity, social class, occupational mobility, and income distribution. A model is presented which links the political behavior of the public, the attitudes and personality qualities relevant to this behavior, and the environmental influences which affect the political participation of the public.

Lipsky, Michael. "Protest as a Political Resource." *American Political Science Review* 62:4 (December 1968): 1144–58. Described in more detail in Lipsky, Michael, *Protest in City Politics*, below.

Using studies of protest groups in a number of different cities, the author develops a conceptual model which illustrates the actors, strategies, and processes involved in protest activity. With this model and the studies of protest groups, the author examines the role of protest leaders and the different strategies that are employed when "relatively powerless groups" engage in protest (defined as a political action oriented toward objection to one or more policies or conditions). The involvement of "third parties" is seen as an essential element in protest strategies.

The author also discusses different methods of reacting to protest activity employed by "target groups" (those groups that the protest activity is designed to influence). The author concludes that protest activity does not produce long-term gains; it can, however, be used for building organizations and gaining bargaining power. Long-term success depends on acquiring stable political resources that do not rely upon the involvement of "third parties."

Lipsky, Michael. *Protest in City Politics: Rent Strikes, Housing and the Power of the Poor.* Chicago: Rand McNally and Company, 1970.

Reviews:

Blake, F. M. *Library Journal* 95 (May 1970): 1750.

Hawley, W. D. *American Political Science Review* 64 (December 1970): 1256.

Novograd, R. J. *Annals of the American Academy of Political and Social Science* 393 (January 1971): 179.

Lowenstein, Edward R. "Citizen Participation and the Administrative Agency in Urban Development: Some Problems and Proposals." *Social Service Review* 45:3 (September 1971): 289–301.

Lowenstein looks at citizen participation from the point of view of the administrative agencies which must organize to accommodate neighborhood people. Their big problem is how to have an efficient program while at the same time incorporating local demands and democratic procedures. Some agencies deal with this situation by manipulating participation to render it ineffective. Other agencies are able to avoid citizen participation entirely. The author makes some recommendations for structuring citizen participation in administrative agencies, including: a negotiated agreement; the structuring of the citizen organization to be representative of, and accountable to, the neighborhood; and the adoption of a belief in citizen participation by the agency.

Lynch, Thomas D., ed. "Neighborhoods and Citizen Involvement: A Public Symposium." *Public Administration Review* 32:3 (May/June 1972): 189–223.

The papers presented at this symposium were somewhat critical of citizen participation and pointed out its limitations. Various aspects of citizen participation were covered. The first paper presents the history of citizen participation in federal government programs and discusses future directions. A paper on citizen participation in metropolitan planning indicates that many metropolitan institutions are irrelevant and thus do not encourage participation. Another subject discussed is how to encourage minority groups to participate. One paper deals with the "new reform" movement which calls for local neighborhood government control over many aspects of life. The role of racism in the quest for citizen participation is raised. Myths and realities of how citizen participation can affect the redistribution of power are discussed. The last paper discusses the role of the academic community as advisor to citizen groups.

The symposium made several recommendations. It recommended that federal legislation provide guidelines that specify the nature of involvement, earmark funds for technical assistance accountable to citizens groups, and confine participation at the metropolitan and regional levels to groups with the power of implementation. It recommends that colleges and universities allow and encourage staff and resources to be involved in the community, offer special degree programs for community people, and establish shared-resource programs with other educational institutions, local officials, and citizen leaders. It is recommended that the American Society for Public Administration encourage better understanding of citizen participation, open itself to community leaders, sponsor a national conference on citizen participation, and draft recommended changes in government programs that would encourage citizen participation.

"A Mini-Symposium: Public Participation in Technology Assessment." *Public Administration Review* 35:1 (January/February 1975): 67–81.

Mogulof, Melvin B. *Citizen Participation: The Local Perspective*. Washington, D.C.: Urban Institute, March 1970.

This study examined seven city- or county-based agencies in the Far West: (1) a neighborhood health services center; (2) a community action agency; (3) an OEO legal services center; (4) a model city agency; (5) a tenants' council; (6) an urban renewal project area committee; and (7) a community mental health center. All were sponsored by one of three agencies: HUD, OEO, or HEW. The projects are described in terms of categories rather than as case studies. The categories are: (1) representation; (2) participation; (3) decision making; (4) relationships with other agencies; (5) aspects of minority community development; and (6) relationship with the federal government. The study found that two factors were significant in determining whether or not an agency had realized the full potential of citizen participation, the character of the minority population and the advocacy behavior of the federal and local staff. The author points out that all the projects had citizen participation because of national policy mandates, but that local factors determined the degree of citizen participation that ultimately occurred.

Mogulof, Melvin B. *Citizen Participation: A Review and Commentary on Federal Policies and Practices*. Washington, D.C.: Urban Institute, 1970.

Mollenkopf, John H. "On the Causes and Consequences of Neighborhood Political Mobilization." Paper prepared for the American Political Science Association meeting, New Orleans, Louisiana, September 8, 1973. Mimeograph.

Nie, Norman H.; G. Bingham Powell, Jr.; and Kenneth Prewitt. "Social Structure and Political Participation: Developmental Relationships, Part I," *American Political Science Review* 63:2 (June 1969): 361–78; "Part II," *American Political Science Review* 63:3 (September 1969): 808–32.

Using data from the five-nation study conducted by Almond and Verba (see Almond, Gabriel A., and Sidney Verba, *The Civic Culture,* above), the authors employ path analysis in attempting to "identify the significant social experiences which explain the growth of political participation in economically advanced nations." In "Part II," the relationships between organizational membership, social status, and several different attitudinal dimensions are explored in depth.

Palay, Miriam G. *Citizen Participation: Issues and Groups, Milwaukee, 1969.* Milwaukee: Milwaukee Urban Observatory, 1972.

Sponsored under the auspices of the urban observatories' first national agenda project, this study analyzes three issue-oriented case studies using the systems framework suggested in the Atlanta study (see Hutcheson, John D., Jr., and Frank X. Steggert, *Organized Citizen Participation in Urban Areas,* above). The issues, selected on the basis of newspaper content analysis and interviews with "knowledgeables," involved low-income housing, the construction of a freeway, and citizen participation in Milwaukee's model cities program. Interviews with group members and public officials were conducted in conjunction with the case studies, and an inventory of existing groups in Milwaukee was classified by type of origin (federally or locally sponsored or self-initiating).

Among the most important conclusions drawn from this study are: (1) self-initiating groups have the highest potential for becoming politically active; (2) the geographical areas most likely to generate "issue-active" groups are areas of the city in the "path of social change"; (3) organizations based on race or community interest are the most active; (4) citizen participation seems to be accepted by public officials as part of the decision-making process; (5) citizen group activities (in the three case studies) seemed to have some effect on changes in officials' positions; and (6) group spokesmen claimed some positive impact on policy, but were not totally satisfied with government responses.

"Participation, Culture, and Personality." *Journal of Social Issues* 5:1 (1949): entire issue.

The first article in this issue is "How Participation Works" by Burt Alpert and Patricia A. Smith. They define participation as a process of destructuring and restructuring which demands the merger and operation of emotion and intellect in the definition, discussion, and action stages. Two types of participation which are identified are formalistic (intellectual but unemotional) and anarchic (emotional but unanalytic). "The Roots of Formalism" by Morris Rosenberg looks at how cultural influences and pressures produce personality structures which lead to formalistic participation. In "Education, Culture, and the Anarchic Worker," Seymour Bellin and Frank Riessman explore what democratic organizations can do in changing behaviors which inhibit participation.

S. M. Miller, in an article entitled "Planning for Participation," writes that productive planning requires participation in formulating plans and working them out. Two-way communication between leaders and members is needed. Various functional forms are suggested for facilitating two-way communication. In "Role Playing as a Participation Technique," Bruce F. Young and Morris Rosenberg describe role playing techniques that could encourage participative behavior. "An Approach to Constructive Leadership," by Sol Levine, describes four types of leadership: charismatic, organizational, intellectual, and informal and how culturally prescribed roles affect these leadership styles. He discusses how roles can be redefined and efforts redirected to encourage more participation.

Report on Citizen Participation in Local Government in the United States. DeKalb: Center for Governmental Studies, Northern Illinois University, 1971. Mimeograph.

This report is an attempt to summarize "what is known about political participation in American local government." The major forms of citizen activity are described and an attempt is made to estimate the proportion of the population which engages in each form. Differences between active and inactive citizens are then described, and demographic and attitudinal correlates of participation are reviewed. The final section describes some of the newer measures adopted by city governments attempting to facilitate increased citizen participation.

Riessman, Frank, and Alan Gartner. "Community Control and Radical Social Change." *Social Policy* 1:1 (May/June 1970): 52–55.

The authors discuss the "goals" of community control and focus on the goal of "changing, redesigning and improving the human services." The authors stress that community control could have different effects in different situations. It could become sociotherapy, or participation for its own sake, or it could increase the accountability of professionals in human service agencies. The authors suggest that if the "dangers" of community control are to be overcome and if it is to produce "radical social change," the movement for community control must escalate its demands, avoid localism, patronage, sociotherapy, and accountability without productivity and develop "an ideology aimed toward the transformation of power and the elimination of basic inequity."

Rothschild, Joan A. "The Role of Alternative Groups in Creating Democratic, Community-Controlled Local Government: Some Thoughts for Further Study." Paper prepared for the American Political Science Association meeting, Chicago, Illinois, August 29–September 2, 1974. Mimeograph.

Rothschild defines alternative groups as "those groups or institutions that have a commitment to member participation and member control of decision and policy making." The ways such groups "may be building-blocks for creating democratic and community-controlled local governments" are discussed and problems which alternative groups might experience are identified.

Rourke, Francis E., ed. *Bureaucratic Power in National Politics.* 2d ed. Boston: Little, Brown, 1972.

The readings in this book focus on how bureaucratic organizations influence public policy. Part Seven, entitled "Citizen Participation in Bureaucracy," contains three selections on the subject. Herbert Kaufman discusses administrative decentralization. Gideon Sjoberg, Richard A. Brymer, and Buford Farris look at the impact of client-centered bureaucracy upon the lower class; and Francis Fox Piven discusses the organization of white middle class civil servants in New York City which seems to pit them against poor blacks and Puerto Ricans.

Rubin, Morton. *Organized Citizen Participation in Boston.* Boston: Boston Urban Observatory, 1971.

This report on citizen organizations in Boston relies upon city documents, newspaper reports, and organizations' materials supplemented by field interviews and observations. A history of organized citizen participation in Boston precedes a review of federally sponsored mechanisms and an analysis of five case studies.

The author concludes that most citizen participation in Boston, in 1969 and 1970, was "token" participation. Some degree of conflict was evident in all of the case studies, leading the author to conclude that "conflict may be essential for fundamental change," and that third parties, acting as advocates, increase the prospects for resolution of such conflict. The process of citizen participation, on the basis of these case studies, is characterized as "episodic," progressing through stages of organization, confrontation, and resolution. Also included are a description of aspects of municipal service delivery systems and a review of the recommendations of the Boston Home Rule Commission which were designed to make decision making more responsive.

Schumaker, Paul D. "Policy Responsiveness to Protest-Group Behavior." *Journal of Politics* 34:2 (May 1975): 488–521.

Defining protest groups as groups "who do not normally interact with governmental officials, but who, under certain conditions . . . organize on an informal, issue-specific basis to make demands on public officials through pressure processes," Schumaker attempts to discern if local political systems are normally responsive to these groups' demands and under what conditions local political systems are most responsive to such demands. Ninety-three case studies of protest activity were examined and 119 mailed questionnaires returned by city government officials were used in the analysis. The author concludes that nonmilitancy in general may enhance policy responsiveness and that some protest groups might profitably appeal directly to protest targets rather than through "third parties" acting as intermediaries between the group and the group's target.

Seeman, Melvin; James M. Bishop; and J. Eugene Grigsby III. "Community and Control in a Metropolitan Setting." *Race, Change, and Urban Society*. Edited by Peter Orleans and William Russell Ellis, Jr. Beverly Hills, California: Sage Publications, 1973, pp. 423–50.

Shelton, Donn. *Regional Citizenship*. Detroit: Metropolitan Fund, 1972.

Chapter 3 of this book discusses citizen participation in regional government. The author believes that there is a need for a mechanism for regional citizen participation and that regional advocacy could be a preliminary form of citizen participation. Ten case studies of metropolitan areas where regional participation and/or advocacy has been taking place are presented: St. Louis, Washington, D.C., Minneapolis-St. Paul, New York City, Seattle, Dallas, Los Angeles, San Francisco, Philadelphia, and cities in southeast Michigan. There is also a discussion of neighborhood government vis-à-vis the regional concept and how the two can complement each other.

Spergel, Irving A., ed. *Community Organizations: Studies in Constraint.* Beverly Hills, California: Sage Publications, 1972.

This book is a collection of nine essays with editorial introductions to sections entitled: "The Structural Context"; "Organizational Strategy and Activity"; and "The Politics of Research." The chapters in the first section focus on the political and social environments which affect community organization. The articles in the second section focus on the strategies employed by community organizations in three different cities, and the third section focuses on community research because "distinctions between research and action become blurred in a community problem-solving process."

Steggert, Frank X. "Community Action Groups and City Governments." Paper prepared for the National Conference of the American Society for Public Administration, Los Angeles, California, April 1–4, 1973. Mimeograph. A summary of the following citation.

Steggert, Frank X. *Community Action Groups and City Governments: Perspectives from Ten American Cities.* Cambridge, Massachusetts: Ballinger, 1975.

Steggert describes some of the findings of the urban observatories' studies conducted under the sponsorship of the first national agenda project and uses some supplemental information from the Urban Observatory Program's Citizen Attitude Survey. All kinds of citizen groups (government-sponsored and self-initiating) attempting to influence local governments (in the Urban Observatory Network's ten cities) were included in the analyses. Group participation rates in the ten cities ranged from 6 to 19 percent of the cities' populations; in most cities membership averaged 13 or 14 percent. Upper class citizens were more likely to participate, while the differences between black and white participation rates were minimal. Long-term residents were found to be more frequently members of groups than relative newcomers. Group membership was also found to be positively correlated with political efficacy.

In most of the cities in the Urban Observatory Network, the issues which most often activated citizen organizations were housing, freeway construction, race relations, taxation and revenue, education, and public welfare. During the interviews conducted by researchers working on this project, race relations often seemed to permeate the discussions—"race relations was a fundamental theme around which a number of other issues revolved." In most cities, administrators and politicians seemed to agree that the concept of citizen participation was good, but that it had certain practical limitations and that elected officials should have final decision-making responsibility. However, the studies do seem to indicate that citizen groups can be effective, particularly if the group has a dedicated leadership cadre within a larger general membership structure.

Steinbacher, Roberta, and Phyllis Solomon. *Client Participation in Service Organization*. Cleveland: Cleveland Urban Observatory, 1971.

The purpose of this study, one of the studies conducted under the auspices of the 1970–1971 National Urban Observatory Agenda Project, was "to examine the characteristics of community residents participating in community groups and to determine the effectiveness of these organizations in relating to community needs." Survey data from the Mount Pleasant area of Cleveland were used in conjunction with other data in order to examine and assess the activities of four organizations in the area. Home ownership and length of residency were found to be positively related to participation, and effectiveness was shown to be related to goal definition and funding.

On the basis of the data from the study of the organizations in Mount Pleasant, the authors construct three "outlines" which consist of descriptions of groups with different organizational goals. These "outlines," the authors feel, can be used by community groups as organizational guidelines.

Stenberg, Carl W. "The History and Future of Citizen Participation: An Overview." Paper presented at the National Conference on Public Administration, Denver, Colorado, April 19, 1971. Mimeograph. Later published as "Citizens and the Administrative State: From Participation to Power." *Public Administration Review* 32:3 (May/June 1972): 190–98.

This paper divides the historical development of citizen participation into three phases: 1949–1963, when nonindigenous citizens acted as advisors but actually had little input; 1964–1968, when indigenous citizens began to become involved in policy making; and 1969–1971, when regionalism and decentralization became issues. The author sees trends in the 1970s as characterized by traditional forms of citizen involvement on the federal level and community control and neighborhood government on the local level. He points out that public administrators will have to adapt to citizen participation.

Strange, John H. "The Impact of Citizen Participation on Public Administration." *Public Administration Review* 32, special issue (September
1972): 457–70.

Strange traces the development of citizen participation from the
revolutionary period through the creation of citizen participation mechanisms in community action and model cities agencies. Emphasizing the
OEO and model cities experiences, the author considers various interpretations of the federal mandates for participation and different problems in
implementing these federal policies. The author then assesses the impact of
participation upon: the participants, the program, and the community.

It is likely, the author feels, that involvement increased hopes for more
government assistance and helped participants learn more about government activities and operations. On the other hand, participation caused
conflict within programs and delays and "forced policy makers to deal with
the problems of race." Additionally, the author points out that participation, in some cases, had negative effects upon planning and coordination,
while participation often led to the employment of more minority group
members. Finally, it is argued that participation broadened the leadership
structure in low income communities and had "important symbolic meaning to minority group communities." The author concludes that citizen
participation can help attain the objectives of programs like community
action and model cities, but he points out that adequate funding is also
necessary.

"Symposium on Alienation, Decentralization, and Participation." *Public
Administration Review* 29:1 (January/February 1969): 2–63.

This symposium consists of six articles on participatory administration. Herbert Kaufman discusses problems, solutions, and trends in making
administrative agencies more representative. S. M. Miller and Martin Rien
describe the process and problems of maximum feasible participation under
the Economic Opportunity Act of 1964 and its effects on agencies. Michael
P. Smith examines the extent to which bureaucratic environment inhibits
the individual's self-fulfillment, starting with a discussion of the philosophy
of French existentialist Gabriel Marcel. Orion F. White, Jr., presents a case
study of a small clientele-centered, nonbureaucratic organization and
suggests this model as a solution to the problem of poor client-agency
relations. William G. Scott discusses managerial ideologies, presents a
proposal for representative government in organizations, and concludes
that chances for the implementation of such a proposal are not good.
Herbert G. Wilcox explores the subject of hierarchy in human organization
and warns that it cannot be easily disregarded.

Thurz, Daniel. "Community Participation: Should the Past Be Prologue?" *American Behavioral Scientist* 15:5 (May/June 1972): 733–48.

The author first presents some rationales for supporting community participation: to arrest the increasing degree of anomie in urban centers; as a solution for problems of the poor; and as a hedge against growth of centralized government and national business conglomerates. He then goes on to assess the state of citizen participation. He bemoans the substitution of politics for research in government programs. He criticizes neighborhood groups as narrow and self-serving and discusses the issue of the legitimacy of groups. He predicts a decline in such groups and a turn toward traditional political practices and the ballot box.

United States Department of Housing and Urban Development. *Citizen Participation Today: Proceedings of a Staff Conference.* Region 4, Chicago, June 3–4, 1968. Washington, D.C.: U.S. Government Printing Office, 1968.

The three major speakers at this conference addressed themselves to different aspects of citizen participation. Francis D. Fisher maintained that citizen participation experiences should be shared. Morris Janowitz argued that there is a need to clarify the goals of citizen participation. James Banks discussed alienation and the role of citizen participation in establishing linkages between people. A panel of two militant leaders and four agency staff persons discussed the citizen participation situations in which they were involved. These case studies are contained in an appendix and include code enforcement in East Cleveland, urban renewal in Detroit, low rent housing in Cincinnati, FHA in Milwaukee, model cities in East St. Louis, and urban renewal in Minneapolis.

United States Senate. Committee on Governmental Operations. Intergovernmental Relations Subcommittee. *Confidence and Concern: Citizens View American Government.* Parts 1–2. Washington, D.C.: U.S. Government Printing Office, 1973.

These documents report the findings of a survey conducted in 1973 by Louis Harris and Associates for the Subcommittee on Intergovernmental Relations. Part One includes narrative interpretations of the data and explanations of survey methodology. Part Two presents cross-tabulations of the responses with demographic characteristics. Chapter 2 of Part One, "Public Involvement in Government," deals, in part, with participation in citizen organizations and perceptions of their influence in governmental decision-making processes.

United States Senate. Committee on the Judiciary. *Responses to Question-naires on Citizen Involvement and Responsive Agency Decision-Making*. Vols. 2, 3. Washington, D.C.: U.S. Government Printing Office, 1971.

These two volumes present survey data obtained by sending question-naires to all heads of executive and independent agencies in the federal government concerning public knowledge of and participation in the processes of the agency and the responses of the agencies. The questionnaire asks each agency to document citizen involvement, citizen contact, and its own responsiveness to citizens.

Verba, Sidney, and Norman H. Nie. "The Organizational Context of Political Participation." *Participation in America: Political Democracy and Social Equality*. New York: Harper and Row, 1972, pp. 174–208.

In Chapter 11 of Verba and Nie's comprehensive study of participation in American political life, the authors consider how organizational involvement affects political activity and how organizations affect the levels of political activity among different status groups. National survey data (1967) are used to describe patterns of organizational affiliation and how organizations participate in politics. Relationships between socioeconomic status, organizational affiliation and activity, and different types of political participation are examined.

The authors conclude that organizational affiliation does increase political activity, and because persons of higher socioeconomic levels are more likely to be affiliated with organizations, organizations increase the gap between the levels of political participation among lower and higher status groups. But Verba and Nie point out that this situation could be changed, noting that "in countries where disadvantaged groups have a better organizational base . . . organizational affiliation and activity do not exacerbate participation inequalities. . . ." Thus, organizations in the United States are viewed as "potential" resources that could be employed in reducing the participation gap between different socioeconomic groups.

Verba, Sidney; Norman Nie; and Jae-on Kim. *The Modes of Democratic Participation: A Cross-National Comparison*. Beverly Hills, California: Sage Publications, 1971.

Four "modes of participation," including "cooperative activity"—participation either in informal groups or in formal organizations—are discussed. Using data from Austria, India, Japan, Nigeria, and the United States, the analysis includes an examination of the relationships between different types of political participation and factor analyses which reveal a "particular set of theoretically relevant modes" of participation. The authors conclude that different modes of participation "have different capacities to carry messages to political leaders and to produce results for the participant."

Weissman, Harold H. *Community Councils and Community Control: The Workings of Democratic Mythology.* Pittsburgh: University of Pittsburgh Press, 1970.

   Weissman attempts to refute the "process" model of community organizations which postulates that if organizational goals are not achieved, it is because the correct process was not followed. As an alternative, the author presents an "exchange" model which views individuals and groups as investing resources in a community organization in order to obtain rewards. The exchange model is used by the author in a case study of a community council which he calls the DuPont Community Council. He chose this council for study because of its longevity and success and because of its location in a "melting pot" urban neighborhood. Data were gathered through interviews with council participants and by observation of the council and the neighborhood. This was done, for the most part, in 1962 and 1963.
   The first section of the book describes the neighborhood and the council, explains the exchange model, and also discusses the "process" model of neighborhood organizations. The second section describes the council in terms of the exchange model. The third section looks at the exchange model and its contribution to practice problems in the field. The epilogue looks at the council five years after the study when "community control" had become an issue in the city. Appendices contain a summary of the utility of the exchange model, an interview schedule for council participants, an outline for field participation, a workers' log, and a description of research procedures.

Wilson, James Q. "The Strategy of Protest: Problems of Negro Civic Action." *Journal of Conflict Resolution* 5:3 (September 1961): 291–303.

   The dilemmas of Negro protest action are discussed in this article. Protest is seen as a process through which powerless groups attempt to bargain with powerful groups. The author points out that powerless groups, such as Negroes, have nothing to bargain with, except withholding disruption. Thus, the author defines protest as the exclusive use of negative inducements (threats) that rely on mass action.

The author then discusses some of the reasons for the relative lack of Negro protest in the North in the 1950s, stressing the lack of resources with which Negroes could bargain. Further, he notes that protest in the 1950s, in the North, did not seem aimed at changing public policy; but it did seem to result in Negroes' becoming the objects of concern to others. The lack of Negro protest in the North, then, was attributable to the "nature of the ends sought, the diffusion of relevant targets, the differentiation of the Negro community along class lines, and the organizational constraints placed on Negroes as they enter into partial contact with the white community."

Wood, Robert C. *Suburbia: Its People and Their Politics.* Boston: Houghton Mifflin, 1959.

> Reviews:
> *Booklist* 55 (February 15, 1959): 304.
> Christman, H. M. *Saturday Review* 42 (February 7, 1959): 37.
> Claiborne, Robert. *Nation* 188 (March 21, 1959): 256.
> Cole, I. W. *Chicago Sunday Tribune* (January 18, 1959): 2.
> Foell, E. W. *Christian Science Monitor* (January 29, 1959): 5.
> Key, V. O. *Yale Review* 48 (March 1959): 403.
> *Kirkus* 26 (November 1, 1958): 843.
> Malone, R. M. *Library Journal* 83 (December 1958): 3522.
> Salisbury, H. E. *New York Times* (January 25, 1959): 5.
> Truman, D. B. *American Political Science Review* 53 (September 1959): 824.
> Weinberger, C. W. *San Francisco Chronicle* (February 22, 1959): 14.

This critique of the American suburb looks at suburban political ideology, its history, values, and consequences. The author is especially struck by the suburban resistance to twentieth-century ideals and values and the fact that suburbanites look to the past for guidance. In Chapter 5, "The Politics of Suburbia," the author deals with the subject of citizen participation. He found that more and more technical functions of suburban government were being handled by bureaucrats and technocrats while popular participation was being limited to the most important local issues— honesty, taxes, and land development. He feels that opinions may become so inbred that the suburbs will come to be "grass roots government run by automation."

Yin, Robert K., and William A. Lucas. "Decentralization and Alienation."
Policy Sciences 4:3 (September 1973): 327–36.

Three forms of decentralization are discussed in terms of their impact on citizen alienation: outreach programs, administrative decentralization, and the development of alternative institutions. Available empirical evidence on the correlates of alienation is reviewed. Three ways in which decentralization might reduce alienation are considered: through increased control over and knowledge about government, through awareness that control is in local hands, and through improved services. No evidence was found to support the theory that decentralization reduces political alienation.

Yin, Robert K.; William A. Lucas; Peter L. Szanton; and J. Andrew Spindler.
Citizen Organizations: Increasing Client Control Over Services. Santa Monica, California: The Rand Corporation, 1973.

The purpose of this study, originally prepared for the Department of Health, Education and Welfare, was "to investigate policy options for citizen participation in the Department of Health, Education and Welfare." Citizen participation is viewed as a part of administrative reform attempting to decentralize programmatic decision making. Thus, the study focuses upon client participation in HEW service delivery systems. In order to serve "an immediate decision-making need," the study relied, for the most part, on an assessment of prior research on citizen participation. (A bibliography of works consulted is appended.) Fifty-one case studies of citizen participation were analyzed using a "checklist methodology," described in an appendix.

Different forms of participation are discussed and evaluated in terms of their potential for adoption by HEW. The authors conclude that "service-linked citizen organizations" are the participatory mechanisms most likely to accomplish decentralization within HEW service delivery systems, and the creation of such mechanisms is within the scope of HEW's authority. The authors then attempt to identify those characteristics of "service-linked citizen organizations" that seem to offer the most potential for accomplishing HEW's objectives of "devolving power, reducing alienation, and improving program effectiveness." A general model for citizen organizations to be formed in HEW is recommended. The "citizen-dominated boards" should have the "following principal characteristics: citizen members are elected, other citizen and community organizations are represented, resources sufficient to support a staff reporting directly to the boards are provided, and each board's formal authority includes at least the power to influence substantially the service program's budget and to investigate citizen complaints." The authors then illustrate how their general model could be applied in six different HEW programs.

Zuzak, Charles A.; Kenneth E. McNeil; and Frederick Bergerson. *Beyond the Ballot: Organized Citizen Participation in Metropolitan Nashville.* Nashville: Urban Observatory of Metropolitan Nashville, 1971.

This study examines the activities of nine citizens groups selected on the basis of a media analysis. Federally and locally sponsored groups as well as voluntary or self-initiating groups were included. Organizational documents, newspaper reports, and over two hundred interviews were used in compiling the information for the report.

Case studies of three citizen groups are used to illustrate a ten-stage "process model for explaining arenas of organized citizen participation." The activities of the remaining six groups are described in order to illustrate "citizen participation problems."

Dissertations

Agger, R. E. "The Dynamics of Local Political Participation." Ph.D., University of Oregon, 1954. (Order no. not available) 244 pp.

Brownlee, Thomas McCue. "Political Participation: Perceptions, Purposes, and the Effects." Ph.D., University of Washington, 1971. (Order no. 72–15,072) 191 pp.

Buckholz, Marjorie Harret. "The Consequences of Co-optation Between a Governmental Body and Civic Groups." Ph.D., New York University, 1967. (Order no. 68–6044) 183 pp.

Chitwood, Stephen Reed. "Group Problem Solving in the Metropolitan Community." Ph.D., University of Southern California, 1966. (Order no. 67–2104) 759 pp.

Clute, William Thomas. "Community Involvement and Associational Participation in a Racially Mixed Urban Area." Ph.D., University of Minnesota, 1969. (Order no. 70–15,714) 453 pp.

Fraser, Stephen Arnsdoff. "Citizen Participation in Decision-Making by Federal Agencies: Selective Service System, Bureau of Land Management, Department of Housing and Urban Development." Ph.D., Johns Hopkins University, 1969. (Order no. 69–21,090) 398 pp.

Grigsby, Jefferson Eugene, III. "Community Analysis: Implications for Citizen Participation." Ph.D., University of California, Los Angeles, 1971. (Order no. 75–5833) 205 pp.

Grossman, Laurence Elliott. "Social Action Ideology and Organizing: A

Comparative Study of Problems and the Criteria for Their Solution in Twenty Social Action Oriented Organizing Projects." Ph.D., Columbia University, 1968. (Order no. 72–0317) 230 pp.

Harris, Marim M. "The Extent, Pattern, and Perceived Effectiveness of Citizen Participation in Decision-Making Under Two Different Types of Power Structures." Ed.D., University of Florida, 1967. (Order no. 68–9474) 167 pp.

James, Leonard Danielson. "Democratic Patterns of Political Participation: The Ideal and the Real." Ph.D., University of Minnesota, 1971. (Order no. 72–345) 270 pp.

Lipsky, Michael. "Rent Strikes in New York City: Protest Politics and the Power of the Poor." Ph.D., Princeton University, 1967. (Order no. 68–02496) 294 pp.

Maccoby, Herbert Henry. "The Relationship Between Participation in the Self-Help Association and Participation in Political Activity." Ph.D., Columbia University, 1965. (Publication no. 13,982; Mic 55–930) 209 pp.

McCall, Charles Herman, Jr. "Paths to Political Participation." Ph.D., Yale University, 1965. (Order no. 65–15,065) 270 pp.

McFatter, William Thomas, Jr. "The Degree, Level, Pattern, and Efficacy of Citizen Participation in Policy Matters Under Different Types of Community Power Structures." Ed.D., University of Florida, 1970. (Order no. 71–12,765) 128 pp.

Nie, Norman Hugh. "Citizen Participators: A Study of the Dimensions of Popular Participation in American Society." Ph.D., Stanford University, 1971. (Order no. 71–23,540) 341 pp.

Riccards, Michael P. "The Concept of Participatory Citizenship: Its Philosophical Background and Systematic Importance." Ph.D., Rutgers—The State University of New Jersey, 1970. (Order no. 71–3095) 197pp.

Richert, Robert Benjamin. "Participation of Citizens in Advisory Committees and Administrative Boards: Selected Michigan Cities." Ph.D., University of Michigan, 1954. (Publication no. 8400; Mic 54–1834) 391 pp.

Robbins, Jane Borsch. "Policy Formation in American Public Libraries: Effects of Citizen Participation." Ph.D., University of Maryland, 1972. (Order no. 73–17,049) 215 pp.

Russell, James Kent. "Analyzing Political Concepts: The Case of Participation." Ph.D., University of Iowa, 1972. (Order no. 73–682) 368 pp.

Sakolsky, Ronald B. "Two Case Studies in the 'Safety Valve' Approach to Citizen Participation." Ph.D., New York University, 1970. (Order no. 71–15,426) 281 pp.

3

Citizen Groups in
Planning and Community Development

The recognition of social disorder and unrest on the domestic scene reflected in national politics after the Korean War stimulated various theoretical explanations for social problems. These theoretical explanations formed the rationale for numerous government programs. The President's Committee on Juvenile Delinquency adhered to the theory that one of the major causes of delinquency was the disintegrated social fabric of communities and that delinquency would decrease with the regeneration of community structures. The ideology implicit in the Community Action Program was similar—that social ills in deprived areas were attributable, at least in part, to the disintegration of the social fabric of those areas. Thus, the Delinquency Demonstration Project, the Community Action Program, and a number of other federally sponsored programs prescribed "community mobilization," "community development," or "community organization" as remedies for various social ills. The formation of citizen groups, sponsored and, in some cases, supported by these programs, sought to facilitate the participation of target populations in decision making within the local administrative structures of such programs and sought to develop community leadership and encourage social and political organization in the target communities.

In other federal community development programs, such as Urban Renewal, where the emphasis was upon the physical development of communities, citizen participation had been required much earlier. The Housing Act of 1954 required citizen participation as a part of the "workable program for community development," necessary for receiving federal funds. Most cities responded to the Housing Act of 1954 by establishing citywide citizen advisory committees made up of "leading citizens." There was little or no representation from the neighborhoods most directly affected by urban renewal. By the mid-1960s, however, the example of other federally sponsored programs encouraged the inclusion of participants from areas directly affected by the program. However, the focus of this participation was upon attempting to influence decision making within the structures of local urban renewal agencies rather than upon efforts to mobilize or organize target communities.

Concurrently, planning agencies and professional planners began to recognize the desirability and utility of obtaining information and impressions from residents of communities potentially affected by their activities. The concept of advocacy planning evolved from this recognition and many planners have encouraged and practiced different forms of more direct citizen involvement in planning, participatory planning. Where participatory planning is practiced in specific, geographically defined areas, it has been referred to as neighborhood or community planning.

The objectives of all of these efforts have been similar—to involve residents in social and physical development decision making which may affect their communities. This chapter includes literature which is concerned with such efforts. It is divided into six sections. The items in the first section deal with efforts to involve citizens and citizen groups in planning. Even though all works dealing with advocacy and participatory planning are not included, references to many of the major recent theoretical and empirical studies concerning advocacy and participatory planning may be found in this section. The second section includes references to materials focusing upon citizen participation in community development in general, community development corporations, and references to materials which deal with two or more federally sponsored community development programs. The following four sections include references to items that concern citizen group involvement in specific federally sponsored community development efforts: Urban Renewal, Juvenile Delinquency, Community Action, and Model Cities.

PLANNING

Aleshire, Robert A. "Planning and Citizen Participation: Cost, Benefits, and Approaches." *Urban Affairs Quarterly* 5:4 (June 1970): 369–93.

Examining the relative costs and benefits of citizen participation in planning, the author sees the costs chiefly in terms of the increased complexity and difficulty of the planning process. Citizen participation makes planning more costly and more time consuming. The benefits that accrue are seen in terms of democratic influence on issues and priorities. Two planning approaches are identified: citizen participation as a part of planning, and planning as a part of citizen participation. Reflecting upon the advantages and disadvantages of citizen participation in planning, the author calls for increased participation in planning processes.

American Society of Planning Officials. "Citizens Planning Groups." ASPO
    Planning Advisory Service Report no. 149. Chicago, August 1961.

This is an attempt to describe the many functions and activities of
citizens planning groups. The article discusses both the potential and the
disadvantages of these groups with reference to the four phases of the
planning process: formulation of goals, studies, plan preparation, and plan
implementation. Four case studies are presented which illustrate particular
problems which may arise from the participation of citizens groups in
planning. The article concludes that planning has become an established
function and that citizens must have input. It says that two types of citizens
planning groups are needed—one made up of community influentials to give
advice and support and one which also includes a wide range of citizens
representing a cross section of the community.

American Society of Planning Officials. "The Planning Agency and the
    Black Community: A Workshop Report." ASPO Planning Advisory
    Service Report no. 274. Chicago, November 1971.

This report is divided into four sections. The first is an introduction by
Frank S. So entitled "The Planning Agency and the Black Community: An
Overview of the Workshop," in which the objective of the workshop is
described. The objective was to offer help to the planning agency as it tries
to improve its relationship with the black community, assuming that the
planning agency rather than the black community is the cause of problems.
    The second section is a paper by Charles C. Allen, "The View from the
Black Community." Allen asserts that the ghetto is a result of the failure of
planning caused by inherent institutional racism in the planning process.
The next section is a paper by Malcolm D. Rivkin called "Adapting
Techniques of Planning to Serve a Fragmented Society: Where Does
Importance Lie?" in which he claims that the real issue is ineffective service
to the many diverse groups within our society, not merely to ghetto
residents. The last paper is "Black Participation in Planning Decision-
Making" by Jack Meltzer. He discusses the role of public planning and the
involvement of active citizens planning groups within the black community.

Barnett, Jonathan. *Urban Design as Public Policy: Practical Methods for
    Improving Cities.* New York: Architectural Record, 1974.

The author presents specific methods for dealing with a number of
urban and environmental problems. Chapter 4 is concerned with neighborhood planning and community participation. The efforts of the author and

his associates to plan with citizens in New York City are described. The author found that the involvement of the community was real but that the city and state governments had trouble responding. He feels that community participation could be most effective if the neighborhood was the unit of government serving target communities.

Batley, Richard. "An Explanation of Non-Participation in Planning." *Policy and Politics* 1 (December 1972): 95–114.

Blecher, Earl M. *Advocacy Planning for Urban Development: With Analyses of Six Demonstration Programs.* New York: Praeger, 1971.

The study reported in this book was conducted by Kirschner Associates and presents a comparative analysis of six demonstration programs in advocacy planning which received funds from the Housing Branch of the Office of Economic Opportunity. The six programs examined were: (1) Architects' Renewal Committee in Harlem (New York City); (2) Community Design Center (San Francisco); (3) Urban Planning Aid (Cambridge, Massachusetts); (4) Model Neighborhood Board (Boston); (5) East Oakland-Fruitvale Planning Council (Oakland, California); and (6) Irish Channel Action Foundation (New Orleans). Data were collected from individual field reports, OEO memoranda, articles and books related to the topic, and interviews with key officials and field investigators. Three program models were developed from the six programs: A, a combination of expert staff and autonomous relationships; B, a combination of nonexpert staff and administrative control by clients; and C, a combination of expert staff and administrative control by clients and organizational executives. Each of these produced different organizational processes. Model A was found to have resulted in viable organizational vehicles, while B and C resulted in internal organizational conflict which detracted from building such vehicles.

Brown, Lance Jay, and Dorothy E. Whiteman. *Planning and Design Workshop for Community Participation: An Evaluative Report.* (Princeton, New Jersey: School of Architecture and Urban Planning, Princeton University, 1973.

"The City Tells Its Story: CLIC Works for Minneapolis—Citizens Help and the City Progresses." *American City* 77:11 (November 1962): 164ff.

CLIC is the City Council's Capital Long-Range Improvement Committee in Minneapolis. It is composed of nineteen citizens from labor, business, government, and the League of Women Voters. This article describes how CLIC works and discusses the advantages of citizen participation in long-range planning. It also describes how CLIC has sparked other citizen action in Minneapolis.

Clavel, Pierre. "Planners and Citizen Boards: Some Applications of Social Theory to the Problem of Plan Implementation." *Journal of the American Institute of Planners* 34:3 (May 1968): 130–39.

Cleaveland, James R. "Planning vs. Participation." *New Generation* 51 (Summer 1969): 27–31.

Cleaveland argues that if the community attempts to "insert itself into every operating decision," government would come to a "standstill." Other arguments against community control are presented.

Davidoff, Paul. "Advocacy and Pluralism in Planning." *Journal of the American Institute of Planners* 31:4 (November 1965): 331–38.

The author introduces the idea of planners acting as advocates of the interests of government and other groups. He believes that planning cannot come from neutral values because it must be based on desired objectives. To further democratic government, he urges citizen participation in planning. Citizen groups and other interests would each have their own advocate planner who would submit plans representing their interests.

Davidoff, Paul; Linda Davidoff; and Neil Newton Gold. "Suburban Action: Advocate Planning for an Open Society." *Journal of the American Institute of Planners* 36:1 (January 1970): 12–21.

Suburban Action, an advocate agency which is attempting to facilitate the use of suburban resources in solving urban problems, is described. It is engaged in formal and informal actions attempting to open up the suburban job and housing markets to people of low and moderate income. The group is located in Westchester County, New York; its programs concerning housing, employment, taxes, land use, and zoning are described.

Earnest, L. E. "Citizen Involvement in Community Planning and Implementation." Paper prepared for the Summer Institute on Urban Problems, State University of New York, Brockport, August 4, 1969. Mimeograph.

This paper describes the participation of various community groups in community planning processes in San Diego. Seventeen groups, representing different sectors of the city, were given "official recognition" by the city, and the author describes their formation, the process through which these groups develop community plans, and how the community plans influence the city planning commission's modification of the citywide plan.

Evans, Bernard. "Planning Aid as a Social Service." *Built Environment* 2:1 (January 1973): 47–48.

Fagence, Michael T. "The Design and Use of Questionnaires for Participation Practices in Town Planning—Lessons from the United States and Britain." *Policy Sciences* 5:3 (September 1974): 297–308.

Fagence discusses the use of questionnaires as mechanisms for facilitating citizen participation in planning. Several examples are used for illustrative purposes, and a number of suggestions for increasing the utility of the technique are made.

Ferebee, Ann. "Successful Cincinnati." *Design and Environment* 3:4 (Winter 1974): 40–45.

In examining the city planning process in Cincinnati, Ohio, this article describes how city officials and citizens participated in drawing up the plans to renew the city's downtown area. The author attributes the success of the plans to citizen participation, because earlier plans had been turned down by the voters. The author feels that the regeneration of the city between 1962 and 1972 was remarkable. She describes the work of the eighteen-member Working Review Committee, which consisted of representatives from city government, the city planning commission, the downtown development committee, and civic organizations. She also describes the plan which divided downtown Cincinnati into a core area for business and office use and the frame area for housing.

Friedmann, John. *Retracking America: A Theory of Transactive Planning.* Garden City, New York: Doubleday, 1973.

The author's theory of transactive planning, which he thinks is appropriate for a postindustrial society, is explained in this book. Transactive planning stresses the importance of human relations and is based on mutual learning and cooperation between experts and clients. The author stresses that the subject of societal guidance is too important to be left to the experts and emphasizes the role of citizen participants in planning processes. In this book, Friedmann presents his theory, its intellectual base, and how a society conducive to transactional planning might be developed.

Gans, Herbert J. *People and Plans: Essays on Urban Problems and Solutions.*
New York: Basic Books, 1968.

Reviews:
Choice 6 (May 1966): 441.
Kapenstein, H. M. *Library Journal* 93 (November 1968): 4275.
Millard, Peter. *Architectural Forum* 131 (July 1969): 99.
Nation 209 (October 6, 1969): 355.
Rossi, P. A. *American Journal of Sociology* 75 (November 1969):
434.
Weisman, S. R. *Commonweal* 90 (April 25, 1969): 173.

Gans argues that planners have been too concerned with creating
orderly and beautiful cities and not concerned enough with how people
actually want to live. He suggests that planners should begin formulating
plans by determining affected communities' goals and problems. In doing
so, he argues, planners can more effectively contribute to the solution of
urban problems.

Gieser, Miriam. "Planning With the People." *Journal of Housing* 25 (July
1968): 298–301.

The West End Task Force in Cincinnati was a group made up of area
residents. Its purpose was to develop a long-range plan and a program for
the area and to advise and recommend action to the city. The organization
and work of the task force are discussed. Some of its short-range projects
were in the areas of recreation, health, beautification, and employment.

Godschalk, David R. "The Circle of Urban Participation." *Taming Megalopolis.* Vol. 2. Edited by H. Wentworth Eldredge. Garden City, New
York: Anchor Books, 1967, pp. 971–79.

The author asserts that cities need "a modus operandi which brings
governmental planners face-to-face with citizens in a continuous cooperative venture." The author introduces the concept of collaborative planning
which emphasizes the collaboration of planners with citizens on a subcom-
munity level. He then suggests a method of operationalizing the concept
through "activities analysis techniques" and describes some examples of the
concept's implementation.

Godschalk, David R. *Participation, Planning and Exchange in Old and New
Communities.* Chapel Hill: Center for Urban and Regional Studies,
University of North Carolina, 1972.

Examining six case studies of citizen participation in community planning processes, the author develops an "exchange-based paradigm of participatory planning." Relating community goals to collaborative principles and concepts, the author examines, through observation and survey research, citizen participation in planning in two new towns—Reston, Virginia, and Columbia, Maryland. The author concludes that, in Reston, participation in planning had been characterized by open conflict, civic innovation, and volunteer activity that produced a competitive exchange relationship between the developer and the citizens' association. In Columbia, the planning process had been characterized by conflict avoidance, professionally accomplished innovations, and limited volunteer activism. Citizens in Columbia had not formed a "countervailing organization" to express their interests and lacked independent "exchange resources." These findings lead the author to conclude that neither Reston nor Columbia had achieved a collaborative planning system but that "they appear to be making progress toward the goals . . ." of collaborative planning.

In the final chapter, the author uses the collaborative paradigm in comparing the participation experience in suburbia, inner cities, and new communities, using Levittown, Oakland, and Philadelphia as well as Reston and Columbia. Using this analysis, the author then speculates about the future of citizen participation in community planning and outlines some alternative strategies that might be implemented by planners and citizen groups.

Godschalk, David R., and William E. Mills. "A Collaborative Approach to Planning through Urban Activities." *Journal of the American Institute of Planners* 32:2 (May 1966): 86–95.

Graves, Clifford W. "Citizen Participation in Metropolitan Planning." Paper presented at the American Society of Public Administration meeting, Denver, Colorado, April 19, 1971. Mimeograph.

Graves argues that citizens participate in civic affairs only when they believe a cause to be important to them and when they feel that their participation will produce desired results. He states that current metropolitan planning often meets neither of these criteria and, therefore, activates few citizens. He notes, however, that effective planning cannot be performed without citizen input.

Harman, Douglas. *Citizen Involvement in Urban Planning: The San Diego Experiment.* San Diego: Public Affairs Research Institute, San Diego State College, 1968.

Hatch, C. Richard. "Some Thoughts on Advocacy Planning." *Architectural Forum* 128:5 (June 1968): 72ff.

The author discusses the beginnings of advocacy planning with the Architect's Renewal Committee in Harlem in 1964. He sees advocacy planning as one response to ghetto pathologies in that it can transfer power to the powerless. Some cases of architects and planners joining with community groups to defeat offensive projects are presented. The author writes that public and private corporate redevelopers cannot do the job because their commitment to sponsors and investors means that they must stick to timetables which preclude "interference" by citizens.

Advocacy planning encounters problems due to the complexity of ghetto communities. The advocacy planner is often involved in conflicts and forced to side with one group against other groups. There is difficulty in including everyone in the planning process because it is the upwardly mobile ghetto residents who tend to become involved. Generally, ghetto organizations are ephemeral, tending to be issue oriented. The author believes that advocacy planners should try to organize stable citizen organizations. He also calls for advocacy planners to encourage ghetto business enterprises that can participate in building and redevelopment.

Hays, Floyd B. *Community Leadership: The Regional Plan Association of New York*. New York: Columbia University Press, 1965.

This book is a description of the institutional role of the Regional Plan Association of New York in the development of community leadership. Data came from minutes of meetings, files, correspondence, memoranda, records, and interviews with staff, directors, and others. In the 1920s the Regional Plan Association formulated a plan and then promoted it among leading citizens. During the development of the 1950s plan, community leaders were involved in the research and planning processes. The author attributes the trend toward citizen involvement in the association to the changed situation of the association in the 1950s: availability of foundation funds; the report of the Advisory Committee on the Harvard Study; and changes in the board and staff of the association.

Hyman, Herbert H. "Planning with Citizens: Two Styles." *Journal of the American Institute of Planners* 35:2 (March 1969): 105–12.

This is a study comparing two planning orientations—elite and pluralistic—and their impact on the development of Boston's South End Urban Renewal Project. It analyzes the work of two different planners involved with the same ten citizens groups in relationship to four factors:

planning orientation, involvement with citizens, relationship to the central office, and uses of influence. It was found that the two models had differing impacts on the planning process, the planner's use of information, the citizen groups with which the planner worked, and the planner's relationship with the central office. The elite planner was more dogmatic in his plans, had minimal contact with neighborhood-based groups and more with community-wide elites, was under the influence of the central office, and focused on the executive committees of community-wide boards. The pluralistic planner was more pragmatic in the planning process, had more contact with neighborhood-based groups, had complete authority in the field, and focused on neighborhood bodies in general meetings. The nature of the plans also differed. The plans of the elite planner were rejected by the community, which later accepted the plans of the pluralistic planner.

The implications of the study are as follows: (1) the planner's style will influence his choice of the segment of the community with which he will identify; (2) where two levels of citizen planning exist, the planner should expect differences in values of the leaders of the two levels; (3) planners working with two levels of citizen interests will need access to different types of resources; (4) the planner working with a community-wide elite should not commit himself until the plan is tested at the neighborhood level; and (5) planning is time consuming.

Jaakson, Reiner. "Decentralized Administration and Citizen Participation in Community Planning." *Long Range Planning* 5:1 (March 1972): 16–22.

The shift from politics to expertise in government is seen as the reason for a lag in citizen participation. The author sees a need to balance demands for centralized bureaucracy with increased concern for local, specialized interests. He defines the planning process and discusses the roles of citizen, government, and planner with reference to the centralization-decentralization question.

Kalba, Kas. "Postindustrial Planning: A Review Forward." *Journal of the American Institute of Planners* 40:3 (May 1974): 147–55.

The author discusses different approaches to planning in "postindustrial society." Each approach described involves some form of citizen involvement.

Kaplan, Marshall. "Advocacy and the Urban Poor." *Journal of the American Institute of Planners* 35:2 (March 1969): 96–101. An expanded version appears in *The Social Work Forum, 1969*.

Kaplan presents and compares two styles of advocacy planning: directed or outside advocacy means that the planner works with a client and nondirected or inside advocacy means that the planner works for an agency and is linked to a constituency rather than a client. Two case studies are presented: Hunters Point in San Francisco, where planning consultants were asked to work with a group fearful of displacement and relocation, and Oakland, where planning consultants assisted a city-county task force in preparing a successful model city application. The author concludes that (1) advocacy is technical assistance rather than the expression of ideology; (2) there are problems in determining local priorities; (3) the white professional in the black ghetto must let his clients define the initial frame of reference; and (4) with regard to citizen participation, the black community is really many communities.

Kennedy, Padriac M. "The Poor and the Planners." *Nation's Cities* 6:9 (September 1968): 24–26.

In this article, VISTA volunteers relate the attitudes of the poor concerning city planners. The volunteers found that the poor are generally hostile and resentful toward planners because planners do not consult them. The author emphasizes the importance of community organizations for defining the needs of the poor. He believes that the poor should be consulted in the initial stages of planning.

Keyes, Langley C., Jr., and Edward Teitcher. "Advocacy Planning: A View From the Establishment." *Journal of the American Institute of Planners* 36:4 (July 1970): 225–26.

The authors present a critique of advocacy planning. They feel that advocacy planning is too concerned with the problems of the poor and not concerned enough with the techniques of planning. They feel that students entering planning schools today already understand the human side of planning and need to concentrate on the "nuts and bolts" of planning. They feel that today's planning graduates lack specialized skills and that these graduates are avoiding establishment jobs and abdicating their responsibility to unimaginative civil servants.

Levine, Aaron. "People and the Plan." *Community Planning Review* 15:2 (Summer 1965): 25–30.

Three reasons for citizen concern with the planning process are presented: planning affects the life of every citizen; citizens can make positive contributions to planning; and citizen participation will help to gain public support for planned projects. Two principles underlying the development of citizen participation in planning are discussed: genuine commitment on the part of public agencies and sound citizen organizations.

Lipsky, Michael. *Radical Decentralization: A Response to American Planning Dilemmas.* Madison: Institute for Research on Poverty, University of Wisconsin, 1968.

Radical decentralization is defined as the distribution of authority to those who are affected by institutions or programs. The author evaluates "conservative" decentralization (distributing authority below the national level) and suggests that the government sponsor experiments in radical decentralization.

Newell, Charldean, and Jerry L. Yeric. "The Citizen: Cared For or Cared About in the Urban Planning Process." Paper presented at the Southwestern Political Science Association meeting, Dallas, Texas, March 23, 1973. Mimeograph.

This paper explores the relationship between participation and planning in council-manager cities in Texas. Recognizing that city managers share in the policy-making processes in these cities and that planning is often done by the city managers' staffs, the authors explore the degree to which city managers and city councils represent the populations of their cities. The data demonstrate that "the values of representativeness and participation may suffer greatly in council-manager communities." Several suggestions for maximizing "community-wide citizen participation" and "expressions of general opinion" are then offered by the authors.

Peachey, Paul. *New Town, Old Habits: Citizen Participation at Fort Lincoln.* Washington, D.C.: Washington Center for Metropolitan Studies, August 1970.

A case study of the Citizens' Planning Council for the Fort Lincoln Project, this work reviews one year's activities of the council which provided input during the initial planning phase of Fort Lincoln New Town. The council eventually failed to meet the demands of the situation and thus lost its mandate and was replaced by an advisory body representing several civic groups.

Peattie, Lisa R. "Drama and Advocacy Planning." *Journal of the American Institute of Planners* 36:6 (November 1970): 405–10.

The imagery of the theater is used as an analogy to describe local community activity. The author feels that this is more appropriate than describing the community as an ecology of games, because in a game all the players must choose sides. She sees main actors, a supporting cast, and staged performances by community organizers. She feels that there is no such thing as an organized community but that there are numerous organizations in any community. Advocate planners should, therefore, select as clients community-based organizations which are building issues and support.

Peattie, Lisa R. "Reflections on Advocacy Planning." *Journal of the American Institute of Planners* 34:2 (March 1968): 80–88.

Written as a result of the writer's experience as a member of Urban Planning Aid, an advocacy planning group in Cambridge, Massachusetts, this article describes that group's work with the Lower Roxbury Community Committee and discusses the problem of how to balance the interests of a heterogeneous community. The author calls for the politicization of planning and sees advocacy planning as a new kind of politics.

Routh, Frederick B. "Goals for Dallas: More Participation than Power-Sharing." *City* 5:2 (March/April 1971): 49–53.

The author describes the philosophy and organization of the Goals for Dallas Program. The process through which the goals were formulated is explained, and the goals enumerated. The author concludes by discussing different community leaders' reactions to the goals and to the program itself.

Seaver, Robert C. "The Dilemma of Citizen Participation." *Pratt Planning Papers* 4:3 (September 1966): 6–10.

Three obstacles to productive citizen-agency exchange are discussed: all parties in the renewal or planning process operate from different sets of imperatives; there is a gap between what renewal and planning can do and what citizens expect them to do; and renewal and planning contain goal conflicts which need to be balanced in the development of specific proposals. The author believes that there is a need for flexibility and responsiveness to concerns outside the scope of renewal and planning and for communication between planners and citizens.

Segal, Morley. *The Million Dollar Misunderstanding: The Interim Assistance Program in the District of Columbia.* Washington, D.C.: Center for Metropolitan Studies, September 1970.

This is a case study of efforts in Washington, D.C., to involve citizens in the planning and construction of three parks in riot-torn areas under guidelines from the Department of Housing and Urban Development's Interim Assistance Program. The process brought out the inherent conflicts between an established bureaucracy and citizen participation which, in this case, manifest themselves in the issue of strict financial accountability.

Shore, William B. *Public Participation in Regional Planning.* New York: Regional Plan Association, October 1967.

In describing the public participation process used in shaping the Second Regional Plan for the tristate region surrounding the Port of New York, the author discusses the role of the public, how the Regional Plan Association tried to work with citizens groups, and the results of those efforts. The goals project involved a series of five meetings with 5,600 persons attending at least one of the meetings.

Smith, Richard Warren. "A Theoretical Basis for Participatory Planning." *Policy Sciences* 4:3 (September 1973): 275–95.

The author first asserts that the "conventional planning process is not structured to allow the natural, positive inclusion of citizen input. What is needed is a theoretical reorientation away from the conventional hierarchial decision-making models toward a 'reticular' structure which allows the continuous inclusion of substantive citizen input." In supporting his contention that participatory planning requires "reticular" planning-decision structures, Smith discusses forms of legitimacy—modes of justifying planning actions; aspects of participatory planning—the rational, personal, and social aspects of participatory planning; and the planning process as a learning system. Drawing from a wide range of literature on participatory and advocacy planning and the social and psychological impacts of different organizational structures, the author argues that participatory planning "increases the effectiveness and adaptivity of the planning process and contributes adaptivity and stability to the societal system."

Spiegel, Hans B. C., and Stephen D. Mittenthal. *Neighborhood Power and Control: Implications for Urban Planning.* New York: Institute of Urban Environment, School of Architecture, Columbia University, November 1968.

This is an exploratory study which looks at the emergent demand for neighborhood power and control from low income communities and what it means for urban planning. Data were gathered during brief visits to some first-round model cities programs, papers solicited from experts, and a three-day conference of people with knowledge about neighborhood power and control in model cities areas. The report discusses the background of the movement for neighborhood control and the new politics of participation, a sociological evaluation of the concepts of neighborhood power and control, and federal programs which sponsor citizen participation. A case study of the model cities program in Oakland, California, is presented. The implications of the movement for neighborhood power and control are discussed in terms of client relationships, planning constituencies, and the planning process. The authors recommend that HUD increase its support for neighborhood control.

Steps Towards Increasing Citizen Participation in City Planning. An Interim Staff Technical Report for the United States Department of Housing and Urban Development. New York: New York City Planning Department, 1974.

Sviridoff, Mitchell. *Planning and Participation.* New York: Ford Foundation, 1969.

Verburg, Edwin A. "Citizen Participation in Open Space and Recreation Planning: The Glendale Experience." *Urban Land* 33:10 (November 1974): 12–21.

The city of Glendale, California, concerned over the disappearance of open space in the nearby mountains, produced a plan to acquire Housing and Urban Development and Bureau of Outdoor Recreation funds for preservation of open space. This article presents a case study of the environmental planning process. It looks at citizen involvement and describes local support for the plan and the process of community review and citizen participation.

Von Eckardt, Wolf. "Getting Into the Act." *Saturday Review* 52 (July 4, 1970): 43–44.

In this article, Von Eckardt discusses several concepts of citizen participation in planning. The Model Inner City Citizens Organization in the Shaw area of Washington, D.C., is involved in "nonviolent land reform," where the government takes slum land from absentee owners so that nonprofit neighborhood corporations can build on it. He then discusses the failure of the Fort Lincoln project, meetings of planners and community people, advocacy planning, and the British system of citizen participation in planning. The author is in favor of the British system in which experts submit plans to the public at large for intensive inspection and approval.

Will, W. H. "Planning with People." *Jersey Plans* (Winter 1966): 48–56.

Willeke, Gene E. "Citizen Participation: Here to Stay." *Civil Engineering* 44:1 (January 1974): 78–82.

Williams, Ruth, and M. Justin Herman. *Collaborative Planning at Hunters Point*. San Francisco: San Francisco Redevelopment Agency, 1967.

COMMUNITY DEVELOPMENT

Aleshire, Robert A. "Power to the People? An Assessment of the Community Action and Model Cities Experiences." Paper prepared for the National Academy of Public Administration Conference on Crisis, Conflict, and Creativity, Airlie House, Warrenton, Virginia, April 23–25, 1970. Mimeograph. Also in *Public Administration Review* 32, special issue (September 1972): 428–43.

Aleshire assesses the costs and benefits of participation of the poor in the community action and model cities programs. He views the costs as time, money, and inefficiency. He then surveys several problems presented by participation: the promise-delivery gap, rational or political decision making, action vs. participation, defining who "the citizen" is, and the necessity of making choices. The author believes that such costs are worthwhile investments. As benefits of participation he lists: extension of the democratic ideal, a check against the idealistic or technocratic theorist, preservation of the individual, provision of a forum for priority setting, leadership development, and issue development. He believes that participation has significantly affected both Model Cities and the Community Action Program.

Biddle, William W., and Loureide J. Biddle. *The Community Development Process: The Rediscovery of Local Initiative*. New York: Holt, Rinehart and Winston, 1965.

Reviews:
Anderson, Nels. *Annals of the American Academy of Political and Social Science* 362 (November 1965): 184.
Lee, Robert. *Christian Century* 83 (June 29, 1966): 833.

This book explains the community development process by first presenting two case studies, a rural Appalachian mining county and a deteriorating urban industrial neighborhood in the North. The authors present and define the concepts and terms relevant to community development. They then outline a process through which a method of community development can evolve. This includes different phases of organization. There are suggestions for solving problems presented by the fact that needs are varied and means of meeting needs are limited. The authors then explore the relationships between community development and different academic disciplines, social welfare work, religion, and education. Finally, the book examines the role of the community development worker as an encourager who initiates a process that eventually makes community groups independent. The book also contains a chapter on how to construct a research design, an appendix on the background of community development in the United States, and a bibliography on current literature.

"Citizens Action in Model Cities and CAP Programs: Case Studies and Evaluation." *Public Administration Review* 32, special issue (September 1972): entire issue.

This special issue contains seven articles on citizen participation in Model Cities and CAP. The first three articles are concerned with the controversy surrounding citizen participation in the model cities program in North Philadelphia. In "Maximum Feasible Manipulation," Sherry Arnstein tells the story from the viewpoint of the North City Area Wide Council, Inc., the model cities citizens group which was dissolved by HUD and the city in a power struggle. "The View From City Hall" tells the same story from the viewpoint of city hall officials. In "Citizen Participation in the Philadelphia Model Cities Program: Retrospect and Prospect," Erasmus Kloman presents an evaluation of the issues involved in the Philadelphia case and appraises the future prospects for citizen participation in the Philadelphia Model Cities Program.

David M. Austin presents the findings from the Study of Community Representation in Community Action Agencies conducted by the Florence Heller Graduate School at Brandeis. The article, entitled "Resident Participation: Political Mobilization or Organizational Cooptation?," presents the results of this study which involved twenty community action agencies in cities of from 50,000 to 80,000 in population. In "Federally Financed Citizen Participation," Howard Hallman reviews the experiences of four federal programs and asks whether federal funds should be used to induce citizen participation, and if so, how? In "Power to the People: An Assessment of the Community Action and Model Cities Experiences,"

Robert A. Aleshire assesses the costs, benefits, and limitations of citizen participation. Richard W. Boone presents his observations about citizen participation, the origins of the concept, and the implementation of citizen participation in the Economic Opportunity Act in "Reflections on Citizen Participation and the Economic Opportunity Act."

Clinard, Marshall B. "Perspectives on Urban Community Development and
    Community Organization." *The Social Welfare Forum, 1962.* Official
    Proceedings, 89th Annual Forum, National Conference on Social
    Welfare, New York, New York, May 27–June 1, 1962. New York:
    Columbia University Press, 1962, pp. 65–89.
    Clinard asserts that a successful program of urban community development is needed as a solution to urban problems. He believes that since problems arise from group practices, they need group solutions. He proposes that departments of urban community development be set up under local governments to elicit citizen participation, develop neighborhood councils, and overcome public apathy.

Downs, Anthony, "Citizen Participation in Community Development:
    Why Some Changes are Needed." *National Civic Review* 64:5 (May
    1975): 237–48.
    The author has examined mechanisms cities have adopted for citizen participation under the Housing and Community Development Act of 1974. In this article he discusses why these arrangements are usually inadequate and suggests ways to improve them. He interviewed public officials and read accounts of citizen participation efforts. Seventeen cities of various sizes were surveyed. The three shortcomings observed were: the cities had to move fast to get community development funds, and shortness of time drastically restricted the possible breadth and depth of citizen participation; the present mechanisms for citizen participation cannot attract private capital into community development; and they also do not give citizens the opportunity to effectively participate because there is no preliminary period of learning about the community. Downs believes that citizen participation should acquaint citizen participants with the basic nature of their communities, form a strong enough consensus behind a recommended program so that it can be carried out, and develop a practical understanding of how to deal with the federal bureaucracy and how to engage in effective planning.

Evans, Howard S. "Encouraging Effective Citizen Participation in Commu-
    nity Development." *Public Management* 43:11 (November 1961): 242–
    45.

The role of citizens in community affairs, as seen by the National Chamber of Commerce, is presented. The chamber recognizes a role for citizens in the analysis of community problems and the formulation of recommendations for solutions. The author describes a demonstration project in Erie, Pennsylvania, in which 300 citizens participated in this way. A second way citizens can participate in community affairs is through the establishment of a mechanism which will allow them to assume leadership in policy making. The chamber calls this mechanism the citizen participation process and divides it into three interrelated functions: fact finding, public discussion, and action.

"From Private Enterprise to Public Entity: The Role of the Community Development Corporation." *Georgetown Law Journal* 57:5 (May 1969): 956–91.

This article traces the community development corporation (CDC) through stages of capitalization, acquisition of land, and investment in enterprises. The economic viability of CDCs is explored and some suggestions for ensuring financial success are made. The political implications of CDCs, in terms of local control of government services, are discussed. The article concludes that the development of a CDC would logically lead to the emergence of a submunicipal corporation or "minicipality." Even without that, it is felt that a community development corporation will be an important integrative and catalytic force within the community and will represent the community in local politics.

Gifford, Kilvert Dun. "Neighborhood Development Corporations: The Bedford-Stuyvesant Experiment." *Agenda for a City: Issues Confronting New York.* Edited by Lyle C. Fitch and Annmarie Hauck Walsh. Beverly Hills, California: Sage Publications, 1970, pp. 421–50.

Gifford provides a detailed, chronological examination of the community development experiment in the Bedford-Stuyvesant community in Brooklyn, New York. It traces the project from its inception through the planning stage to its implementation and also discusses the future of the project and its implications for New York City. The project was not planned as an attempt at neighborhood self-government, but rather as an experiment in local organization and institution building. Eight programs sponsored by the project are described, and future plans are outlined. The author lists the major ingredients that contributed to the survival of the project: (1) the influence of Robert Kennedy; (2) management ability; (3) realism; (4) continuity; (5) community control; (6) an ad hoc approach to dealing with the jurisdictional problems posed by bureaucratic rigidities; and (7) flexible federal funds. The author concludes that such projects "have a place in the future of New York City."

Goodpaster, Gary S. "An Introduction to the Community Development Corporation." *Journal of Urban Law* 46:3 (1969): 603–65.

The author believes that municipal institutions have failed to meet current problems and sees the lack of citizen participation as one of the sources of this failure. He reviews organizational strategies and remedies: direct action including community organization, legal services for the poor, and the war on poverty which includes participation of the poor. There is a discussion of urban social conditions: poverty, inequality, social discrimination, and race. Turning to business in the ghetto, the author feels that efforts to support black capitalism do not address the scale of the problem. He sees a need for community development corporations on a large scale. In his opinion such a program would attack problems of discrimination, poverty, lack of citizen participation, and the failure of governmental institutions and would, at the same time, move to satisfy demands for black power and contribute to the process of racial integration.

Hallman, Howard W. *Community Corporations and Neighborhood Control.* Washington, D.C.: Center for Governmental Studies, 1970.

This pamphlet is based on a study of community corporations conducted by the author in 1968 and 1969. He describes and contrasts two generations of community corporations—the community action agencies in Washington, D.C., and New York City and the model cities agencies in Oakland, California, and Dayton, Ohio. He sees leadership, unity, and technical know-how as the major factors in achieving success with community corporations. Methods of achieving representativeness and accountability are discussed.

Hallman, Howard W. *Neighborhood Control of Public Programs: Case Studies of Community Corporations and Neighborhood Boards.* New York: Praeger, 1970.

The author analyzes the operations of community corporations and neighborhood boards. The study is based on the author's experiences with about thirty such organizations of varying forms and styles. Many are connected with the Community Action Program. They are, for the most part, decentralized operations of a program funded by a central agency. Background information on citizen participation in public programs is provided through information about New Haven, Connecticut. The case studies cover community corporations in New York City, Washington, D.C., Newark, New Jersey, and Columbus, Ohio, and community action agencies in Appalachia, other rural areas, and on Indian reservations. They also include studies of groups in St. Louis, Washington, D.C., San Francisco, and Philadelphia; studies of citizen participation in urban renewal in Washington, D.C., New Haven, San Francisco, and Philadelphia; and studies of citizen participation in model cities in Dayton, Ohio, and Oakland, California.

The author believes that these organizations represent promising starts. He says that the common ingredients in most successful community corporations are neighborhood unity, technical know-how, and effective leadership. The most important problems faced by these groups are the questions of representativeness and accountability.

Howard, Ian McLeod. "The Saving of Savannah: How an All-American City Faced Up to Its All-American Problems." *Atlanta Economic Review* 19:7 (July 1969): 10–14.

Howard describes the rehabilitation and restoration of Savannah, Georgia, and the instrumental roles played by Atlanta banker Mills B. Lane, Jr., and his deputy Bill Van Landingham. The first phase of the project was the Spring Clean Program, in which volunteers helped slum residents clean up their neighborhoods. Phase two involved setting up a community development corporation to help poor families buy homes, to help landlords improve buildings, and to help poor people start businesses. The Historical Savannah Foundation's role in the restoration effort is also described.

Kotler, Milton. "Two Essays on the Neighborhood Corporation." *Urban America: Goals and Problems*. Report of the Subcommittee on Urban Affairs, Joint Economic Committee, United States Congress. Washington, D.C.: U.S. Government Printing Office, 1967, pp. 170–92.

In the first of these two essays, the author argues that the lack of neighborhood control contributed to the unrest that resulted in the urban riots of the mid-1960s. The author then suggests that the federal government provide initial funding for neighborhood corporations that are locally initiated. The second essay responds to some of the most often cited arguments against the neighborhood corporation idea.

Krause, Elliot A. "Functions of a Bureaucratic Ideology: 'Citizen Participation.' " *Social Problems* 16:2 (Fall 1968): 129–42.

This study explores the bureaucratic use of the ideology of citizen participation and the intended and unintended consequences of accepting or rejecting such an ideology. The author sees bureaucracies as potential proponents of ideology; i.e., as political actors who, in this case, use the ideology of citizen participation to achieve their ends. Planning activities of two government agencies were analyzed: the U.S. Housing and Home Finance Agency with its urban renewal agencies and the Community Action Program of OEO. The author feels that target groups did not appear to have benefited from citizen participation. The benefits accrued instead to the bureaucratic proponents of citizen participation and their businessmen clients. He sees the ideology as a powerful bureaucratic tool.

Mogulof, Melvin B. "Coalition to Adversary: Citizen Participation in Three Federal Programs." *Journal of the American Institute of Planners* 35:4 (July 1969): 225–32.

Mogulof traces the development of citizen participation in federal programs from its role in the public-private coalitions of the juvenile delinquency demonstration programs to a larger role in the policy coalitions of the Community Action Program to the "adversary" citizens organizations involved in the Model Cities Program.

Mogulof, Melvin B. "Federal Action for Citizen Participation in Social Action." *The Social Welfare Forum, 1969.* Official Proceedings, 96th Annual Forum, National Conference on Social Welfare, New York, New York, May 25–29, 1969. New York: Columbia University Press, 1969, pp. 86–107.

Citizen involvement in three federal programs is discussed: the Juvenile Demonstration Program, the Community Action Program, and Model Cities. Each program is seen as incorporating concepts and practices of community organization and citizen participation. The author discusses each program in terms of self-determination for poor black communities.

"Notes: The Inner-City Development Corporation." *Virginia Law Review* 55:5 (June 1969): 872–908.

In a discussion of the establishment of business enterprises in urban poverty areas, problems facing ghetto-based businesses are identified: high cost of land and insurance, high rate of taxation, lack of skilled labor pool, and lack of market. Existing private efforts and federal programs are then surveyed. There are two categories of private efforts: corporations with plants or wholly owned subsidiaries in the ghetto which provide employment but do not involve residents in decision making, and corporations which build plants they intend to turn over to local interests through granting stock options to employees and selling shares to community residents. Federal efforts consist of small business assistance under four programs: Title IV of the Economic Opportunity Act of 1964, the Small Business Assistance loans to local development corporations, the Public Works and Economic Development Act of 1965, and the Special Impact Program.

The article focuses on two contrasting programs. The Bedford-Stuyvesant redevelopment project in Brooklyn, New York, demonstrates the potentials of minority-staff organizations which can administer federal funds and utilize outside expertise to create resident-owned businesses. The Community Self-Determination Act proposed the creation of federally chartered, locally controlled development corporations which combine political and social functions with ownership of, or assistance to, local businesses. The authors prefer the Bedford-Stuyvesant approach and see the community self-determination approach as detrimental to business development.

Rhodes, Alfred H., Jr. "Case Presentations in Community Development, I. Rural Mississippi." *The Social Welfare Forum, 1969.* Official Proceedings, 96th Annual Forum, National Conference on Social Welfare, New York, New York, May 25–29, 1969. New York: Columbia University Press, 1969, pp. 149–62.

Rhodes describes the Mississippi Project of the National Federation of Settlements and Neighborhood Centers, begun in 1966 to give technical consultation to autonomous neighborhood organizations. Several of the activities of the project are described. Existing black organizations in Rankin County were pulled together to form the Rankin County Assembly. A neighborhood center was built in Bolton. The OEO-funded summer project provided youth recreational and job training opportunities. Political participation of blacks was increased when the author ran an unsuccessful campaign for the state legislature.

Rosenbloom, Richard S., and Robin Marris, eds. *Social Innovation in the City: New Enterprises for Community Development.* Cambridge, Massachusetts: Harvard University Press, 1969.

This is a report on work in progress conducted (in 1969) by the Research Group on Technology, Business, and the City, one of the research groups of the Harvard University Program on Technology and Society. The group attributes urban problems to technological advances and to the inability of the social structure to use technology for problem solving. The group has concentrated on designing new institutions and social technologies. Chapters deal with the potentials of local government and business as urban problem solvers, urban development corporations, black power, a typology of community organizations, institutional change, housing, and the status of the group's work. Rather than specifying solutions to urban problems, the group focused on organizations designed to solve problems. Its most specific recommendation was for the establishment of local and state development corporations which would provide mechanisms for increasing citizen participation.

Selznick, Philip. *TVA and the Grass Roots: A Study in the Sociology of Formal Organization.* Berkeley: University of California Press, 1949.

> Reviews:
> *American Sociological Review* 14 (December 1949): 824.
> *Booklist* 46 (September 1, 1949): 7.
> Collins, Orvis. *American Journal of Sociology* 55 (January 1950): 419.
> Pritchett, C. H. *Annals of the American Academy of Political and Social Science* 265 (September 1949): 176.
> Sayre, W. S. *American Political Science Review* 43 (October 1949): 1031.
> Uhlig, R. H. *San Francisco Chronicle* (July 3, 1949): 16.

This book analyzes the TVA's official policy of decentralization and grass roots administration as it attempted to function with and through existing institutions in the area. The relationship of the TVA to the farm interests in the area is explored in detail. The TVA was able to coopt new elements (i.e., the farm leadership) into its leadership and policy-making structure which ensured its stability. At the same time, however, the TVA had to accommodate its coopted elements in various ways, such as in its stand against the utilization of public ownership of land as a conservation measure.

Specht, Harry. "Community Development in Low Income Negro Areas." *Social Work* 11:4 (October 1966): 78–89.

Opposing the Alinsky model of community organization, the author advocates a method similar to that used in underdeveloped countries. Such a method unites the efforts of people with those of government to improve conditions and integrate the community into the mainstream. The author describes the efforts of the Richmond (California) Community Development Demonstration Project, which uses that approach.

Spiegel, Hans B. C., ed. *Citizen Participation in Urban Development.* Vol. 1. *Concepts and Issues.* Washington, D.C.: National Training Laboratory Institute for Applied Behavioral Science, 1968.

This is a collection of papers stressing the theoretical and value aspects of the participation of low and moderate income citizens in urban life. The first section consists of a bibliographic survey of citizen participation by Hans B. C. Spiegel and Stephen D. Mittenthal. The second section contains papers discussing citizen participation in urban renewal and model cities by James Q. Wilson, Robert C. Seaver, and Harold Goldblatt and also includes HUD publications on the subject. The third section is made up of papers on the Office of Economic Opportunity, the Community Action Program, and maximum feasible participation by Louis A. Zurcher, Frances F. Piven, and Peter Marris and Martin Rein. The fourth section concerns Saul Alinsky's approach and presents excerpts from *Reveille for Radicals* and criticisms of Alinsky by Stephen C. Rose and Richard C. Murray and Thomas D. Sherrar. The implications that citizen participation has for community decision making are the subject of the last section. Articles in this section are by Edgar S. and Jean Camper Cahn, Harold Edelson and Ferne Kolodner, and Robert Crain and Donald Rosenthal.

Spiegel, Hans B. C., ed. *Citizen Participation in Urban Development.* Vol. 2. *Cases and Programs.* Washington, D.C.: National Training Laboratory Institute for Applied Behavioral Sciences, 1969.

This book presents twenty-nine readings on the experience and practice of citizen participation in various situations. The readings are divided into three sections: patterns of citizen participation, with articles focusing on neighborhood organization, the black caucus, and urban renewal; crisis situations that catalyze citizen action, such as school decentralization, roads, civil disorders, and housing; and use of external agents such as advocate planners, community development catalysts, and training for participation.

Spiegel, Hans B. C., ed. *Citizen Participation in Urban Development.* Vol. 3. *Decentralization.* Fairfax, Virginia: Learning Resources Corporation/ National Training Laboratory, 1974.

Strange, John H. "Citizen Participation: An Outline of the OEO-Model Cities Experience." Paper prepared for the National Academy of Public Administration Conference on Participation of the Poor and Public Administration, Holly Knoll Conference Center, Williamsburg, Virginia, May 21–23, 1970. Mimeograph.

Van Til, Jon, and Sally Bould Van Til. "Citizen Participation in Social Policy: The End of the Cycle." *The New Urban Politics: Cities and the Federal Government.* Edited by Douglas M. Fox. Pacific Palisades, California: Goodyear, 1972, pp. 210–21. Originally published in *Social Problems* 17:3 (Winter 1970): 313–23.

Examining participation in urban renewal, the war on poverty, and model cities, this paper presents six forms of citizen participation and the patterns in which they appear. The typology distinguishes between two aspects of participation: range of citizenry involved and the focus of their participation. When the range of participation includes only elites and the focus is administration only, an elite coalition form emerges. When the focus is politics and administration, the form is the politics of renewal (in urban renewal) or the politics of reform (in the antipoverty program). When elites and nonelites participate and the focus is administration, a citizen-advice form emerges. When the focus is politics and administration, a pluralist-participation form emerges. When only nonelites participate and the focus is administration, client participation is the result. When the focus is politics and administration, grass roots politics is the result.

URBAN RENEWAL

Alinsky, Saul D. "Citizen Participation in Planning and Urban Renewal." Paper prepared for the National Association of Housing and Redevelopment Officials' meeting, Chicago, Illinois, January 29, 1962. Mimeograph.

Beagle, Danny; Al Haber; and David Wellman. "Turf Power and the Tax Man: Urban Renewal, Regionalization and the Limits of Community Control." *Leviathan* 1 (April 1969): 26–33.

Bellush, Jewel, and Murray Hausknecht. "Planning, Participation, and Urban Renewal." *Urban Renewal: People, Politics and Planning.* Edited by Jewel Bellush and Murray Hausknecht. Garden City, New York: Anchor Books, 1967, pp. 278–86.

Attacking the idea that all citizens of a community are equally able to participate in local affairs, the authors argue that the middle class will always predominate, because the poor do not have the capacity for organizational activity, the leadership, the knowledge, or the awareness for participation. They also feel that uncritical acceptance of the ideology of citizen participation can raise unrealistic expectations and lead to illegitimate interferences in planning.

Berger, Curtis J., and Joel Cogen. "Responsive Urban Renewal: The Neighborhood Shapes the Plan." *Urban Law Annual* 1 (1968): 75–117.

Berger and Cogen discuss how site residents and neighborhood organizations can have a voice in urban renewal plans for their community. The first section presents aspects of the urban renewal process with which people should be familiar: agency structure, stages of the urban renewal process, and constraints which bear on the plan's responsiveness to site residents. The second section discusses the kinds of political efforts that a neighborhood organization can undertake in order to become active in urban renewal. The third section is a case study of Pulaski, Tennessee, where citizens were able to block a plan that they felt was inimical to the interests of the community. The authors conclude that if urban planning is to be responsive to the community, the community must be involved throughout the planning process.

Brewer, Garry D. "Accommodating Increased Demands for Public Participation in Urban Renewal Decision-Making." Conference paper P–4868. Santa Monica, California: The Rand Corporation, July 1972.

This paper presents a model for citizen input into the urban renewal process. The first step is a survey of citizens, policy makers, and experts to find clues about alternative uses of renewal. Then verbal and visual representations of each plausible use are prepared by experts and analyzed by citizens and decision makers to head off future trouble and to keep attention focused on the right issues. Third, citizens and decision makers are resurveyed on remaining options, and information is collected on the selected option. Fourth, progress reports are made available to citizens.

Brignac, Ronald L. "Public Housing Official Reacts to Citizen Participation Messages With One-Man Drama." *Journal of Housing* 26:11 (December 1969): 604–05.

This article discusses the case of New Orleans, where citizens were so involved in urban renewal that the program was halted. Two examples, model cities and scattered site public housing, are discussed and used to support the author's reservations about citizen participation.

Burke, Edmund M. "Citizen Participation is a Necessity." *Journal of Housing* 26:11 (December 1969): 599–602.

Burke argues that citizen participation in urban renewal has become a practical necessity because of legal requirements and demands of the people. He sees the problems of citizen participation as: (1) definition of interests; (2) the place of community organization; (3) the question of reconciliation of public and private interests; (4) the need for incentives to provide motives for participation; and (5) the confused expectations of what citizen participation can do. He suggests the separation of the citizen participation function and the political decision-making function. Elected neighborhood commissions are suggested as a method of decentralization.

Burke, Edmund M. "Citizen Participation in Renewal." *Journal of Housing* 23:1 (January 1966): 18–22.

Data were gathered by submitting questionnaires to 113 local planning agencies (85 percent replied). Four renewal agencies were then analyzed in detail. Interviews were conducted with local planning agency directors, administrative staff, community organization workers, and citizens from the renewal areas. The survey found that few agencies employed community organization specialists. Generally, more citizen participation was found in rehabilitation programs than in clearance programs. One case where citizens did participate in clearance is described. Citizen participation was not found to be widespread but was seen as increasing.

"Citizen Participation Issue." *Journal of Housing* 20:8 (September 1963): entire issue.

This issue is devoted to what was being done in cities around the country to involve citizens in public housing, urban renewal, and code enforcement programs. The articles survey some of the methods through which citizens and agencies were working together. Thirteen programs in twelve cities around the country are described. The various programs include examples of involvement of the business community, social work professionals, city government, local housing authorities, tenants associations, and citizens housing associations. The author then provides a comparison of types of citizen participation and a description of a program for training citizens for participation.

"Citizen Participation in Renewal." *Journal of Housing* 23:1 (January 1966): 23–25.

This article describes six cases of citizen participation in urban renewal in five cities: Kansas City, Missouri; Cooper Square, New York City; Oakland, California; Central Brooklyn, New York City; Los Angeles; and Charlestown, Boston.

"Citizen Participation in Urban Renewal." *Civil Engineering* 38:11 (November 1968): 28–31.

This article presents highlights of discussions from two meetings of civil engineers on efforts of civil engineers and planners to work with citizen groups to develop renewal plans. The first section reviews the problems of the ghetto. Human needs are discussed in terms of building a sense of community and self-esteem for ghetto residents. Professionals are warned of the dangers of making promises to ghetto residents without carrying through. The importance of preserving and building neighborhoods is emphasized. In the second section, two cases of urban renewal programs in San Francisco are presented. In one case there was conflict between citizens and the agency, and in the other case there was cooperation.

"Citizen Participation in Urban Renewal." *Columbia Law Review* 66:3 (March 1966): 486–607.

In examining the role of citizen participation in urban renewal, this article outlines legislation relevant to citizen participation in renewal. Five case studies showing different forms of citizen participation in different contexts are presented. The studies focus on the formation of groups, articulation of local needs, and impacts on governmental action. The impact of citywide citizen groups is analyzed and seen as being limited to articulation of broad goals. The article is devoted, primarily, to the discussion of neighborhood groups. The community organization process is described, and successes and failures of renewal agencies in initiating citizen groups are analyzed. The interactions between citizen groups and city officials are also analyzed. The article recommends that citizen input come in the early stages of renewal planning so that neighborhood participation will not mean a shifting of the locus of power from city agencies to private hands.

Clark, Terry N. "Community Structure, Decision-Making, Budget Expenditures, and Urban Renewal in 51 American Communities." *American Sociological Review* 33:4 (August 1968): 576–93.

A systematic investigation of community decision making, this article presents propositions relating community structure characteristics to decision-making patterns and to budget and urban renewal expenditures. Community decision-making structure was measured by examining the number of major actors involved in each decisional area and the degree to which decision makers overlapped from one issue to the next. Interviews were conducted with a standard panel of community informants in fifty-one communities with populations of 50,000 to 750,000. The interviews covered issues such as urban renewal, elections of mayors, air pollution, and the antipoverty program.

The study hypothesized that the greater the horizontal and vertical differentiation in a social system, the greater the differentiation between political elites, the more decentralized the decision-making structure, and without the establishment of integrative mechanisms which leads to loss of coordination between sectors, the lower the level of output. The data supported the hypothesis. Cities with more economic diversification and with structures favoring citizen participation displayed more decentralization of decision making which led to higher levels of community expenditures and a larger urban renewal program.

Dahl, Robert. "The Rituals of Participation." *Urban Renewal: People, Politics and Planning.* Edited by Jewel Bellush and Murray Hausknecht. Garden City, New York: Anchor Books, 1967, pp. 302–14.

This excerpt from *Who Governs?* describes the Citizens Action Commission, the twenty-five-member citizens group of the New Haven (Connecticut) Redevelopment Agency. The commission, made up of community influentials, never opposed any action of the redevelopment agency. It became a mechanism for avoiding, rather than settling, disputes.

Davies, J. Clarence, III. *Neighborhood Groups and Urban Renewal.* New York: Columbia University Press, 1966.

> Reviews:
> Ascher, C. S. *Annals of the American Academy of Political and Social Science* 368 (November 1966): 240.
> Lebeaux, C. N. *American Sociological Review* 31 (October 1966): 741.
> Roth, H. L. *Library Journal* 91 (January 1966): 270.

Davies presents three case studies of neighborhood groups involved in urban renewal projects in New York City: Seaside-Hammels, the West Side, and the West Village. Seventy-five neighborhood leaders, government officials, and informed observers were interviewed in an attempt to examine the roles of neighborhood groups. The three cases are presented and then analyzed in terms of the formation of neighborhood attitudes, roles of neighborhood and nonneighborhood actors, access of neighborhood groups to levels of government, and the relationship between neighborhood participation in urban renewal and the public interest.

Davis, Lloyd. "With Citizen Participation." *Journal of Housing* 22:3 (March 1965): 132–35.

This article describes community organization in the Dixwell renewal and redevelopment project in New Haven, Connecticut. The Dixwell program and the community are described. The program started when residents of this low income area urged its initiation. The Dixwell Renewal Committee functions more like a board of directors than an advisory body. Some techniques used for encouraging citizen involvement were newsletters, monthly forums, annual dinners, and block discussions and socials.

Galphin, Bruce. "The West End Story." *Nation's Cities* 5:1 (January 1967): 18–20.

This article describes a $15 million urban redevelopment project in Atlanta's West End community. The emphasis of the program was on renovation of existing structures. The author feels that this program is an example of an ideal program in which community education led to community involvement and community enthusiasm. He describes the funding of the project, the changes it proposed, and the services that were provided to the people of the area.

Greer, Scott. *Urban Renewal and American Cities: Dilemma of Democratic Intervention.* Indianapolis: Bobbs-Merrill, 1965.

> Reviews:
> *Choice* 4 (March 1967): 68.
> Schroth, R. A. *America* 114 (May 21, 1966): 744
> Seasholes, Bradbury. *American Political Science Review* 61 (June 1967): 517.

Urban renewal programs in fourteen American cities are surveyed in this book. Data were gathered through observation and interviews done in 1961 and 1962. Urban renewal is discussed in terms of its history and theory. Programs are analyzed with emphasis on the local public authority as the center of action, and the impact of social trends on programs is discussed. The author attributes much of the confusion surrounding urban renewal to an unsystematic mixture of three goals: increase in low cost housing, revitalization of the central city, and creation of a planned city through community renewal. He feels that urban renewal lacks the powers, the precedents, and the knowledge to achieve its aims, and calls for more and better evaluation of renewal programs.

Hartman, Chester. *Yerba Buena: Land Grab and Community Resistance in San Francisco.* San Francisco: Glide Publications, 1974.

This book chronicles the attempts of a resident organization, Tenants and Owners in Opposition to Redevelopment, to halt an urban renewal project in San Francisco. The development of the Yerba Buena plan, the formation of the opposition to the plan, the residents organization's activities, and the ensuing legal battle are described in detail.

Herman, M. Justin. "Renewal Official Responds to Citizen Participation Statements of Messrs. Burke and Rutledge." *Journal of Housing* 26:11 (December 1969): 602.

Problems of agencies in working with citizens are cited: discontinuity of community leadership, infighting among neighborhood groups, and people who exploit the situation for their own political advantage. The author is cautious about the concept of a citizen veto over programs and plans and is concerned about the selection methods used in choosing citizen representatives.

Homman, Mary. *Wooster Square Design.* New Haven, Connecticut: New Haven Redevelopment Agency, 1965.

This describes the experiences of an urban renewal project in New Haven, Connecticut, which redeveloped and rehabilitated a unique historical area known as Wooster Square. The history of the area is presented and the project is discussed in terms of planning and execution. Case histories of residential and nonresidential rehabilitation are included, and they are accompanied by many photographs and sketches.

Kaplan, Harold. *Urban Renewal Politics: Slum Clearance in Newark.* New York: Columbia University Press, 1963.

Reviews:
Adrian, C. R. *American Political Science Review* 58 (June 1964): 431.
D. B. C. *Architectural Forum* 120 (January 1964): 129.
Hemdahl, R. G. *Annals of the American Academy of Political and Social Science* 354 (July 1964): 172.
Holleb, Doris. *Journal of Political Economy* 72 (August 1964): 424.

Kaplan describes the Newark (New Jersey) Housing Authority (NHA) and how it launched nine clearance projects in the first ten years of Title I of the 1949 Federal Housing Act. The study looks specifically at the political environment of NHA and its efforts to function within that environment. It focuses on the roles of the major actors in the renewal system—the "politicos," realtors, corporation executives, city planners, and grass roots organizers—and the patterns of interaction among them. The urban renewal system in Newark was found to be a relatively closed circle with limited membership and relative impermeability. The origins of the stability of the system were traced to the negotiations between NHA and each of the participants.

Krasnowiecki, Jan Z. *Materials on Community Participation in Urban Renewal and Federal Low-Cost Housing Programs.* Philadelphia: University of Pennsylvania Law School, 1967.

Lewis, Gerda. "Citizen Participation in Renewal Surveyed." *Journal of Housing* 16:3 (March 1959): 80–87.

Two surveys were conducted in order to determine whether the citizen participation in urban renewal provision of the Housing Act of 1954 was serving its purpose. Questionnaires were submitted to local urban renewal officials in ninety-one cities to determine the status of citizen participation. Another questionnaire was submitted to local adult education directors in the ninety-one cities to determine the extent of use of public adult education facilities in cooperation with urban renewal. Forty-one percent of the urban renewal directors replied, and 55 percent of the public school adult education directors replied. The findings indicated a low level of development in the roles of citizen participation and adult education in urban renewal. The author recommends the following: (1) clarification of objectives of citizen participation; (2) at least one professional staff member devoted to community organization; (3) neighborhood advisory committees with direct ties to the citywide advisory committee and the renewal agency; (4) participation from all segments of the community; (5) greater participation in more elements of the urban renewal program; (6) more cooperation from other agencies; and (7) better use of communication techniques and media.

Loring, William C., Jr.; Frank L. Sweetser; and Charles F. Ernst. *Community Organization for Citizen Participation in Urban Renewal.* Prepared by the Housing Association of Metropolitan Boston for the Massachusetts Department of Commerce. Cambridge, Massachusetts: Cambridge Press, 1957.

This is a presentation of materials on citizen participation in urban renewal projects in the Boston area. The book describes selected cases ranging from federally assisted projects to projects of voluntary rehabilitation and experiences of neighborhood associations and district councils and efforts to develop citizen participation at the citywide level. Dominant aspects of renewal are identified as economic, domestic, educational, religious, governmental, and the welfare and civic elements of the urban community. The study drew two conclusions about leadership: citizen participation in urban renewal must be guided by leaders who are experienced and competent in the skills of community organization; in blighted areas, effective community organization for citizen participation in urban renewal will require the services of professionally competent community organization workers to guide and assist groups fighting blight. The last chapter presents some "lessons" gleaned from the study and puts citizen participation in perspective for professionals in various fields.

National Urban League Urban Renewal Demonstration Project. *Toward Effective Participation in Urban Renewal*. New York: National Urban League, 1974.

Nixon, William B. *Citizen Participation in Urban Renewal*. Nashville, Tennessee: State Planning Commission, 1957.

Rosenberg, Albert G. "Baltimore's Harlem Park Finds Self-Help Citizen Participation is Successful." *Journal of Housing* 18:5 (May 1961): 204–09.

Rosenberg describes urban renewal in Baltimore's Harlem Park, a high density, low income area. The original urban renewal decisions were made without community input. Professional community organizers later came into the area and through their efforts the neighborhood council was completely reorganized so that real participation could take place. Absentee landlords and renters both became involved in neighborhood improvements. The article describes some of the problems that have been attacked.

Rossi, Peter H., and Robert A. Dentler. *The Politics of Urban Renewal: The Chicago Findings*. Glencoe, Illinois: Free Press, 1961.

> Reviews:
> *Booklist* 58 (April 1, 1962): 514.
> Buck, Thomas. *Chicago Sunday Tribune* (April 15, 1962): 4.
> Goldhor, Herbert. *Library Journal* 87 (June 1962): 2152.

Liel, J. T. *American Sociological Review* 27 (August 1962): 374.
Lynd, Staughton. *New Republic* 146 (April 23, 1962): 27.
Scaffer, Albert. *Social Forces* 41 (October 1962): 95.
Sjoberg, Gideon. *American Journal of Sociology* 68 (November 1962): 374.

This study attempts to ascertain the part actually played by citizens in developing an urban renewal program for the Hyde Park-Kenwood community in Chicago. Interviews were conducted with persons most active in local planning and community problem solving and with organizational leaders. This was supplemented with data from conference records, newspapers, observations, and the National Opinion Research Center. The study examines the history and the social characteristics of Hyde Park-Kenwood, the alternatives available to Hyde Park-Kenwood, and the roles of the University of Chicago and the Hyde Park-Kenwood Community Conference. Two cases in which the conference mediated between citizens and planners are analyzed. The opposition of a metropolitan opponent to the plan is described, and the roles played by city officials and municipal agencies are discussed. The authors assert that the case of Hyde Park-Kenwood is unique because the community was already well organized and because of the involvement of the conference and the University of Chicago. The conference was found to have its greatest success in sparking the movement toward change and creating popular acceptance of the renewal plan. Other less successful roles which the conference played were shaping goals and functioning as policy makers. An appendix contains the survey instrument used in Hyde Park-Kenwood.

Rutledge, Edward. "Citizen Participation." *Journal of Housing* 26:11 (December 1969): 603.

Rutledge asserts that the only issue involved in citizen participation in housing is racial segregation. He blames public housing for creating segregation in many communities where it had not previously existed. More participation by blacks is seen as a solution.

Schaller, Lyle E. "Is the Citizen Advisory Committee a Threat to Representative Government?" *Public Administration Review* 24:3 (September 1964): 175–79.

The author discusses citizen advisory boards in general but focuses, in some cases, specifically upon citizen boards in the urban renewal program. After describing the functions of and problems with citizen advisory boards, the author concludes that citizen advisory boards can "make a significant contribution to the governmental process if both the appointing officials and the committee members clearly understand the limited authority which properly can be vested in such a group," but that citizen boards have "failed to adequately bridge the widening gulf between government and the growing body of alienated citizens."

Schaller, Lyle E. "Ten Suggestions for Citizen Advisory Boards." *Tennessee Planner* 25:4 (Summer 1964): 115–21.

Ten suggestions for citizens advisory committees in urban renewal programs are presented: (1) each member should represent the public interest; (2) the committee should be a two-way channel of communication; (3) the committee should discover what the people want; (4) the committee should realize that it *advises* governmental officials who have the major responsibility in the area; (5) the committee should work to reconcile differences between people and their government; (6) the committee should take firm positions on controversial issues; (7) the committee should not make political decisions, rather its report should contain alternatives and recommendations; (8) meetings should be convenient and public; (9) the committee should be representative along social and economic lines as well as along racial, ethnic, and geographic dimensions; and (10) the committee should not try to "grab power."

United States Department of Housing and Urban Development. "The Citizen in Urban Renewal." *Urban Renewal Notes.* Washington, D.C.: Department of Housing and Urban Development, January/ February 1962.

This pamphlet discusses citizen participation as a requirement in urban renewal programs. It presents specific instances of what citizens are doing in sixteen places. Suggested readings are included.

United States Office of Urban Renewal. *Adams-Morgan: Democratic Action to Save a Neighborhood.* Washington, D.C.: U.S. Government Printing Office, 1964.

This is a description of an attempt to upgrade the Adams-Morgan community in Washington, D.C. The application for the demonstration project was made by the Board of Commissioners of the District of Columbia to the Housing and Home Finance Agency in February 1958 at the urging of the Adams-Morgan Better Neighborhood Conference. The project proposed to involve residents and government in improving the neighborhood and organizing ongoing community groups. This was to be done through citizen participation, conservation and rehabilitation, and city government participation. This report describes the kinds of work done during the two-year project. It describes how the project was organized and how people were encouraged to participate through block groups, community organizations, special purpose organizations, and larger organizations such as churches and civic associations. The various programs instituted by the different departments of the government of the District of Columbia are summarized. Planning with citizen involvement and types of housing improvements are discussed. The Citizens Planning Committee together with the National Capital Planning Commission and the District of Columbia Redevelopment Land Agency drew up an urban renewal plan that would exclude industry and heavy commerce from the area.

Wilson, James Q. "Planning and Politics: Citizen Participation in Urban Renewal." *Journal of the American Institute of Planners* 29:4 (November 1963): 242–49. Reprinted in Bellush, Jewel, and Murray Hausknecht, eds. *Urban Renewal: People, Politics and Planning.* Garden City, New York: Anchor Books, 1967, pp. 287–301.

Wilson discusses the need for citizen participation in urban renewal and points out two different types of citizen organizations. Upper and middle income people are described as "public regarding." They view the long-range interests of the community as a whole and articulate positive goals for their community urban renewal projects. Low income people, with no skills in participation and a lower sense of personal efficacy, are described as "private regarding." They organize against what they perceive as specific threats against themselves. The implications of this are that middle class people will be consulted by planners in setting urban renewal goals, while lower class people will not be consulted.

Wilson, James Q., ed. *Urban Renewal: The Record and the Controversy.* Cambridge, Massachusetts: MIT Press, 1966.

Reviews:
Abrams, Charles. *New York Times Book Review* (July 16, 1967): 6.
Choice 3 (December 1966): 962.
Christian Century 83 (May 18, 1966): 656.
Potts, R. S. *Library Journal* 91 (July 1966): 346.

This is a collection of writings on urban renewal from different points of view. Materials are included on history, theory and practice, and on legal, political, social, economic, and design issues. The eight parts of the book cover the following topics: (1) the economics of cities; (2) the history, goals, and accomplishments of urban renewal; (3) three cases of development of local renewal programs; (4) relocation of families and businesses; (5) citizen participation and federal-city relations; (6) response of city planning to urban renewal; (7) criticisms of urban renewal and replies; and (8) views of three experts on the future of urban renewal.

JUVENILE DELINQUENCY

Brager, George A. "Organizing the Unaffiliated in a Low-Income Area." *Social Work* 8:3 (April 1963): 34–40.

Barriers to organizing low income communities are discussed. The author feels that characteristics of community life, lower income life, and the structure of community organizations hinder low income community integration. He then discusses the efforts of the Organizing the Unaffiliated program of Mobilization for Youth. It makes use of the existing social structure and indigenous organizers to stimulate participation of low income residents.

Brager, George A., and Francis P. Purcell, eds. *Community Action Against Poverty: Readings from the Mobilization Experience.* New Haven, Connecticut: College and University Press, 1967.

Reviews:
Mitrisin, Sophie. *Library Journal* (January 1968): 93.
Shostak, A. B. *American Sociological Review* 33 (June 1968): 473.

This collection of papers presents reports of observations and experiences by staff members of Mobilization for Youth. The first section of papers discusses the participants in the antipoverty program—the poor and public and private agencies. The second section presents the demonstration project as an answer to the failure of public and private agencies, with Mobilization for Youth as an example. The last four sections discuss the concepts of social action by the poor, the employment of clients, new roles for social workers as advocates, and the use of law and legal services in social action.

Brager, George A., and Harry Specht. "Mobilizing the Poor for Social Action." *The Social Welfare Forum, 1965.* Official Proceedings, 92d Annual Forum, National Conference on Social Welfare, Atlantic City, New Jersey, May 23–25, 1965. New York: Columbia University Press, 1965, pp. 197–210.

Brager and Specht discuss how the poor can best be organized for social action. The authors examine two kinds of problems in mobilizing the poor—ideological and institutional. Three strategies used by the Mobilization for Youth community development program are presented: social brokerage to increase participation, integrative mechanisms to strengthen organizations, and social protest to support social movements.

Grosser, Charles F. "Community Development Programs Serving the Urban Poor." *Social Work* 10:3 (July 1965): 15–21.

The experience of the Mobilization for Youth program is used to identify some of the issues involved in trying to organize the poor. First, problems inherent in organizing the poor are presented. Next, the several roles of the community worker are explored: the enabler, the "broker," the advocate, and the activist. Third, the author looks at the issue of organizational forms of neighborhood development programs. He feels there is a need to determine the effectiveness of various strategies.

Grosser, Charles F. *Helping Youth: A Study of Six Community Organization Programs.* Washington, D.C.: U.S. Government Printing Office, 1968.

This report presents in-depth case studies of six projects designed to develop comprehensive community action programs to deal with the basic causes of juvenile delinquency. All of the projects assumed that social, structural, and environmental pathology were the causes of juvenile delinquency and that neighborhood residents and recipients needed to be involved in planning and implementing social services. The six case studies presented are: (1) Mobilization for Youth on New York City's Lower East Side; (2) Syracuse Crusade for Opportunity in Syracuse, New York; (3) United Planning Organization, Washington, D.C.; (4) Houston Action for Youth, Houston, Texas; (5) Action for Appalachian Youth, Charleston, West Virginia; and (6) HARYOU-ART, Harlem, New York City. The concluding chapter offers suggestions to other community organizers and social planners drawn from the experiences of these programs.

Mogulof, Melvin B. "Involving Low-Income Neighborhoods in Anti-Delinquency Programs." *Social Work* 10:4 (October 1965): 51–57.

Mogulof reports on the efforts of demonstration programs of the President's Committee on Juvenile Delinquency and Youth Crime to involve neighborhood leadership in policy making and to organize neighborhoods to have an impact on policy making. The author points to three ways of facilitating participation of the poor: convenient meetings, clarification of the right to sanction policy, and knowledge of when to involve people and whom to involve.

COMMUNITY ACTION

Alinsky, Saul D. "The War on Poverty—Political Pornography." *Journal of Social Issues* 21:1 (1965): 41–47.

The author views the poverty program as sanctimonious and a political blunder. He points out that we cannot treat the poor as though they were a foreign nation. He also feels that the poverty program does not recognize that poverty includes poverty of power. He concludes that the poverty program is a huge political pork barrel in which poverty funds are used for political patronage.

"Antipoverty Community Corporations," *Columbia Journal of Law and Social Problems* 2 (June 1967): 94–104.

This article argues that the poor can control and administer antipoverty programs through community corporations. To support this argument, two examples of community corporations are described.

Austin, David M. "Resident Participation, Political Mobilization, or Organizational Cooptation? Findings from the Study of Community Representation in Community Action Agencies." Paper prepared for the National Academy of Public Administration Conference on Participation of the Poor and Public Administration, Holly Knoll Conference Center, Williamsburg, Virginia, May 21–23, 1970. Mimeograph. Also in *Public Administration Review* 32, special issue (September 1972): 409–20.

The findings of comparative evaluations of community action agencies are presented. Twenty community action agencies in cities with populations from 50,000 to 80,000 were studied in 1967 and 1968. The focus of the study was target area members on community action agency policy boards and the activities of target area groups sponsored by the community action agency. The study found that participation on community action agency boards, through target area associations, and through employment of nonprofessionals, was similar in the agencies studied. Also similar was the impact of participation, which was relatively limited. Variations among community action agencies were numerous despite federal provisions, leading to the conclusion that local variables were more important than the federal constant. Four participation patterns were identified: (1) limited organizational participation; (2) active organizational participation; (3) organizational adversary participation; and (4) one type of political participation, political adversary participation. The study found that citizen participation had not spread from the community action agencies to other areas of government.

Avery, Robert W., and Herbert A. Chesler. *A Community Organizes for Action: A Case Study of the Mon-Yough Region in Pennsylvania.* University Park: Pennsylvania State University Institute for Research on Human Resources, June 1967.

This is a case study of the Mon-Yough Community Action Committee (MYCAC) in a steel mill area in Allegheny County, Pennsylvania. The study presents a description and analysis of the process of organization, an analysis of the goals and activities of the organization, and an economic and demographic profile of the area. The evolution of community action in this case is described as a synthesizing process in which parts of other organizations are recruited and merged to form a synthetic organization (i.e., MYCAC).

Bachrach, Peter. "A Power Analysis: The Shaping of Anti-Poverty Policy in Baltimore." *Public Policy* 18 (Winter 1970): 155–86.

Disagreeing with the pluralist interpretation of community power, Bachrach asserts that the community political system is closed or partially closed to certain groups. He says that power, though not demonstrated in the decision-making process, may, nonetheless, be used to prevent political conflict. He calls this non-decision making. As an example, he presents the case of blacks in Baltimore, Maryland, as they sought to gain access to the political system.

Berry, Theodore M. "O.E.O.: Making Citizen Participation Work." *Public Management* 51:7 (July 1969): 21–22.

A positive assessment of "maximum feasible participation" in community action agencies is presented in this article. The author believes that, for the first time, ghetto residents have been given the opportunity to participate in aspects of community life that affect them. He also believes that public and private agencies have become more responsive to the needs of the poor.

Bloomberg, Warner, Jr., and Henry J. Schmandt, eds. *Power, Poverty, and Urban Policy.* Beverly Hills, California: Sage Publications, 1968.

Part Three of this book contains five selections on participation of the poor in urban politics. The first article, by Sanford Kravitz, looks at the origins of the participation concept of OEO, its implementation, and impact. The next selection presents an interpretive analysis of the community action program prepared for the Senate Subcommittee on Employment, Manpower, and Poverty, by Howard Hallman, director of a study which investigated community action agencies and operations in thirty-five communities. The study found the poor had real power in only three cases. The third article, by Warner Bloomberg and Florence W. Rosenstock, asserts that the increase in participation of the poor through the war on poverty may force the upper and middle classes to encourage a more effective antipoverty program. The last two selections focus on two developing areas of the world: Africa, discussed by Peter C. W. Gutkind, and South America, discussed by William Mangin.

Boone, Richard W. "Reflections on Citizen Participation and the Economic Opportunity Act." Paper prepared for the National Academy of Public Administration Conference on Crisis, Conflict, and Creativity, Airlie House, Warrenton, Virginia, April 23–25, 1970. Mimeograph. Also in *Public Administration Review* 32, special issue (September 1972): 444–56.

This paper discusses the history of the concept of "maximum feasible participation" of the poor, how it came to be implemented in the Economic Opportunity Act of 1964, and how it was received at the local community level. The author feels that participation of the poor under the Community Action Program has led to demands for participation in government from all sectors of the society. However, he believes that the power to participate cannot be given; rather, that institutions need to be restructured to open them up to participation by all citizens.

Bowen, Don R., and Louis H. Masotti. "Spokesmen for the Poor: An Analysis of Cleveland's Poverty Board Candidates." *Urban Affairs Quarterly* 4:1 (September 1968): 88–110.

The authors analyze an election to select representatives of the poor for five newly created seats on the Council for Economic Opportunities in Greater Cleveland (Ohio). Three hypotheses about the candidates were presented: that the candidates were located near the center of a center-periphery continuum of social dimensions; that the candidates' personal organization would be stronger and more effective than that of most of the poor; and that this election has aroused and flushed out the ideologues among the poor. Forty-three of the forty-eight candidates were interviewed. The first two hypotheses were confirmed, but the third was not supported by the data.

Brody, Stanley J. "Maximum Participation of the Poor: Another Holy Grail?" *Social Work* 15:1 (January 1970): 68–75.

Brody criticizes "maximum feasible participation" of the poor as defined and implemented by the Office of Economic Opportunity. He points out that voting for poverty representatives has not achieved "maximum" participation because voter turnout is very low, that few people are actually served by the programs, and that "the poor" are not a homogeneous group. He categorizes the poor as upper class poor with special needs exceeding their income, middle class poor characterized by underemployment, and the poor-poor who are isolated and rarely visible on poverty boards. He asserts that poverty programs are geared to the problems of the upper and middle class poor and that they are the ones who participate. The author believes that efforts must be made at the federal level to define the nature and goals of citizen participation and to establish mechanisms for its implementation.

Cobb, Paul. "Comments on Events in Oakland, California." Paper prepared for the National Academy of Public Administration Conference on Crisis, Conflict, and Creativity, Airlie House, Warrenton, Virginia, April 23–25, 1970. Mimeograph.

Cobb presents a chronological account of attempts by the Alameda (California) County Republicans to destroy the Oakland Economic Development Council, Inc., the official Oakland community action agency. Because the council had been so successful in organizing the poor and involving them in politics, the Republican mayor was trying to gain control of the council. The purpose of this was, obviously, to prevent the diluting of Republican control in the county.

Dare, Robert. "Citizen Participation in NSC Advisory Committees." *A Comprehensive and Systematic Evaluation of the Community Action Program and Related Programs Operating in Atlanta, Georgia, Final Report, Special Reports.* Edited by Fred R. Crawford. Atlanta: Center for Research in Social Change, Emory University, 1969, pp. 37–55.

This is a report on the involvement of the poor in the antipoverty program in Atlanta in 1965 and 1966. Ninety citizen advisors from four of twelve neighborhood service centers were interviewed. It was found that the poor were involved more in an advisory capacity than as policy makers; i.e., their involvement did not begin until most of the policy decisions had been made. However, more poor were involved in 1966 than in 1965.

Davis, Lawrence. "Syracuse: What Happens When the Poor Take Over."
Reporter 38:6 (March 21, 1968): 19–21.

Davis describes the case of Syracuse, New York, where representatives of the poor were able to gain control over the local community action agency and its program. The author gives a chronological account of how the poor gained power and antagonized the city power structure and OEO in the process. OEO finally cut off funds for the agency.

Description and Evaluation of Neighborhood Centers. Springfield, Virginia: National Technical Information Service, 1965.

This is a segment of a report by Kirschner Associates which analyzed and interpreted aggregate data on the Community Action Program's neighborhood service centers. Five hundred field interviews were conducted with officials, staff, and clients of twenty representative centers. Relevant aspects of each center such as origins, purposes, organizational arrangements, budget, community action, and participation of the poor are discussed.

Dubey, Sumati N. "Community Action Programs and Citizen Participation: Issues and Confusions." Social Work 15:1 (January 1970): 76–84.

Four rationales for resident participation are presented: (1) program irrelevance and inadequacy; (2) creation of a power base; (3) improved service delivery; and (4) the value of participatory democracy. Three predominant patterns of participation are identified: residents as policy makers on boards, residents serving in staff positions, and residents in constituent groups providing feedback. Methods of promoting participation are seen as: containment, cooptation, and codetermination. The author feels that the main issues involved in citizen participation are: (1) lack of consensus on goals; (2) the degree of participation of residents; (3) their right to sanction policy; and (4) the credentials of the participants.

Gilbert, Neil. Clients or Constituents: Community Action in the War on Poverty. San Francisco: Jossey-Bass, 1970. Aspects of this study also reported in Gilbert, Neil. "Maximum Feasible Participation? A Pittsburgh Encounter." Social Work 14:3 (July 1969): 84–92; and Gilbert, Neil. "Neighborhood Coordinator: Advocate or Middleman?" Social Service Review 43:2 (June 1969): 136–44.

The author describes and analyzes the development of Pittsburgh's community action program over a three-year period, particularly its efforts to elicit citizen participation. Six elements of the program are examined: organizational structure, strategy for change, professional leadership, solidarity, opposition, and goal achievement. Data were gathered through participant observation, examination of program related documents, and a survey of 256 citizen board members and 26 professional staff members. The poor were found to have had little influence in creating the structure of the program. The role of the coordinator was seen as one fraught with conflict. He must act as both advocate and middleman. Citizen participation was found to be functioning more as education and therapy than as a strategy for social change. The Mayor's Committee on Human Resources was privately committed to building a strong citizens' confederation but was unable to do so. Opposition to the program was negligible because it was viewed as nonthreatening. There was a low degree of internal solidarity, and the program was not successful in achieving its objective of democratizing social welfare.

Gilbert, Neil, and Joseph W. Eaton. "Who Speaks for the Poor?" *Journal of the American Institute of Planners* 36:6 (November 1970): 411–16.

This article describes the results of a survey of resident assessments of conditions in eight antipoverty program neighborhoods in Pittsburgh. The survey found that leaders who claimed to speak for the neighborhood displayed a high degree of discontent while the majority of residents were satisfied with neighborhood conditions (i.e., the status quo). The authors caution planners who seek "community support" not to be fooled into thinking that support from such leaders is democratic planning.

Gilmore, Mary H. "Playing for Keeps." *Neighborhood Organization for Community Action*. Edited by John B. Turner. New York: National Association of Social Workers, 1968, pp. 212–20.

This chapter discusses the case of Operation Breakthrough, a community action program funded by OEO and directed by a statewide antipoverty agency in a southern college town of 80,000. Its purpose was to provide health and welfare services with citizen participation. The discussion describes the organizing of public housing tenants and tenant gains.

Gove, Walter, and Herbert Costner. "Organizing the Poor: An Evaluation of a Strategy." *Social Science Quarterly* 50:3 (December 1969): 643–56.

An effort by the Central Area Motivational Program of Seattle, Washington, to develop local neighborhood self-improvement associations through the efforts of indigenous community organizers is described. Organizers were nonprofessional local black women and the nineteen clubs that were organized had memberships consisting of mostly black women. One hundred twelve residents of the area (all available club members) and five community organizers were interviewed. The study concluded that this strategy of community organization was a failure and that more professional help was needed in such efforts.

Greenstone, J. David, and Paul E. Peterson. *Race and Authority in Urban Politics: Community Participation and the War on Poverty.* New York: Russell Sage Foundation, 1973. Aspects of this study also reported in Greenstone, J. David, and Paul E. Peterson. "Reformers, Machines, and the War on Poverty." *City Politics and Public Policy.* Edited by James Q. Wilson. New York: Wiley and Sons, 1968, pp. 267–92.

This book is a comparative analysis of citizen participation in community action agencies in the five largest American cities: New York, Chicago, Los Angeles, Philadelphia, and Detroit. The book begins with an analysis of the five case studies which illustrates the differences between the five cities and describes the studies' analytic frameworks. The authors use a "role-interest approach" in comparing group behavior across cities and over time. Using this approach, the authors then discuss specific role interests and associated ideologies of groups involved in community action. This analysis leads to an emphasis on the racial dimensions of the citizen participation controversy.

After having identified the differing roles of classes, races, and authorities in the participation controversy, the authors attempt to identify those factors which explain variations in the degree of participation in the cities studied. They argue that the manner of selecting participants and whether or not the city has a "relatively autonomous bureaucracy" influence the degree of participation. Power structures and policy-making processes that produced variations in participation policies are then examined. In the concluding chapter, the authors discuss "participation as public policy" and examine some major objections to participation as practiced by community action agencies.

Grossman, David A. "The Community Action Program: A New Function for Local Government." *Urban Planning and Social Policy.* Edited by Bernard J. Frieden and Robert Morris. New York: Basic Books, 1968, pp. 432–47.

Seven major features of the Community Action Program are discussed: (1) federal grants in aid coupled with local funds; (2) community based programs; (3) the community-wide "umbrella" agency; (4) federal funds for both public and private agencies; (5) broad range of eligible community activities; (6) CAP as a coordinator of other federal programs; and (7) resident participation. The two most important elements are seen as the effort to develop comprehensive service programs to attack poverty and maximum feasible participation.

Kramer, Philip. "The Indigenous Worker: Hometowner, Striver, or Activist." *Social Work* 17:1 (January 1972): 43–49.

Kramer presents a three-part typology of indigenous community workers from an exploratory study of indigenous community workers in two Boston agencies—the Roxbury Multi Service Center and the Brockton Community Action Agency. The three types are: the hometowners who are older, female, less educationally motivated, neither militant nor moderate organizer members, and who look at problems individually; the strivers who are female, younger, motivated toward future education, reject the militant media, belong to moderate organizations, and who look at problems clinically; and the activists who are male, younger, educationally but not professionally oriented, believe in social action, and who view problems as resulting from a lack of political power. The article goes on to examine each group's problems vis-à-vis loyalty identification, task requirements, and vocational advancement.

Kramer, Ralph M. *Participation of the Poor: Comparative Case Studies in the War on Poverty.* Englewood Cliffs, New Jersey: Prentice-Hall, 1969.

This book presents case studies of five California community action agencies: Berkeley, Contra Costa County, Oakland, San Francisco, and Santa Clara County. Data were gathered through observation and interviews in 1965 and 1966. Comparative analyses were done in the areas of control, representation, power, service vs. organization, and participation. The author concludes that the extent of independence and political power of the community action agencies are not as great as some believe.

Kramer, Ralph M., and Clare Denton. "Organization of a Community Action Program: A Comparative Case Study." *Social Work* 12:4 (October 1967): 68–80.

In this comparative case study of six San Francisco Bay Area communities, the authors look at the process of organizing a community action program, the steps taken, and the sources of influence behind the implementation. Interviews were conducted with key participants in the organizational process (as identified by the reputational method). The study found that the process was similar in all six communities. Four separate phases were identified: (1) initiation and the convergence of interests; (2) inception and expansion of the action system; (3) decision making in which the action system operated; and (4) the transformation of the action system.

Kravitz, Sanford, and Ferne K. Kolodner. "Community Action: Where Has It Been? Where Will It Go?" *Political Power and the Urban Crisis*. 2d ed. Edited by Alan Shank. Boston: Holbrook Press, 1973, pp. 486–500. Originally appeared in *Annals of the American Academy of Political and Social Science* 385 (September 1969): 31–40.

A history and critique of the Community Action Program are presented in this article. The Ford Foundation's Gray Areas Program and the President's Committee on Juvenile Delinquency are discussed as precursors, and the emergence of community action and its problems and successes are described. The relationship of the community action agencies to the decentralization movement is discussed, and criticisms of the agencies are presented. The author believes that the next step in poverty relief should be in the direction of income redistribution.

Lyden, Fremont James, and Jerry V. Thomas. "Citizen Participation in Policy-Making: A Study of a Community Action Program." *Social Science Quarterly* 50:3 (December 1969): 631–42.

This is a report on a nineteen-month study of the Seattle-King County (Washington) Economic Opportunity Board to determine whether the representatives of the poor were able to participate in policy making and whether a viable decision-making entity could be developed by community leaders, public officials, and the poor. Data were gathered through observation of the regular monthly meetings of the board. It was concluded that while all groups participated, the poor participated in smaller numbers. However, a viable decision-making entity was developed.

Marris, Peter, and Martin Rein. *Dilemmas of Social Reform: Poverty and Community Action in the United States*. New York: Atherton Press, 1967.

Reviews:
Choice 5 (September 1968): 880.
Levitan, S.A. *American Sociological Review* 33 (August 1968): 646.
Peterson, P.E. *American Journal of Sociology* 73 (March 1968): 640.

Marris and Rein discuss the community action movement in the context of American reform. The historical background and the social and political contexts of community action are described. The Community Action Program and problems it encountered are described. The underlying assumptions of the community action movement were the apathy of the poor and the stultification of bureaucracy. However, many problems encountered by the program were beyond the scope of the agencies. One problem encountered was the diffusion of power, i.e., the problem of integrating institutions around a common plan. The authors found that, after five years, the reformers had still not been able to solve the problems of the intransigent autonomy of public and private agencies, how to use social science for the practical formulation and evaluation of policy, and how to increase the power of the poor under government auspices.

Marshall, Dale Rogers, *The Politics of Participation in Poverty: A Case Study of the Board of the Economic and Youth Opportunities Agency of Greater Los Angeles.* Berkeley: University of California Press, 1971.

> Reviews:
> Hudson, J. R. *American Journal of Sociology* 78 (September 1972): 441.
> Silverman, William. *Library Journal* 96 (July 1971): 2326.

This study analyzes what happens when the poor become members of a community action agency. The study focused on the process of interaction between poor and nonpoor members of the Board of the Economic and Youth Opportunities Agency of Greater Los Angeles. Information was collected from interviews with board members, observation of meetings, and examination of written information about the board. The author concluded that although the community members were coopted, their level of participation in the system was increased and their dissatisfaction with the system remained. Thus, leaders in movements for social change were being created. Agency representatives on the board became more tolerant of the community viewpoint, but did not experience as much change in attitudes as did the community representatives.

Marshall, Dale Rogers, "Public Participation and the Politics of Poverty." *Race, Change, and Urban Society.* Edited by Peter Orleans and William Russell Ellis, Jr. Beverly Hills, California: Sage Publications, 1973, pp. 451–82.

Using evidence from the available literature, the author places "the public participation ideology in historical perspective," then traces the role of public participation in the "War on Poverty" through its origins, implementation, and results. The author then attempts to evaluate the experience of the "War on Poverty" in terms of its implications for urban reform.

"Maximum Feasible Participation in the Austin Community Action Program." *A Comprehensive Evaluation of the Community Action Program in Austin and Travis County, Texas, Final Report*. Vol. 2. Austin: TRACOR, 1969, pp. 64–184.

Moynihan, Daniel P. *Maximum Feasible Misunderstanding: Community Action in the War on Poverty*. New York: Free Press, 1969.

> Reviews:
> Bliven, Naomi. *New Yorker* 45 (June 7, 1969): 143.
> *Choice* 6 (October 1969): 1064.
> Conlin, J. J. *Best Sellers* 28 (February 15, 1969): 457.
> Forslund, M. A. *Library Journal* 94 (February 1969): 741.
> Gannon, T. M. *America* 121 (November 29, 1969): 530.
> Goldwasser, Thomas. *Saturday Review* 52 (March 8, 1969): 30.
> Greely, A. M. *Critic* 27 (June 1969): 86.
> Greene, Wade. *Newsweek* 73 (February 10, 1969): 82.
> Pierce, Francis. *New Republic* 160 (February 22, 1969): 23.
> Riecken, H. W. *Science* 164 (May 9, 1969): 663.
> Thernstrom, Stephen. *Commentary* 47 (May 1969): 87.
> *Virginia Quarterly Review* 45 (Summer 1969): 113.
> Walinsky, Adam. *New York Times Book Review* (February 2, 1969): 1.
> Wolman, Harold. *Commonweal* 90 (May 16, 1969): 267.

This book contains a critical account of the war on poverty of the 1960s. The author describes the origins of the maximum feasible participation concept in sociological theory and then explains how an idea originating in the social sciences became a political reality. He charges that the antipoverty program was a failure chiefly because the government did not know how to implement such an idea.

Moynihan, Daniel P. "What is 'Community Action'?" *Public Interest* 5 (Fall 1966): 3–8.

The author questions the definition, meaning, and intent of the Community Action Program. He presents four definitions: (1) the Bureau of the Budget concept which focuses on the coordination of programs; (2) the Alinsky concept of community organization for power; (3) the Peace Corps concept of community development; and (4) the Task Force concept of a pragmatic program that would be enacted by Congress. The author charges that pluralism runs rampant in the Community Action Program and that diversity has led to misunderstandings, confusion, and a sense of betrayal.

Peterson, Paul E. "Forms of Representation: Participation of the Poor in the Community Action Program." *American Political Science Review* 64:2 (June 1970): 491–507.

Using Hanna Pitkin's categorization of representation (formal, descriptive, substantive, or interest representation), the author analyzes the process of representation in the Community Action Program during its initial formative period (1964–1966) in Chicago, Philadelphia, and New York City. The following hypotheses were supported: representation of universalistic interests of low status groups was associated with (1) organized relationships between formal representatives and the low status groups, (2) political competition between those seeking to be representatives, (3) formal representatives who are related to the low status group but not socially descriptive of it, and (4) substantial influence of formal representatives over the operation of the program. Representation of particularistic interests was associated with (1) little competition, (2) few if any organizational links, (3) ample opportunity for representatives to distribute material benefits to their constituents, (4) moderate influence of representatives over program, and (5) representatives who were socially descriptive of the low status group.

Piven, Frances. "Participation of Residents in Neighborhood Community Action Programs." *Social Work* 11:1 (January 1966): 73–80.

The author asserts that poor people are hindered from participation in community life because of their lack of resources and that strategies for participation of the poor will have to overcome this problem. She discusses certain strategies and problems: (1) provision of services; (2) help for existing low income organizations; (3) engagement of professional community organization staff; (4) use of ethnic, religious, occupational, or residential groups as basis for affiliation; and (5) participation in social protest. The author also presents different forms of participation and the problems associated with them: resident participation on policy-making boards, resident employment as staff, and residents as members of active constituent groups.

Pollinger, Kenneth J., and Annette C. Pollinger. *Community Action and the Poor: Influence vs. Social Control in a New York City Community.* New York: Praeger, 1972.

Review:
Greene, Kenneth R. *American Political Science Review* 68 (March 1974): 286–87.

Examining twenty-six community action agency target areas in New York City and conducting an in-depth case study of one area, the authors conclude that inadequate financial and technical resources prevent community residents from effectively influencing the administration of the poverty program. It is then suggested that the community action agency acted as an agent of social control rather than as an advocate for the poor.

Rein, Martin, and S. M. Miller. "Citizen Participation and Poverty." *Connecticut Law Review* 1:2 (1968): 221–43.

This article describes several methods used to facilitate citizen involvement: sociotherapy, social action, employment of the poor, seeking legal redress, policy development (economic development and control of service systems), and the redistribution of political power.

Rein, Martin, and Frank Riessman. "A Strategy for Antipoverty Community Action Programs." *Social Work* 11:2 (April 1966): 3–12.

The authors discuss the Community Action Program's strategy against poverty in light of other third party intervention strategies which serve as a bridge between the citizen and bureaucracy: the traditional welfare council approach, the British system of using citizens advice bureaus, and the ombudsman. They see the Community Action Program as both a spokesman for the poor and an agent of established power.

Segalman, Ralph. "Dramatis Personae of the Community Action Program: A Built In Conflict Situation." *Rocky Mountain Science Journal* 4:2 (October 1967): 140–50.

Segalman describes stereotypes of the participants in the power struggle over community action programs: the poor, including the pseudo-poor, the surrogates of the poor, and the activists; and the representatives of the community, including lay leaders, professionals, and politicians. The author believes that, if programs are to survive, poor participants must be willing to compromise with "the system."

Shingles, Richard D. "Experimenting With Quasi-Experimentation: Effects of Participation in Voluntary Associations (CAA's) on Political Attitudes." Paper presented at the American Political Science Association meeting, Chicago, Illinois, August 29–September 2, 1974. Mimeograph.

Using respondents residing in St. Paul, and employing a pretest-post-test nonequivalent control group design and a cross-lagged panel design, the author examined the impact of participation in a community action agency project upon the respondents' personal and political alienation. No significant reduction in alienation could be attributed to participation in the project; but the author suggests that there are other, perhaps much more significant, benefits to be obtained from organizing the poor in self-help organizations.

Shostak, Arthur B. "Promoting Participation of the Poor: Philadelphia's Antipoverty Program." *Social Work* 11:1 (January 1966): 64–72.

This is a report on the efforts of poor people in Philadelphia to elect their own representatives to the Philadelphia Antipoverty Action Committee. The author reviews the background of the committee, its town meetings, the antipoverty election, and the record of the representatives of the poor. Also discussed are questions concerning the relationship between race and poverty. The author is optimistic about the Philadelphia experiment and calls for other cities to follow suit.

Slavin, Simon. "Community Action and Institutional Change." *The Social Welfare Forum, 1965*. Official Proceedings, 92d Annual Forum, National Conference on Social Welfare, Atlantic City, New Jersey, May 23–25, 1965. New York: Columbia University Press, 1965, pp. 147–61.

The author discusses the chances that community organization sponsored by OEO will result in institutional change. He discusses three aspects of "maximum feasible participation" of the poor: participation in policy making and administration, training and employment programs for the poor, and organizational mobilization of the poor. He feels that antipoverty programs are treating the symptoms rather than the causes of poverty and that community action programs are not enough to restructure the institutions and social patterns which result in poverty.

Social Welfare Planning Council. *Community Organization in Low-Income Neighborhoods in New Orleans*. New Orleans: Social Welfare Planning Council, December 1968.

This study examined Total Community Action, New Orleans' community action agency, and the effects of its maximum feasible participation program. Sixteen neighborhood groups were studied in one target area. Data came from structured interviews with participants, observations of meetings, reports, records, and news articles. Three groups of variables were isolated in an attempt to see if and how the organization accomplished its objectives: program variables which included goals, community organization staff, and community organization methods; intermediate variables including the number of neighborhood residents involved, the number of groups formed, the type of groups formed, and the strength of the group and its leadership; and dependent variables related to the outcomes of the program. The study makes a number of recommendations for administrative improvements, such as a rethinking of primary program areas, agreement on strategies and direction, and additional administrative staff to provide more control over the program.

Strange, John H. "Community Action in North Carolina: Maximum Feasible Misunderstanding, Mistake or Magic Formula?" *Publius* 2:2 (Fall 1972): 51–73.

Sundquist, James L., ed. *On Fighting Poverty: Perspectives from Experience.* New York: Basic Books, 1969.

> Reviews:
> Candeub, I. A. *Saturday Review* 52 (October 25, 1969): 60.
> *Choice* 6 (November 1969): 126.
> Forslund, M. A. *Library Journal* 94 (June 1969): 2454.
> *New Yorker* 45 (August 23, 1969): 96.

This book consists of a collection of papers from a series of seminars at the American Academy of Arts and Sciences in 1966 and 1967. The papers are concerned with the war on poverty, its origins, its workings, and its politics. Topics covered are the historical background of the antipoverty program, the development of the Community Action Program, two case studies of community action, the politics of the war on poverty, an evaluation of the Office of Economic Opportunity, and issues confronting the Nixon administration. Contributing authors are: Robert Coles, Gregory Farrell, Sanford Kravitz, Robert Levine, Peter H. Rossi, William C. Selover, James L. Sundquist, John G. Wofford, and Adam Yarmolinsky.

Theodore, Eustace D., and Carol N. Theodore. "Citizen Awareness and Involvement in Poverty Action." *Social Problems* 19:4 (Spring 1972): 484–96.

The history and growth of the Community Action Program are described. Interviews were conducted with a sample of 801 target and nontarget area black and white citizens in a city of 250,000 people. Blacks were found to be more aware of the city's community action agency and its work than whites. The young were more aware than the old. Respondents with higher socioeconomic status were more likely to think of the agency as a source of aid. Eighty-eight percent of the population had heard of the agency and 38 percent knew what it was. The authors conclude that the program clearly made an impact vis-à-vis awareness but suggest that new methods of raising awareness and participation are needed.

United States Office of Economic Opportunity. *The First Step . . . On a Long Journey.* Vol. 1. Congressional Presentation, April 1965. Washington, D.C.: U.S. Government Printing Office, 1965.

This is a report on the first six months of the war on poverty. All of the antipoverty programs are described, and budget and administration information is included. A section on citizen participation describes national volunteer group cooperation with, and support for, the antipoverty effort.

Vanecko, James J. "Community Mobilization and Institutional Change: The Influence of the Community Action Program in Large Cities." *Social Science Quarterly* 50:3 (December 1969): 609–30.

Vanecko reports the preliminary results of the first national evaluation of the Community Action Program. The findings reported here are from fifty cities with populations of 50,000 or more. The National Opinion Research Center conducted interviews with persons connected with all aspects of the local programs. The primary hypothesis was that when community action agencies emphasized community organization and mobilization, institutions would become more responsive to the poor than when agencies emphasized education, welfare, and employment services. This was confirmed by the data. The study concluded that an effective community action program had central office support for community organization, had neighborhood centers involved in community organization but uninvolved in militant activities, and did not spend time pressing specific demands on other institutions. Such programs were in cities with high levels of political activity in poverty areas.

Waits, Marilyn. "Dialogue and Response in San Diego." *Communities in Action* 5:2 (April 1969): 3–9.

This is a description of the local poverty program in San Diego, California, and the impact it has had on this traditionally conservative city. The Economic Opportunity Commission, the local community action agency, has encouraged the poor and minorities to speak out in the city. The author points to several developments which signal changes in the city: (1) a black had been appointed to the city council and more nonwhites and poor were participating in city government; (2) the city had secured model cities funds and a surplus food program; (3) the United Community Service, the charity fund raising agency, was reevaluating its role in serving the poor and reordering its priorities; (4) the Economic Opportunity Commission and the Welfare Rights Organization had succeeded in improving welfare policy; (5) the Navy became involved in supporting youth activities for the poor; and (6) changes in the State Employment Agency opened new jobs to the poor.

Waterman, Kenneth S. "Local Issues in the Urban War on Poverty." *Social Work* 11:1 (January 1966): 57–63.

The author describes types of poor people and suggests ways that they can be involved in solutions to their own problems. He believes that real political participation cannot be facilitated by the Office of Economic Opportunity (OEO). He suggests that private agencies and organizations provide seed money for grass roots organizations which could then contract with the government for services. OEO money could be used to hire indigenous people.

Wilson, Charles Z., and Adrienne S. Bennett. "Participation in Community Action Organizations: Some Theoretical Insights." *Sociological Inquiry* 37:2 (Summer 1967): 191–203.

The authors discuss the Barnard-Simon motivation model in terms of its usefulness in providing theoretical insights into participation in community action organizations. The model states that: an organization is a system of the interrelated social behaviors of a number of persons (participants) in the organization; inducements are payments made by or through the organization to its participants (i.e., wages, services, income); and contributions are "payments" to the organization (work, fee, capital).

Yankelovick, Daniel (Inc.). *Study of the Effects of Sections 210 and 211 of the 1967 Amendments to the Economic Opportunity Act as Required Under Section 233(c) of the Amendments.* Vol. 1. *Summary and Conclusions.* Springfield, Virginia: National Technical Information Service, February 1969.

Reporting the results of a ten-month research project which looked at the effects of the Green amendments on community action agencies, the author concludes that the amendments gave state and local governments some measure of control over the community action agencies. Six thousand personal interviews were conducted with community leaders and the poor and 53 community action agencies in 37 states were investigated and analyzed. The study found that the amendments had no negative effects on the community action agencies. In addition to presenting the conclusions of the study, the report discusses the climate before implementation of the amendments, factors affecting compliance decisions by communities, and reasons why no statewide community action agencies were created. An appendix contains the text of the amendments.

Zurcher, Louis A. "Functional Marginality: Dynamics of a Poverty Intervention Organization." *Southwestern Social Science Quarterly* 48:3 (December 1967): 411–21.

This study examined the Topeka (Kansas) Office of Economic Opportunity as it worked toward accomplishing the goals of the war on poverty. Seventy meetings were observed and two-hundred unstructured interviews were conducted. The Topeka OEO was found to be working to maintain a "functional marginality" between the poor and the nonpoor and trying to bring them together in order to implement an "Overlap Model" for social change.

Zurcher, Louis A. "The Leader and the Lost: A Case Study of Indigenous Leadership in a Poverty Program Community Action Committee." *Genetic Psychology Monographs* 76 (August 1967): 23–93.

Using data from an Indian community action committee of the Topeka (Kansas) Office of Economic Opportunity, the author explores the conflicts resulting from differing interpretations of the role of citizen participants. Data were gathered through participant observation and unstructured interviews. The study found that the indigenous leader experienced stress as he worked to maintain a marginal position between his followers and the organization. This was caused by a conflict between the two groups' expectations of his behavior. Some suggestions for training such indigenous leaders to cope with this type of situation are presented.

Zurcher, Louis A. "Poverty Program Indigenous Leaders: A Study of Marginality." *Sociology and Social Research* 53:2 (January 1969): 147–62.

Zurcher examines the process of role enactment among a small sample of volunteer indigenous leaders involved in the Topeka (Kansas) Office of Economic Opportunity. Interviews were conducted with twenty-three elected officers of the target neighborhood committees in Topeka. The study found that the indigenous leaders were more oriented toward the poor and saw themselves as less marginal than expected by the program's professional staff. The author feels that this finding questions the role of indigenous leaders as "bridges" between the poverty agency and the poor.

Zurcher, Louis A. "Socio-psychological Changes among OEO Indigenous Leaders as a Result of 'Maximum Feasible Participation'." Paper presented to the Society for the Study of Social Problems, American Sociological Association meeting, Boston, August 25, 1968. Mimeograph.

Zurcher, Louis A. "Walking the Tightrope—Some Role and Value Conflicts Experienced by a Poverty Program's Indigenous Leaders." Paper presented at the American Sociological Association meeting, Miami Beach, August 28, 1966. Mimeograph.

MODEL CITIES

Arnstein, Sherry R. "Maximum Feasible Manipulation." *Public Administration Review* 32, special issue (September 1972): 377–90; and "The View From City Hall," in the same special issue, pp. 390–402.

This is a case study told first from the perspective of the members of the North City Area Wide Council (Philadelphia model cities program) and then from the perspective of "City Hall." The first section was written by Sherry Arnstein with the understanding that she would write what the council "told her to write." The second segment was "approved by City Hall officials." From the council members' point of view, the case study is described as a two-and-a-half-year struggle for power that ended in "the power structure" withdrawing recognition and support from the council because of "the degree of power we [the Council] managed to achieve over the program." From the perspective of "City Hall," HUD and the model cities administration were to retain ultimate authority for the program and citizen boards were to serve in primarily advisory capacities.

Bourgeois, A. Donald. "Citizens Role in St. Louis Model Cities Program Described." *Journal of Housing* 24:11 (December 1967): 613–17.

Burke, Barlow, Jr. "The Threat to Citizen Participation in Model Cities." *Cornell Law Review* 56:5 (May 1971): 751–78.

Burke describes citizen participation in federal programs since the 1930s, the legislative background and the administration of the Model Cities Program, and the role the courts can play in disputes arising over the role of citizen participation in the program. The author feels that the role of the courts may well be to enforce contractual agreements. He sees the ambiguity of bureaucratic regulations as a major threat to Model Cities.

Gilbert, Neil; Harry Specht; and Charlane Brown. "Demographic Correlates of Citizen Participation: An Analysis of Race, Community Size and Citizen Influence." *Social Service Review* 48:4 (December 1974): 517–30.

Using data from model cities throughout the country, the authors assess the impact of race and community size upon the degree of citizen influence in model cities decision making. The data reveal no relationship between racial composition and citizen influence, but do indicate "a moderate positive correlation between community size and degree of citizen influence."

Harrison, Bennett. "Research Report: The Participation of Ghetto Residents in the Model Cities Program." *Journal of the American Institute of Planners* 39:1 (January 1973): 43–55.

This study investigated variation in the rates of employment of ghetto residents and in the salaries of all model cities employees during the program's planning period in 77 first-round community development agencies. Among the findings were: (1) citizen boards were active in most cities, but did not seem to have sole or primary control over important decisions; (2) model neighborhood residents were often employed as paraprofessionals, but not as professionals or in clerical office jobs; (3) higher salaries went with seniority; (4) even after removing the effects of age, sex, education, hours, and occupation, model neighborhood residents received $800 to $1,300 less per year than outsiders; and (5) more model neighborhood women than men were employed. Where model cities employees were under civil service, fewer residents were employed, and, in large cities, more residents were employed. The author concludes that the urban poor have not received as large a share of the benefits of this program as might be desired.

Hyde, Floyd K. "HUD Builds Partnership for Participation." *Public Management* 51:8 (July 1969): 17–19.

Hyde describes the statutory provisions for citizen participation in the Model Cities Program and the rationale behind them. He describes how citizen participation was shaping up in the initial planning period of the first-round cities and presents observations on the future directions of citizen participation in model cities programs.

Kaplan, Marshall. "HUD Model Cities—Planning Systems." Paper prepared for the National Academy of Public Administration Conference on Participation of the Poor and Public Administration, Holly Knoll Conference Center, Williamsburg, Virginia, May 21–23, 1970. Mimeograph.

An examination of the planning stages of model cities programs in eleven cities identifies five types of planning systems (illustrating each with descriptions of different model cities agencies in different cities) based on the degree of staff or resident participation in the planning process: (1) staff dominance/resident legitimization; (2) staff influence/resident sanction; (3) staff/resident parity; (4) resident influence/staff sanction; and (5) resident dominance/staff legitimization.

Kloman, Erasmus H. "Citizen Participation in the Philadelphia Model Cities Program: Retrospect and Prospect." *Public Administration Review* 32, special issue (September 1972): 402–08.

This article is preceded in this special issue of *Public Administration Review* by descriptions of citizen participation in the Philadelphia Model Cities Program from the perspectives of members of the North City Area Wide Council and representatives of "City Hall." (See Arnstein, Sherry, "Maximum Feasible Manipulation," above.) Kloman describes the initiation of the program and the origins of the divisions that ultimately led to the split between the area wide council (AWC) and city hall and the limiting of citizen participation to an advisory role. The author concludes that "there is a serious residue of bitterness and racial mistrust, but the bitterness has not prevented many former AWC personnel from continuing to work in constructive ways for their cause."

Mann, Seymour Z. "Participation of the Poor and Model Cities in New York City: The Impact of Participation and Has Participation Made a Difference?" Paper prepared for the National Academy of Public Administration Conference on Participation of the Poor and Public Administration, Holly Knoll Conference Center, Williamsburg, Virginia, May 21–23, 1970. Mimeograph.

A critical analysis of participation of the poor in the Model Cities Program in New York City, this paper examines data obtained during a number of different studies. One report prepared by the Hunter College

Urban Research Center found that the final authority in the model cities structure was at the top while the major policy and planning decisions were left to those at the bottom. This created administrative confusion in the whole city government. A Columbia University study of the model cities program in the South Bronx found considerable conflict between the city and the community. Interviews with the staff of the Harlem-East Harlem Policy Committee pointed to restlessness and dissatisfaction. The author felt that, at the time of his writing, the impact of participation was "negative and counterproductive," but he was optimistic about the continuation of the program and the prospects for positive impacts resulting from participation.

Mogulof, Melvin B. "Black Community Development in Five Western Model Cities." *Social Work* 15:1 (January 1970): 12–18.

The author examined five predominantly black model cities agencies in Seattle, Portland, Fresno, Richmond, and Oakland to see if decision making was characterized by a coalition between residents and administrators or if an adversary relationship developed. The adversary model describes a situation where two separate authorities exist with independent rights to block policy development or program action. Coalition is characterized by a situation where authority is divided among public agencies, the private sector, and the affected neighborhood. The author suggests that adversary relationships would be conducive to racial separation and that coalition would be conducive to racial integration. Programs in each of the five cities are described. They were all seen as characterized by adversary relationships and conducive to racial separation.

Patlan, Juan J. "The Model Cities Program, II. A Mexican-American View." *The Social Welfare Forum, 1971.* Official Proceedings, 98th Annual Forum, National Conference on Social Welfare, Dallas, Texas, May 16–21, 1971. New York: Columbia University Press, 1971, pp. 158–67.

In discussing the experience of the Model Cities Program in San Antonio, the author points out the lack of all of the "four C's—citizen participation, comprehensiveness, coordination, and concentration." Next he describes the Mexican American Unity Council, a community-based organization which he feels is effective. Three of its activities are discussed: the council obtained a National Institute of Mental Health Grant to extend the services of the mental health center; it brought together McDonald's, a bank, and the Small Business Administration to obtain the first McDonald's franchise for a Mexican-American; and it sponsored a project to tutor Mexican-American schoolchildren.

United States Commission on Civil Rights. *T.W.O.'s Model Cities Plan.* Washington, D.C.: U.S. Government Printing Office, 1969.

This booklet describes the Woodlawn Organization of Chicago, its origins, its involvement with model cities, and its relationship with the University of Chicago. The model cities proposal is described along with its strategy for citizen involvement, the strategic framework of the plan, and specific program proposals. Six factors underlying the Woodlawn approach are: (1) delivery of services; (2) evaluation as a management instrument; (3) ordering of goals; (4) environment; and (5) new techniques.

United States Department of Housing and Urban Development. *Citizen Participation in the Model Cities Program.* Community Development Evaluation Series, no. 2. Washington, D.C.: U.S. Government Printing Office, 1972.

The objectives of the study reported in this "summary" were "to develop an objective snapshot of citizen participation in the Model Cities Program; to assess the effect of existing HUD citizen participation policy and practice; to analyze the impact of citizen participation on individuals, projects and programs, and institutions; and to provide guidance to HUD on citizen participation in Model Cities programs." The authors describe the types of citizen participation groups found in model cities programs, the different decision-making roles these groups have in different localities, and the types of conflict arising between citizen groups, agency administrators, and city officials.

HUD policies were found to ensure that citizen participation existed to some degree in each of the cities examined, but that, in no case, did citizen control of the program result. In some cities HUD policies were found to have had "little or no impact on the development of citizen participation."

Citizen participation, the report concludes, has resulted in employment of residents of the model neighborhoods, increased political awareness among residents, and sometimes, increased disillusionment with government programs; but the report also notes that these impacts are limited to small segments of model neighborhood populations. Citizen participation seemed to have had little impact upon the development of applications for model cities programs and little effect upon the administration of the programs; but citizen participation did seem to influence the setting of priorities and the selection of projects after model cities efforts were initiated. Citizen participation seemed to have little impact upon city officials and institutions, but the authors feel that such impacts may be increasing.

The study concludes that "the results of citizen participation are generally consistent with [Model Cities'] goals," but that HUD's citizen participation policies and guidelines have, in some communities, been difficult to implement; and many local communities and HUD's regional and area offices have difficulty in "interpreting and implementing citizen participation policy."

United States Department of Housing and Urban Development. *The Model Cities Program: A Comparative Analysis of Participating Cities; Process, Product, Performance, and Prediction.* Washington, D.C.: U.S. Government Printing Office, 1973. Parts of this report are also described in Kaplan, Marshall, "HUD Model Cities," above.

This report is one of a series of analyses done by Marshall Kaplan, Gans, and Kahn for HUD. Information came from interviews with HUD staff and CDA directors and from questionnaires completed by model cities officials at federal and local levels. Five patterns of resident and staff influence, in planning and action, were identified: (1) staff dominant, (2) staff influence, (3) parity, (4) resident influence, and (5) resident dominant. Of 147 cities, nearly 60 percent were staff dominant and less than 20 percent were resident dominant. Factors influencing model city response patterns were size, form of government, and city patterns of behavior. Factors associated with the development of quality planning products were chief executive support and political integration, and the parity-type systems. There was little association between quality of program and implementation. The study also found that HUD's predictions on which cities would be able to meet the requirements were either no better than random or proved to be the opposite of what happened.

Warren, Roland L. "Model Cities First Round: Politics, Planning, and Participation." *Journal of the American Institute of Planners* 35:4 (July 1969): 245–52.

The International Study Project of the Florence Heller Graduate School at Brandeis University gathered reports from nine cities concerning the planning period for the cities' model cities programs: Oakland, Denver, San Antonio, Detroit, Columbus, Atlanta, Newark, Boston, and Manchester (New Hampshire). It was found that disputes arose between residents of the target areas and city halls over who should have how much power or control over the programs. The agencies were relatively quiet during this period. Reverse cooptation seemed to take place, i.e., agency experts were coopted by the model cities programs. Examples of resident participation are cited, and the roles of antipoverty agencies, urban renewal agencies, boards of education, and health and welfare councils are briefly discussed.

Warren, Roland L. "The Model Cities Program, I. An Assessment." *The Social Welfare Forum, 1971.* Official Proceedings, 98th Annual Forum, National Conference on Social Welfare, Dallas, Texas, May 16–21, 1971. New York: Columbia University Press, 1971, pp. 141–58.

An analysis of the successes and failures of the Model Cities Program is presented. The program is discussed in terms of the "four C's—comprehensiveness, concentration, coordination, and citizen participation." The author believes that citizen participation in model cities has never been given a fair trial, that the cards were stacked against it. Even so, he sees the program as having some modest gains: extremely modest improvement in social services, some experience for city administrators in social planning, and a modest but important experiment in citizen participation.

Williams, Junius W. "The Impact of Citizen Participation." Paper prepared for the National Academy of Public Administration Conference of Participation of the Poor and Public Administration, Holly Knoll Conference Center, Williamsburg, Virginia, May 21–23, 1970. Mimeograph.

Williams discusses two citizen participation mechanisms in Newark, New Jersey, the Housing Council and the Model Cities Neighborhood Council. The Model Cities Neighborhood Council was described as completely controlled by city hall and as having only the form of citizen participation, not the substance. The Housing Council was an outgrowth of an agreement between the black community and the government resulting from the extension of a medical college into the black community. The Housing Council was formed as a broad based umbrella group to distribute sixty-three acres of land. The author feels that this group demonstrates the positive impacts of citizen participation.

Dissertations

Austin, David M. "Organizing for Neighborhood Improvement or Social Change? A Descriptive Study of the Action Methods and Action Issues of Black Resident Associations Sponsored by Community Action Agencies." Ph.D., The Florence Heller Graduate School for Advanced Study in Social Welfare, Brandeis University, 1969. (Order no. 70–19,967) 354 pp.

Ball, Ian Traquair. "Institution Building for Development: O.E.O. Community Action Programs on Two North Dakota Indian Reservations." Ph.D., Indiana University, 1968. (Order no. 69–4723) 175 pp.

Barndt, Michael Guernsey. "Decision-Making in a Community Corporation: Sources of Cleavage Among Actors." Ph.D., Case Western Reserve University, 1972. (Order no. 72–26,137) 578 pp.

Boo, Sung Lai. "A Description and Analysis of the Concept of Participation of the Poor in a Southern Rural Community Action Program." Ph.D., Florida State University, 1970. (Order no. 71–13,487) 94 pp.

Buell, Emmett Harold, Jr. "Uncertain Warriors: The Political Roles of Members of an Antipoverty Agency Governing Board." Ph.D., Vanderbilt University, 1972. (Order no. 72–26,092) 341 pp.

Burke, Edmund M. "A Study of Community Organization in Urban Renewal: Social Work Method in a Non-social Work Setting." Ph.D., University of Pittsburgh, 1965. (Order no. 66–08106) 306 pp.

Christensen, Terry Lynn. "Citizen Participation and the Participation of the Poor in the Community Action Program." Ph.D., University of North Carolina at Chapel Hill, 1972. (Order no. 73–16,458) 275 pp.

Clavel, Pierre. "The Genesis of the Planning Process: Experts and Citizens Boards in Sullivan County, New York." Ph.D., Cornell University, 1966. (Order no. 66–10,242) 195 pp.

Cloud, Ralph Martin. "The Management of an Anti-Poverty Program: A Case Study of Economic Opportunity Atlanta, Incorporated." Ph.D., University of Georgia, 1967. (Order no. 67–16,206) 181 pp.

Cruthrids, Chalmers Thomas, Jr. "The Community Action Program Agency and Voluntary Delegate Organizations: Issues in Interorganizational Contracting." D.S.W., Tulane University School of Social Work, 1972. (Order no. 72–30,074) 289 pp.

Dare, Robert Clark. "Involvement of the Poor: A Study in the Maintenance of Organizational Values." Ph.D., Emory University, 1967. (Order no. 68–4479) 319 pp.

De'Ath, Colin Edward. "Patterns of Participation and Exclusion: A Poor Italian and Black Urban Community and Its Response to a Federal Poverty Program." Ph.D., University of Pittsburgh, 1970. (Order no. 71–7991) 285 pp.

Dobbs, Carolyn Elizabeth. "Community Development: A Proposal for Involving Citizens in the Planning Process." Ph.D., University of Washington, 1971. (Order no. 72–15,084) 178 pp.

Eisinger, Peter Kendall. "The Anti-Poverty Community Action Group as a Political Force in the Ghetto." Ph.D., Yale University, 1969. (Order no. 70–2726) 321 pp.

Gilbert, Neil. "Clients or Constituents: A Case Study of Pittsburgh's War on Poverty." Ph.D., University of Pittsburgh, 1968. (Order no. 68–12,664) 164 pp.

Godschalk, David Robinson. "Participation, Planning and Exchange in Old and New Communities: A Collaborative Paradigm." Ph.D., University of North Carolina at Chapel Hill, 1971. (Order no. 72–18,400) 330 pp.

Guy, Joseph Lawrence. "Citizen Participation in Model Cities: The Role of Federal Administrators." Ph.D., State University of New York at Albany, 1973. (Order no. 73–24,356) 348 pp.

Hallenbeck, Howard Braun. "Factors Influencing Citizen Participation in Survey and Planning of Group Work and Recreation Services to Suburban Areas." D.S.W., Washington University, 1959. (L.C. Card no. Mic 59–5268) 121 pp.

Hoffman, Richard Lee. "Community Action: Innovative and Coordinative Strategies in the War on Poverty." Ph.D., University of North Carolina at Chapel Hill, 1969. (Order no. 70–3245) 351 pp.

Hruza, Franklyn Lee. "Seattle Model Cities Program: A Case Study of Citizen Participation in the Planning Process During the Initial Planning Year 1967–68." Ph.D., University of Washington, 1972. (Order no. 73–13,834) 249 pp.

Hutcheson, John D., Jr. "Social Position, Alienation and the Impact of the War on Poverty." Ph.D., University of Georgia, 1969. (Order no. 70–10,198) 89 pp.

Kass, Henry De St. Leu. "Citizen Participation in a Technically Oriented Governmental Decision-Making Process: A Study of the Development of a Neighborhood Plan for the Adams-Morgan Project Area, Washington, D.C." Ph.D., American University, 1969. (Order no. 69–19,353) 525 pp.

Klinck, Thomas Cottingham. "Assessing Organizational Effectiveness and Developing a Strategy of Change for a Community Action Agency Board of Directors." Ph.D., University of California, Los Angeles, 1969. (Order no. 70–8163) 258 pp.

Larson, John Albert, Jr. "Community Participation in Locating Industries in Nonmetropolitan Tennessee." Ph.D., Northwestern University, 1956. (Publication no. 19,008; Mic 57–633) 599 pp.

Lombard, Rudolph Joseph. "Achieving 'Maximum Feasible Participation' of the Poor in Anti-Poverty Elections." Ph.D., Syracuse University, 1970. (Order no. 70–24,093) 208 pp.

Milne, James Stephen. "Feasibility in Poverty Politics: Participation or Paternalism?" Ph.D., Temple University, 1972. (Order no. 72–17,705) 312 pp.

Morgan, Julia Elizabeth. "A Study of the Wild Rose Community Council as a Medium for Community Development." Ph.D., University of Wisconsin, 1960. (L.C. Card no. Mic 60–3243) 266 pp.

Muller, John Alfred. "Community Organization, Neighborhood Redevelopment, and Local Politics: The East Tremont Neighborhood Association 1954–65." Ph.D., Fordham University, 1971. (Order no. 71–26,986) 546 pp.

Nelsen, William Cameron. "Participation, Alienation, and Renewal in an Urban Community." Ph.D., University of Pennsylvania, 1971. (Order no. 71–26,062) 238 pp.

Owen, Raymond Edward. "Community Organization and Participatory Democracy: A Study of the Ghetto Corporation." Ph.D., State University of New York at Buffalo, 1971. (Order no. 72–241) 267 pp.

Perrota, John. "Representation of the Poor in the Community Action Program in Providence, Rhode Island: 1965–1969." Ph.D., New York University, 1971. (Order no. 71–24,763) 439 pp.

Rivera, Jose A. "Community Control of Economic Development Planning: A Study of the Recipient Beneficiaries of Change as the Actors of Change." Ph.D., The Florence Heller Graduate School for Advanced Studies in Social Welfare, Brandeis University, 1972. (Order no. 72–26,330) 244 pp.

Ruoss, Meryl Hocker. "A Participatory Planning Model for Voluntary Associations." Ph.D., University of Southern California, 1972. (Order no. 73–766) 110 pp.

Seferi, Maria Louise. "Resident Participation in Relocation Planning: The Case of the Denver Neighborhood of Auraria." Ph.D., University of Colorado, 1970. (Order no. 71–5928) 329 pp.

Sheehan, Joseph Connor. "Community Participation in Urban Renewal Planning." Ph.D., University of Maryland, 1969. (Order no. 70–11,640) 301 pp.

Tellis-Nayak, Jessie B. "Community Organization in Redevelopment Areas (A Case Study of the Application of Community Organization Principles in Urban Renewal)." D.S.W., Catholic University of America, 1965. (Order no. 65–7864) 256 pp.

4

Citizen Involvement in
Service Delivery Systems

Closely following the citizen participation mechanisms provided by federally sponsored community development programs, federally sponsored categorical service delivery programs began requiring citizen participation in local agencies receiving federal funds. The 1964 amendments to the Hill-Burton Act, for example, required that health consumers compose 50 percent of the state hospital construction council, and the Comprehensive Health Planning and Public Health Services Act of 1966 required that state plans designate a health planning council, 51 percent of which must be representatives of consumers of health services. In 1968, an Office of Citizen Participation was established in the Social and Rehabilitation Service to serve as a focal point for developing the idea of recipient involvement in Social and Rehabilitation Service programs and services.

Concurrently, demands for participation in local programs and local policy making have increased. Some local programs and agencies have responded to these demands by establishing different forms of citizen participation mechanisms. Local health, education, welfare, and housing programs were, in most locales, the first to experience and react to demands for increased citizen access to policy and decision-making processes. Policy areas such as criminal justice, the environment and natural resources, and transportation, as a rule, have been the targets of such demands more recently.

This chapter contains seven sections, each of which includes references to literature focusing on different types of service delivery systems or different policy-issue areas. The sections are entitled:

1. Criminal Justice
2. Education
3. Environment and Natural Resources
4. Health
5. Housing

6. Social Welfare
7. Transportation

A large portion of the literature cited in these sections is descriptive, often focusing on citizen participation in one program or agency. Little research analyzing the impacts of participation on participants, communities, or the quality of service delivery has been reported in the literature. Some observations about the impacts of participation upon participants are reflected in the literature, but few researchers have focused upon the impact of citizen participation upon the quality of services rendered. One notable exception is work analyzing the educational impacts of decentralized educational facilities in New York (see, for example, Guttentag, Marcia, "Children in Harlem's Community Controlled Schools," below), but such research has been limited and its findings less than conclusive. The service and program impacts of citizen participation, then, seem to be an important area which might be the subject of future research efforts.

CRIMINAL JUSTICE

Allen, Robert F., and Saul Pitnick. *Conflict Resolution: Team Building for Police and Ghetto*. Union, New Jersey: Scientific Resources, 1968.

American Correctional Association. "Community Services and Citizen Participation." *Proceedings of the 97th Annual Congress of Corrections*. Washington, D.C.: American Correctional Association, 1967, pp. 45–63.

This is a collection of five papers presented at the Congress of Corrections on the subjects of community services and citizen participation. In "Community Services for Parole," Harry W. Poole calls for coordinated efforts among community agencies to absorb the parolee into the community. Poole feels that specialized agencies are not needed because more effective use of existing agencies could handle the job. In "The Half-Way House," George P. Denton urges the establishment of criteria for setting up half-way houses. In a paper entitled "Uses of Community Mental Health Centers," Dr. Alfred Oevre, Jr., describes how a community mental health center in Kansas City, Missouri, came to serve the correctional psychiatry needs of the city, county, and state. Keith Stubblefeld's paper, "Use of Volunteers," describes the work, data, and findings of the Joint Commission on Correctional Manpower and Training. The paper urges a unified national approach to correctional rehabilitation. Robert R. Hannon describes the past and present roles of private agencies in corrections in a paper called "Vocational Placement."

Kelly, Rita Mae. *The Pilot Project: A Description and Assessment of a Police-Community Relations Experiment in Washington, D.C.* Washington, D.C.: American Institute for Research, January 1972. Last chapter of this study also available as (by the same author) *On Improving Police-Community Relations: Findings from the Conduct and Evaluation on an OEO Funded Experiment in Washington, D.C.* Washington, D.C.: American Institute for Research, January 1972. This chapter contains the findings and conclusions of the study.

A pilot project, in Washington, D.C., that attempted to improve police-community relations by changing the attitudes and behavior of police and citizens and by involving citizens in law enforcement is described in this publication. The goals of the project were to establish a representative community advisory board, to partially decentralize police functions, to use more civilians and more minority group policemen from the area, and to redefine the role of the police officer to fit the needs of the community. This study concludes that the community must be involved as much as the police department in efforts to improve police-community relations. Recommendations for ways to improve police-community relations are included.

Knopf, Terry Ann. *Youth Patrols: An Experiment in Community Participation.* Waltham, Massachusetts: The Lemberg Center for the Study of Violence, Brandeis University, 1969.

The author examines ghetto youth patrols which were active in trying to control violence during the civil disorders of 1967 and 1968. In most cases, the impetus for formation of such groups came from the black community. The evidence seems to show that the patrols were successful in maintaining or restoring order and that they were an important factor in improving communications with the larger community. Patrols in twelve cities were studied by examining newspaper clippings, official reports and documents, and through telephone interviews.

Marx, Gary T., and Dane Archer. "Citizen Involvement in Law Enforcement Processes: The Case of Community Police Patrols." *American Behavioral Scientist* 15:1 (September/October 1971): 51–72.

Marx and Archer examine descriptive data on twenty-eight self-defense groups. Issues, and how groups dealt with them, are discussed in terms of five organizational problems: (1) the relationship of the group to the police and the legal system; (2) its legitimacy in the eyes of the community; (3) the recruitment and management of personnel; (4) the choice of appropriate operations; and (5) the maintenance of resources, incentives, and motivation for the groups' survival. Most groups face many difficulties, including a short life span and the lack of resources and mandate. Some groups, however, survive because of crisis, charismatic leadership, or their evolution into formal organizations with financial support. The authors believe that such groups work best when a relatively homogeneous population lives within well-defined boundaries.

Myren, Richard A. "Decentralization and Citizen Participation in Criminal Justice Systems." *Public Administration Review* 32, special issue (October 1972): 718–38.

The underlying assumption of this article is that the criminal justice system in the United States is in trouble and that citizens are worried. The author discusses the pros and cons of decentralization and citizen participation in three phases of the criminal justice system: police agencies, prosecution and adjudication, and corrections. He distinguishes between administrative decentralization which involves decentralization of the bureaucracy and political decentralization which gives increased power to citizens.

The major part of the article is devoted to police agencies because the author feels that the impact of decentralization and citizen participation has been greater there and that the police have the greater impact on the whole of the criminal justice system. Four ways in which citizens can participate in police work are presented: support of police agencies, assumption of duties under police officers, evaluation of police performance, and setting policy. The author concludes that there is more administrative than political decentralization in this area and that there is little citizen participation in the determination of policies and procedures.

The author identifies two kinds of citizen participation in prosecution and adjudication—volunteers in probation and citizen input in the charge determination of the prosecutor. However, the author feels that there is little evidence of either administrative or political decentralization in this field. In the field of corrections, a trend was found toward decentralization of program and centralization of organizational structure.

Nelson, Harold A. "The Defenders: A Case Study of an Informal Police Organization." *Social Problems* 15:2 (Fall 1967): 127–47.

This case study describes the efforts of blacks in a small Southern town to provide for themselves protective services normally provided by law enforcement agencies. This informal police organization was able to provide protection, challenge the traditional Southern relationship between blacks and whites, and force a redistribution of power in the community.

O'Leary, Vincent. "Some Directions for Citizen Involvement in Corrections." *Annals of the American Academy of Political Science* 381 (January 1969): 99–108.

The author describes the lack of citizen participation in corrections and the lack of recognition of the roles that citizens can play in corrections. He examines four roles which citizens might play in the corrections system: (1) correctional volunteers who work with clients; (2) "social persuaders" who are community influentials who can help shape workable programs; (3) "gatekeepers" of opportunities such as employers, school administrators, and welfare directors; and (4) "intimates" who are members of the peer groups and communities of the offenders. Programs that incorporate these roles are described.

Ostrom, Elinor; William H. Baugh; Richard Guarasci; Roger B. Parks; and Gordon P. Whitaker. *Community Organization and the Provision of Police Services.* Beverly Hills, California: Sage Publications, 1973.

In attempting to identify the impact of different forms of community organization upon police performance in different neighborhoods in the Indianapolis area, the authors compared three "independent" communities with their own relatively small police departments to neighborhoods in Indianapolis served by the city's police department. They found that there was "a great deal more communication between citizens and their police in the three independent communities than in the Indianapolis neighborhoods." They then "postulate that this higher communication level results in greater community control of local police in the independent communities."

Ostrom, Elinor, and Gordon Whitaker. "Does Local Community Control of Police Make a Difference? Some Preliminary Findings." *American Journal of Political Science* 17:1 (February 1973): 48–76.

A comparative study of large-scale and small-scale police organization in urban neighborhoods, this study focuses on three city neighborhoods in Indianapolis and three matched adjacent communities with independent police forces. It was hypothesized that higher levels of police output would be found in the communities with small independent police forces. Data were collected through a survey of 722 respondents in which information on citizen experience with and evaluation of police was sought. The data indicated a pattern of higher levels of police output in independent neighborhoods. The authors concluded that small police forces, under local control, are more effective in meeting citizen needs.

Perry, David C., and Paula A. Sornoff. *Politics at the Street Level: The Select Case of Police Administration and the Community.* Beverly Hills, California: Sage Publications, 1973.

Presenting findings from a study of police behavior in Rochester, New York, this study describes the interaction between: "(1) the beat patrolman, (2) the dominant/white community, and (3) the minority/poor communities." Research encompassed a period of a year and a half and involved interviewing over 400 people. The authors describe the roles of the Rochester Police Advisory Board and compare different actors' perceptions of the utility of the board. Minority/poor community residents' views of the board were, generally, more positive than those of other groups of actors.

Riley, David. "Should Communities Control Their Police?" *Civil Rights Digest* 2:4 (Fall 1969): 26–35.

The author analyzes the two-way prejudice between the black community and the police and catalogues incidents of hostility and trouble between blacks and police. The author feels that the police are isolated from the community they are supposed to be serving. He focuses on the police as a political force and on the extent of civilian control of the police. Attempted solutions to the problem, such as hiring more blacks, community relations programs, and citizens advisory committees, have had little success. This situation has been especially hard on black policemen. The author calls for community control of the police to ensure that the police will be more familiar with the community they serve.

Viteritti, Joseph P. *Police, Politics, and Pluralism in New York City: A Comparative Case Study.* Beverly Hills, California: Sage Publications, 1973.

EDUCATION

Berube, Maurice R., and Marilyn Gittell, eds. *Confrontation at Ocean Hill-Brownsville: The New York School Strikes of 1968.* New York: Praeger, 1969.

Reviews:
Choice 6 (September 1969): 877.
Fowler, Austin. *Library Journal* 94 (August 1969): 2769.

This is a collection of documents and analyses of the controversy surrounding the experiment in community control of schools in New York City. Part One covers the prelude to the controversy. Part Two deals with the issues involved in the confrontation: due process, anti-Semitism and racism, and decentralization and community control. Each section is comprised of relevant documents and the viewpoints of participants and observers. The editors have written a prologue and an epilogue which present their generally favorable position on school decentralization and the experiment. A chronology of events is included at the end of the book.

Bloom, Janet. "Street School Scene." *Architectural Forum* 138:5 (June 1973): 38–45.

The Human Resources Center in Pontiac, Michigan, is described in this article. It is a community service school planned with community cooperation. The community was especially influential in site selection and has continued to support the school. The author discusses the purpose and philosophy of the design of the center. She also discusses the financing of the center which involved a combination of federal, state, county, city, and school board funds.

Burnes, Donald W. "Community Controlled Schools: Politics and Education." *Civil Rights Digest* 2:4 (Fall 1969): 36–41.

Assuming that local control is a fundamental tenet of public schools, the author contrasts the present realities of local control in the suburbs and in the ghettos and argues that black demands for local control of schools are logical rather than radical demands. He says that a double standard permits affluent whites to participate in their schools and prohibits others from doing likewise. He then describes the failures of urban schools and provides some examples of community control of city schools that have been successful—Ocean Hill-Brownsville in New York and Morgan in Washington, D.C. The author refutes arguments that low income blacks are not capable of controlling their schools and that they will be racist in outlook, and cites evidence from these two school districts. He argues that participation will improve the self-concept of poor blacks.

Chamberlayne, Prue. "Teachers Versus the Community." *New Society* 26 (November 15, 1973): 398–400.

The author of this article argues that community control of the schools in New York has increased the conflict between teachers and community groups. The author describes several confrontations between black and Puerto Rican community groups and the teachers' union.

Cloward, Richard A., and James A. Jones. "Social Class: Educational Attitudes and Participation." *Education in Depressed Areas.* Edited by A. Harry Passow. New York: Teachers College Press, 1968, pp. 190–216.

This study focuses on the impact of involvement in educational matters upon attitudes toward education. Also, the authors attempt to identify differences in the attitudes of individuals of different social strata. Nine hundred eighty-eight adults residing in the Lower East Side of New York City were interviewed. Respondents were classified, by income, as middle, working, or lower class. A three-part categorization of involvement in schools was used: no contact with the school, visits to the school, and P.T.A. membership.

Significant differences by social class were found in attitudes toward the schools. The two general findings of the study were: that evaluations of the importance of education in the lower and working classes seemed to be influenced by occupational aspirations, and that participation in educational activities does influence evaluations of the importance of education and attitudes toward the school as an institution; participation increases one's perception of the importance of education, especially among lower class individuals. The study suggests that more lower class involvement in education would increase lower class interest in school achievement.

"Community Participation in Public Elementary Schools: A Survey Report." Washington, D.C.: Center for Governmental Studies, September 1970. Mimeograph.

The information described in this report was collected from questionnaires sent to the 545 largest school districts in the country of which 75.8 percent replied. Ten percent of the responses indicated that parents and/or community representatives had control of at least one function in one or more elementary schools, most frequently in after-school programs and community uses of the school. Five out of six replies indicated that parents and/or community representatives had advisory roles in at least one out of ten listed functions, with larger systems providing a larger variety of advisory roles. The areas in which advisory roles were most frequently exercised were after-school programs and adoption of curriculum. Citizens were least involved in personnel selection.

Coy, Roger L. *A Study of Lay Participation in the Public Schools.*
Middletown, Ohio: Southwestern Ohio Research Council, August
1969. ERIC ED056–401.

This report explores the use of community school councils to increase
citizen participation in school planning. The objectives of the study are: (1)
to present a logical basis for the formation of community school councils; (2)
to describe some of the hazards to the smooth operation of the school
system; (3) to offer guidelines for councils and suggest first-year activities; (4)
to provide a possible list of specific objectives for councils; and (5) to cite
current programs. Two case studies are presented: Paul Lawrence Dunbar
High School in Baltimore, where in 1969 a cadre of citizens formulated
plans for a new high school, and the Educational Component of the Dayton
(Ohio) Model Cities Program, which planned a community-school council.

Cronin, Joseph M. *The Control of Urban Schools: Perspectives on the Power
of Educational Reformers.* New York: The Free Press, 1973.

Reviews:
Saturday Review of Education 1 (May 1973): 88.
Wadsworth, C. E. *Library Journal* 98 (January 1973): 149.

Cronin traces the historical development of urban school structures in
fourteen American cities in light of the present move toward decentralization and community control of the schools. The author's thesis is that the
schools were actually "decentralized" prior to the urban school reforms of
the late nineteenth century. Those reforms attempted to separate education
from ward politics and thus moved urban school systems toward becoming
highly centralized, bureaucratized systems. Cronin argues that the reformers succeeded too well. By the 1960s urban school bureaucracies were so
insulated that they failed to respond to the needs of some segments of the
communities they served. Thus new reformers began to call for a return to
decentralized community-based education.

In case studies of the fourteen cities, the author examines the
historical development of school governance in each city and discusses the
merits and problems of different structures, elected vs. appointed boards,
for example. He also devotes some discussion to the community control
experiments in New York City and Detroit and to the idea of an educational
voucher system. The author concludes that big city school systems can only
survive by breaking the hold of the professional bureaucracy and allowing
parents and community people to share in educational decision making. He
also concludes that the states should have much more responsibility for local
education.

Cunningham, Luverne L., and Raphael O. Nystrand. *Citizen Participation in School Affairs: A Report to the Urban Coalition.* Washington, D.C.: The Urban Coalition, June 1969. ERIC ED035–070.

A study team at Ohio State University conducted this assessment of mechanisms facilitating citizen participation in educational decision making in thirteen cities. The chosen cities were identified by the "grapevine method." Two or more members of the team spent at least two days in each city interviewing school system personnel, involved citizens, and knowledgeable observers.

For each mechanism, an effort was made to learn the following: Who participates and whom do they represent? What is the forum for participation? What issues are considered? What tactics are employed? What sanctions are available? What happens? Who responds? How are programs changed? What is the relationship of the mechanism to traditional decision makers? How are the strengths and weaknesses of the mechanisms perceived by the citizen participants?

Four functions of participation were identified: to develop community support for and understanding of educational objectives, to supplement school staff members in pursuit of educational objectives, to articulate citizen expectations of school performance, and to insist on accountability for educational objectives. Three school system responses were identified: paternalistic, supportive, and change oriented.

The appendices contain descriptions of the mechanisms studied in each city. The cities included in the study are: Atlanta, Boston, Chicago, Columbus (Ohio), Detroit, Duluth, Huntsville (Alabama), Los Angeles, New York, Philadelphia, Rochester (New York), Rockford (Illinois), and San Francisco.

Eddy, Susan. "Case Study/Washington, D.C.: Community Control Guides Morgan School." *Public Management* 51:7 (July 1969): 11–13.

This article is a brief description of the Morgan Community School in Washington, D.C. There is some discussion of the rationale for community control of schools. The article describes the Morgan Community School Board, its functions, and its relationship to the central board of education.

Education for the People: Guidelines for Total Community Participation in Framing and Strengthening the Future of Public Elementary and Secondary Education in California. Vols. 1, 2. Sacramento: California State Department of Education, 1972. ERIC ED066–822.

Fatini, Mario; Marilyn Gittell; and Richard Magat. *Community Control and
the Urban School.* New York: Praeger, 1970.

> Reviews:
> *New York Times Book Review* (September 20, 1970): 36.
> Wadsworth, C. E. *Library Journal* 95 (July 1970): 2467.

After tracing the development of a theory of community participation
in schools, the authors describe and analyze the community control
experiments in New York City and examine subsequent developments and
implications. The authors do not pretend to be objective. They all served as
advisors or staff members on the Mayor's Advisory Panel on the Decentralization of the New York City Schools and were advocates of the community
control experiments. The bulk of the book seems to be devoted to defending
the experiments from criticisms they encountered.

The authors defend community control as a democratic concept that
is not threatening to professionalism. They envision community control as a
partnership in public education. Through community control, the schools
can serve as the agent of a new social order rather than the reflection of the
prevailing social order.

Fredericks, Steven J. "Curriculum and Decentralization; The New York
City Public School System." *Urban Education* 9:3 (October 1974):
247–56.

During the 1969 upheavals in the New York City schools, curriculum
development policy making was taken away from the central board of
education and given to the communities. In 1973 the author conducted a
survey in order to gain information on the relationship between curriculum
development and decentralization.

Questionnaires were sent to district superintendents and community
school board members in thirty-one local school districts. The questions
were designed to elicit information on curriculum development, curriculum
change, participation in curriculum development, and general comments
about curriculum development in the individual districts.

The author found that there was little grass roots participation and
that there was a great deal of pessimism about the effectiveness of
decentralization. He believes that the local districts lack direction but that a
demand exists for more participation in curriculum development.

Gittell, Marilyn. "Decentralization and Citizen Participation in
Education." *Public Administration Review* 32, special issue (October
1972): 670–86.

As background information, the author describes the move toward centralization of the public schools, the bureaucratization and professionalization of the schools, the role of boards of education, and the failure of school integration. She discusses the events that led to the community control experiments in New York City, the Bundy Plan, and the conflict that occurred at Ocean Hill-Brownsville. Despite problems, she believes that decentralization and citizen participation in education can work and points out some of the successes of the projects in New York. She outlines a three-stage plan for more successful community participation: early public participation in the planning stage, a balancing of community and professional roles and of central and local powers, and greater citizen participation in the implementation of the plan.

Gittell, Marilyn. *Participants and Participation: A Study of School Policy in New York City*. New York: Praeger, 1967. Aspects of this study also reported in Gittell, Marilyn. "Professionalism and Public Participation in Educational Policy-Making: New York City, a Case Study." *Public Administration Review* 27:3 (September 1967): 237–51.

The result of a three-year study of decision making in the New York City public schools, this book examines five major decision-making areas—budget, curriculum, selection of the superintendent, teachers' salaries, and school integration—in an effort to explore the political forces affecting educational decision making in New York City and to evaluate the relative openness of the system.

Three models for participation in school affairs are presented: the *closed* system, where only professionals participate; the *limited* system, where the board of education, the mayor, or special interest groups may participate; and the *wide* system, where groups not wholly concerned with school policy participate. The author conducted extensive interviews with system personnel at every level and cross-referenced what she found with newspaper articles concerning school policy.

Gittell found that in the areas of curriculum and budgeting the headquarters supervisory bureaucracy had complete control. In the areas of selection of the superintendent and teachers' salaries, participation could be described as limited. Participants were the mayor, the United Federation of Teachers, and some local union leaders. The widest participation was in the area of integration policy. Parent groups, civil rights groups, and public officials all participated. The study concludes that policy making had been taken away from the lay board of education and the public and was monopolized by the professional bureaucracy and special interests.

Gittell, Marilyn, et al. *Local Control in Education: Three Demonstration School Districts in New York City.* New York: Praeger, 1972.

This evaluative history of the three experimental local school boards in New York City was done by the Institute for Community Studies at Queens College and funded by the Ford Foundation. Most of the data were gathered through participant observation. The study looked at the effects of the experiment on the participants and on school policy.

Effects of the experiment on school governing-board members were found to be increased knowledge of school matters, greater militancy in seeking reforms, and stronger sense of efficacy and self-esteem. An opinion survey found that parental attitudes in the Ocean Hill-Brownsville district had changed. Parents had a stronger sense of efficacy in running the schools, were more knowledgeable, and had developed positive feelings toward the schools. Local boards were found to have effected changes in personnel policy. More paraprofessionals and community-oriented blacks were hired. The authors feel that the local boards were moving toward having significant impacts on the education of students. A study done in the Intermediate School 201 District found that students had greater feelings of self-esteem.

Grant, William R. "Community Control vs. School Integration—the Case of Detroit." *Public Interest* 24 (Summer 1971): 62–79.

This article addresses itself to the conflict between community control of schools and racial integration. The author's conclusion that the two are not compatible is based upon the experience of the Detroit school system. The author explores the recent history of school politics in Detroit beginning in 1964 and also the history of the community control concept. The liberal board of education, first elected in 1964, chose to support the idea of integrated education rather than community control. The idea of community control was first espoused by black groups and was later adopted by the state legislature. Whites soon came to see an advantage in community control. The board was recalled and a more conservative board elected. In confrontations with local schools, this newly elected board always backed down.

The results of community control in Detroit were: (1) racial polarization and a backlash vote which led to a conservative victory on the board; (2) blacks who had pressed for decentralization lost power; (3) disruption lasted for at least a year; and (4) whites were able to coopt community control for segregationist purposes.

Green, Philip. "Decentralization, Community Control, and Revolution; Reflections on Ocean Hill-Brownsville." *Massachusetts Review* 11:3 (Summer 1970): 415–41.

The author presents his analysis of the central meaning of the battle over community control of schools in New York City. He believes that the issue involved was the assertion of minority rights and that the sentiments of the minority in this case were revolutionary. He sees only two possible solutions to the problem: repression of the minority by the majority or decentralization of governmental control. He feels that the confrontation at Ocean Hill demonstrates the injustice of applying the same rules (e.g., due process) to the powerless minority and to the powerful majority. In such situations the majority will always win, and the minority will never be able to make progress.

Gustafson, Thomas John. *A Procedure to Discriminate Between Successful and Unsuccessful Pressure Groups Which Have an Interest in Education, Final Report.* Albuquerque: University of New Mexico, January 31, 1970. ERIC ED037–819.

Gustafson attempts to identify characteristics common to pressure groups interested in education. Eight variables that may have a bearing on effectiveness are discussed: (1) the critical situation; (2) the leadership of the group; (3) the prestige of the group; (4) the control of the group over economic goods; (5) the channels of communication with local, state, and national officials; (6) attitudes shared by the group and the community; (7) group solidarity; and (8) the group's strategy for implementing change. Interviews with fifty-six pressure group leaders and forty-two educational officials were completed. Pressure groups were divided into two groups: lay persons interested in education and groups connected directly with education.

The study found that four of the variables were significantly related to effectiveness: (1) the critical situation; (2) prestige; (3) channels of communication; and (4) strategy. The group's strategy was found to be the most important factor in determining the level of group effectiveness. The study also found differences between the two kinds of pressure groups. The critical situation, channels of communication, and strategy were important to both groups, but prestige and effectiveness were important only to the lay group.

Guttentag, Marcia. "Children in Harlem's Community Controlled Schools." *Journal of Social Issues* 28:4 (1972): 1–20.

This is a summary of a series of studies on community control of schools done at the request of the community school governing board of the Intermediate School (I.S.) District 201 in New York City. The research was supported by grants from the Faculty Research Award Program of the City University of New York and the Carnegie Corporation and by a contract from the New York City Board of Education.

The studies compared the I.S. 201 community school district with a neighboring and similar but centrally controlled school district. The organizational climate study used Stern's Organizational Climate Index as a measure of the environmental press experienced by individuals in an organization. I.S. 201 was found to have a stronger expressive climate and was stronger in developmental press. The parent involvement study measured the use of the school building by six categories of visitors. I.S. 201 had parents in the schools more frequently, for a variety of constructive purposes. Community use of schools was measured, and it was found that I.S. 201 was used more for community activities. A study of innovative programs measured numbers and effectiveness of such programs and found that I.S. 201 was ahead in both. Teacher/pupil classroom interaction was analyzed using the Flanders-Dunbar Technique and was found to be more positive in I.S. 201 schools. The Clark and Clark doll preference and racial identification studies found I.S. 201 children to be more positive in racial identity. Standardized testing and a study of I.S. 201 by the Psychological Corporation showed student achievement in I.S. 201 to be somewhat higher. Expectancies of what children think will happen to them were measured by an expectancy questionnaire. I.S. 201 children were found to have more external expectancies.

Hamlin, Herbert M. "Organized Citizen Participation in the Public Schools." *Review of Educational Research* 23:4 (October 1953): 346–52.

Discussing various aspects of citizen participation in schools, the author lists seven fundamental research questions: (1) What are the effects of various types of organizations on the schools? (2) What are the arrangements for participation? (3) What is the relationship between citizen groups and the board, administration, teachers, nonacademic employees, and students? (4) What are the relative merits of independent and school-sponsored citizen groups? (5) What are the results of different procedures in selecting members of citizen groups? (6) How do these education citizen groups affect the thinking of other citizens? (7) What are the effects of school-sponsored citizen committees upon other groups in the community?

Literature is reviewed in two areas: background on organized citizen participation and reports of studies of citizen groups in action. The studies indicate that participation is extensive and growing, that principles of organizing and operating groups are gaining acceptance, and that the most fundamental questions concerning citizen participation have been asked and are being discussed. The author asserts that the following are accepted statements on citizen participation in the schools. The best arrangement for public relations is to allow the public to participate in decision making. In the United States, laymen are helpful in making public policy. Members of boards of education are inadequate representatives of the public. Special groups of citizens organized to work with schools are needed. School-sponsored committees are usually effective. Citizen groups need broad community representation, knowledge of facts, and an ability to work through constituted school authority. The organization of board committees should be preceded by consultation with those whom the committees would affect. The board should have detailed policy statements for the operation of committees.

Hendricks, Glenn. "La Raza en Nueva York: Social Pluralism and Schools." *Teacher's College Record* 74:3 (February 1973): 379–93.

Hendricks discusses the situation of Spanish-speaking Americans in New York City, the development of their culture, the concept of cultural and social pluralism, and the effect of all this on the public schools. A number of bilingual programs are now operating in the New York City schools. The author feels that community control of schools will lead to all-Spanish local school districts which will further divide the city along ethnic lines.

Hentoff, Nat. "Ocean Hill-Brownsville: Augury for the Nation." *Motive* 29:5 (February 1969): 50–55.

The author describes the failures of public schools in the ghettos of New York City and praises the idea of community control of schools. He characterizes the community control experiment at Ocean Hill-Brownsville as a success and defends the concept. He believes that the experiment has had positive effects on the community as a whole.

Katz, Arthur J. "Clients Participation in Institutional Change." *The Social Welfare Forum, 1971.* Official Proceedings, 98th Annual Forum, National Conference on Social Welfare, Dallas, Texas, May 16–21, 1971. New York: Columbia University Press, 1971, pp. 182–94.

Institutional change is seen as a process resulting in institutions becoming more sensitive to the consumers of services. Head Start's policies directed at accomplishing this objective are described: the policy advisory committees at the local center level, the advisory councils at the city or county-wide level, and the parent involvement program.

Lachman, Seymour P., and David Bresnick. "An Educational Ombudsman for New York City?" *School and Society* 99:2332 (March 1971): 168–70.

The author discusses how public schools could benefit from an ombudsman. The function of the ombudsman would be to accept complaints from citizens, including parents and teachers, alleging arbitrary or unjust treatment by the educational system. He outlines a plan for an ombudsman in New York City and discusses grievance procedures, the powers of an educational ombudsman, and the ombudsman's general investigatory powers and reports.

La Noue, George R., and Bruce L. R. Smith. "The Political Evaluation of School Decentralization." *American Behavioral Scientist* 15:1 (September/October 1971): 73–93.

An examination of the politics of school decentralization in four cities—New York, Los Angeles, Detroit, and Washington, D.C.—reveals that leadership did not come from established politicians or parties, that federal agencies had intervened to promote community control, and that local conflicts involved traditional school interest groups. The issues that caused the most conflict were found to be district boundaries and personnel procedures. The potential effects of decentralization are discussed in terms of the costs in money and foregone benefits such as special schools, integration, and equality of education. The authors see a slowing down of the trend toward decentralization of schools.

La Noue, George R., and Bruce L. R. Smith. *The Politics of School Decentralization.* Toronto: D. C. Heath and Company, 1973.

This study of school decentralization presents data from twenty-nine cities with populations of over 50,000 in 1965. Questionnaires were sent out, one-third of the cities were visited, and data from other studies were used. Twenty-five hypotheses related to demographic and political variables and school decentralization were presented. The variables included size, minority group presence, integration, alienation and achievement, and political forces.

The study found that (1) large cities were more likely to move toward decentralization; (2) the size of nonwhite populations was significantly correlated with decentralization; (3) the degree of student and faculty integration was weakly correlated with decentralization; (4) decentralization does not seem to be related to dropout rates; and (5) there was a slight correlation between the degree of minority representation on the city council and decentralization. Data gathered over a three-year period are presented in case studies of five cities: St. Louis, Los Angeles, Washington, D.C., Detroit, and New York. Field research in these cities was done in the summer of 1969 (see La Noue, George R. and Bruce L. R. Smith, "The Political Evaluation of School Decentralization," above).

Lauter, Paul. "The Short, Happy Life of the Adams-Morgan Community School Project." *Harvard Educational Review* 38:2 (Spring 1968): 235–62.

This article describes the difficulties and failures of the first year of the Adams-Morgan Community School Project in Washington, D.C. Problems arose because the project was planned by white activists rather than by the low income blacks served by the school. Another problem area was the inexperience of those people working in the project. The project was hastily conceived and little understood by the school faculty or the community.

Levin, Henry M., ed. *Community Control of Schools*. Washington, D.C.: Brookings Institution, 1970.

Reviews:
Adelson, H. L. *Library Journal* 95 (June 1970): 2144.
Gross, Ronald. *New York Times Book Review* (September 20, 1970): 36.
Kraft, Ivor. *Nation* 210 (June 29, 1970): 790.

This is a collection of papers presented at the Brookings Conference on the Community School at the Brookings Institution in December 1968. The ten papers cover three general areas: objectives and social implications of community governance of city schools; redistribution of power in decision making between the community, school personnel, students, and government; and organizing and financing a decentralized school system. A summary of conference discussions is also included.

Lopate, Carol, et al. *Some Effects of Parent and Community Participation in Public Education*. ERIC-IRCD Urban Disadvantaged Series, no. 3.

New York: ERIC Clearinghouse on the Urban Disadvantaged, Teachers College, Columbia University, February 1969. ERIC ED027–359. Also published as "Decentralization and Community Participation in Public Education." *Review of Educational Research* 40:1 (February 1970): 135–50.

This paper reviews literature relating to parent participation in education. The first three sections cover background material pertinent to the subject: the historical shift from lay to centralized school administration, the issue of centralization and participation in the public schools of New York City, and some correlates of organizational size and participation in decision making. The last two sections deal with the central issues of the effects of parent involvement on pupil achievement and the effects of community identity on achievement. The author concludes from the literature that parent involvement has a positive effect on the academic achievement of children and that it creates positive changes in the effective and instrumental behavior of the parent participants. About fifty references are cited in the paper.

Mayer, Martin. *The Teachers Strike: New York, 1968.* New York: Harper and Row, 1968.

> Reviews:
> Berube, M. R. *Commonweal* 90 (May 2, 1969): 209.
> *Choice* 6 (September 1969): 881.
> Fowler, Austin. *Library Journal* 95 (April 1969): 1479.
> Kraft, Ivor. *Nation* 208 (May 26, 1969): 670.
> Le Veness, F. P. *America* 120 (April 5, 1969): 418.
> *New York Review of Books* 12 (March 13, 1969): 31.

This is Mayer's account of the events surrounding the New York City teachers strike of 1968. Mayer feels that the strike was the worst disaster that New York City experienced in his (Mayer's) lifetime. He does not believe that the strike was inevitable, and he attempts to explain how it could have been avoided. He describes the role of the Ocean Hill governing board, the development of the confrontation at Ocean Hill, and the events during the three teachers strikes. Mayer points the finger of blame at the foundations which backed the experimental school districts and at the mayor's office, the board of education, and Mayor Lindsay, in that order.

McDill, Edward L.; Leo Rigsby; and Edmund D. Meyers, Jr. "Educational Climate of High Schools: Their Effects and Sources." *American Journal of Sociology* 74:6 (May 1969): 567–86.

Assuming that few schools actually exhibit consistent and powerful educational environments, the authors attempt: to identify some dimensions of the educational and social climates of high schools; to assess the contextual effects of these environmental dimensions on the academic performance and college plans of students; and to investigate the climate's effects on the students' achievement and college plans. Twenty public high schools were selected from eight states in seven geographical areas. Self-administered questionnaires were submitted to students, teachers, and principals. Two Project Talent tests were administered to students. School climate was measured using Selvin and Hagstrom's procedure for classifying large formal groups in terms of a large number of variables. Individual level variables were measured by six items on the student questionnaire.

The study found that achievement level was influenced by: father's educational level, student's academic values, and student's ability. Parental involvement in the school appeared to function as a source of climate effects. The authors feel that the results indicate "that the critical factor in explaining the impact of the high school environment on the achievement and educational aspirations of students is the degree of parental and community interest in quality education." The educational and social climate of the school was found to have a moderate effect on the academic behavior of the students.

Moore, Charles H., and Ray E. Johnston. "School Decentralization, Community Control, and the Politics of Public Education." *Urban Affairs Quarterly* 6:4 (June 1971): 421–46.

The author believes that the myth of political neutrality of schools has permitted educators to legitimize their power and thus to establish educational norms. He explores why participation has become an issue in the 1970s and presents arguments for and against school decentralization. Opponents argue that decentralization will encourage apartheid, further alienate the white working class from governmental agencies, further encourage the suburbanization of whites, and divert liberal attention from urban problems. Proponents argue that it will increase citizen participation, give blacks a more positive orientation to government, build the self-concepts of blacks, and increase the public's satisfaction with government.

The author discusses the politics of school decentralization in Detroit in 1970 and 1971. He points out how race was injected into the issue of decentralization. He believes that the plan of the Michigan legislature was biased in the direction of upper and middle class political practices, because only registered voters can vote in school elections and because petitions with 500 signatures are needed for nominating regional school board candidates. The Detroit Board of Education was finally faced with the dilemma of decentralization or integration. The author says that hard choices will have to be made in this area. He sees the basic issues inherent in decentralization as finances, social class, quality of education, and mass participation.

Moorefield, Story. "Morgan Follows Through." *American Education* 6:1 (January/February 1970): 31–33.

A description of the Morgan Community School in Washington, D.C., is presented in this article. It is an urban slum school, locally controlled by a fifteen-member board made up of seven parents, six nonparent community residents, and two school staff members. The board operates within the general policy directives of the central school board, but it otherwise controls the school. It is responsible for the budget, hiring, curriculum, and teaching methods. The school also has the Head Start Follow Through Program, a federal program which provides intensive instruction and comprehensive services for low income children in the primary grades. The program requires parental involvement. The author is the Follow Through Information Officer for the Office of Education.

National Education Association, National Commission on Professional Rights and Responsibilities. *Central Issues Influencing School-Community Relations in Atlanta, Georgia.* Washington, D.C.: National Education Association, 1969.

In describing the history of school-community conflict in Atlanta in the 1950s and 1960s, this report catalogues the racial inequities in the Atlanta school system, especially with respect to salary and per pupil expenditure differentials. It describes the rigidity of the board of education and its resistance to public pressures such as the grievances of the black community. The commission describes efforts of public oriented organizations including Better Schools Atlanta, the Community Relations Commission, and the Metropolitan Summit Leadership Conference and their inability to have any impact on school policy. The commission makes several recommendations for improving school-community relations: a public information procedure for citizens, a staff information program, an experimental community control school district, citizen advisory boards at each school, and greater teacher participation in school affairs.

New York (City) Mayor's Advisory Panel on Decentralization of the New York City Schools, McGeorge Bundy, Chairman. *Reconnection for*

Learning: A Community School System for New York City. New York: Praeger, 1969.

The Advisory Panel on Decentralization of the New York City Schools was created by Mayor John V. Lindsay under a 1967 act of the New York State Legislature which directed him to prepare a plan for decentralization of the New York City schools. The plan, submitted to the legislature but never implemented, calls for the complete reorganization of the New York City public schools into a community school system. It provides for greatly increased participation for parents and community residents while reducing the power of the board of education, the school bureaucracy, and the teachers and administrators. The plan includes details on how the proposed system could be organized and financed.

Nyquist, Ewald. "All the Isms are Wasms: Self-Renewal in an Age of Discontinuity." *Vital Speeches of the Day* 37:21 (August 15, 1971): 645–50.

This is the text of a speech by the Commissioner of Education of New York State delivered at the 30th Annual Superintendents' Work Conference at Teachers College, Columbia University, on July 15, 1971. In the speech, Nyquist describes New York State's Project Redesign. Its goal is the reexamination and radical reform of the public education system. It is an attempt to move toward a more humanistic educational system. The project involves the community in the reexamination of all aspects of the schools. The State Education Department provides guidance but not control. At this time, four prototype school districts were participating in the project. The State Education Department was helping them in the following areas: (1) assessment of readiness for redesign; (2) formulation of redesign strategy; (3) organizing specific new educational programs; (4) organizing a program for community-wide education about the new system of education; (5) developing organizations to manage redesign; and (6) management and evaluation.

Peebles, Robert W. "The Community School: Then and Now." *Phylon* 31:2 (Summer 1970): 157–67.

The author examines an early experiment in community control of schools in light of the more recent movement for decentralization and community control. The article focuses on Benjamin Franklin High School in East Harlem, which functioned as a community school in the 1930s and 1940s under Principal Leonard Covello. The author describes the school and the community and discusses Covello and his philosophy of community involvement.

Ravitch, Diane. "Community Control Revisited." *Commentary* 53:2 (February 1972): 69–74.

   The author attempts to assess the educational impacts of the community control experiment at Ocean Hill-Brownsville two years after the demise of the project. There has still been no evaluation of the project, and the author sees a conscious effort to avoid such an evaluation. The participants and supporters of the experiment claimed substantial academic achievements, but they would not use standardized tests. The author claims that they manipulated figures concerning student achievement. One year after the experiment standardized tests were given. The reading scores showed that the schools involved in the experiment were ranked below the 45th percentile. The scores were lower than the pre-experiment scores of 1967. Also, records showed a serious attendance problem. The author maintains that no one gained, educationally, from the Ocean Hill-Brownsville experiment in community control of schools.

Rich, Leslie. "Newark's Parent-Powered School: Springfield Avenue Community School." *American Education* 7:10 (December 1971): 35–39.

   Springfield Avenue Community School is a predominately black ghetto school in which the parents are the power base. Parents are involved in both the administrative and educational processes of the school. All parents are members of the Parent's Action Council, which meets once a month to consider recommendations of its fifteen-member board. The author visited the school and interviewed parents and staff members. She describes "academic innovations" at the school and thinks academic progress at the school has been "remarkable."

Roaden, Arliss L. "Citizen Participation in Two Southern Cities." Paper presented at the American Research Association, Los Angeles, California, February 5–8, 1969. ERIC ED028–511.

   This is a study of mechanisms for citizen participation in the schools of Atlanta, Georgia, and Huntsville, Alabama. Data were gathered from interviews and examination of printed materials. The author identified two levels of citizen participation in the schools—system-wide and neighborhood—and two types of mechanisms—those initiated by the schools and those initiated by citizens. He asked two questions in assessing the groups: How influential is the mechanism for effecting school policy? How stable is the mechanism for sustained influence? (Is it dependent on one or two influential people?)

In Atlanta he found that neither type of mechanism at the system-wide level was successful. At the local level both types showed uneven success. In Huntsville the major mechanism (which was system-wide) was judged very effective. The author attributed this to the fact that it was run by community leaders, that it dealt with fundamental issues, and that it had the confidence of the school system. In Huntsville the mechanisms at the local level were mostly federally sponsored, but the administration seemed to go beyond minimum requirements. The author concluded that the impact of citizen participation in the schools in the South was limited because blacks were still docile and because of the elitist power structures.

Rosenfeld, Raymond A. "Membership Characteristics of Voluntary Organizations: Two Groups Involved in Atlanta School Desegregation." *Georgia Political Science Association Journal* 1 (Fall 1973): 77–99.

The author compares two voluntary organizations formed in response to the desegregation of teachers in the Atlanta Public Schools in 1970. HANDS (Help Atlanta's Neighborhood Schools) was formed to fight teacher desegregation. HOPE (Help Our Public Schools) supported desegregation. The two groups were compared with respect to social characteristics, political characteristics, and issue perceptions and opinions of members. The author hypothesized that social and political characteristics as well as issue perceptions and opinions of the members of the two groups would differ. The hypothesis is based upon the theory that organizations having different issue positions will attract members with different characteristics.

Interviews were conducted in 1970 with a random sample of the members of each group and with all formal leaders of the two groups. It was found that certain characteristics clearly differed: education; occupation; age, race, and religion; community ties, evaluation of local government, and party identification.

Sigel, Roberta S. "Citizen's Committees—Advise and Consent." *Trans-Action* 4:6 (May 1967): 47–52.

The author spend eighteen months observing a citizens advisory committee which was making recommendations for a community high school in a quasi-slum neighborhood of a large city. The citizens advisory committee produced a comprehensive plan that went beyond the original intentions for the community high school. The author observed the decision-making process of the committee and she found the committee slow, accepting of administration goals, dependent on experts, and unable to generate its own ideas. The committee was also characterized by an absence of conflict and little use of negotiating techniques.

Sigel, Roberta S. *Detroit Experiment: Citizens Plan a New High School.* Inter-University Case Program no. 95. Indianapolis: Bobbs-Merrill, 1966.

Steinberg, Lois S. "Some Structural Determinants of Citizen Participation in Educational Policy-Making in Suburbia: A Case Study." Paper for the American Educational Research Association Convention, Washington, D.C., February 1971. ERIC ED046-841.

The author examines the institutional arrangements in school board-community and school parent-administration relationships. Data were gathered during two and a half years of observation of school board meetings in one suburb, content analysis of newspaper articles and letters, participant observation of formal and informal meetings, and the testimony of elite and nonelite informants. The study identified five participation channels: voting, the nominating process, board appointed committees, board meetings, and ad hoc groups.

The study found that citizen involvement in this suburb was episodic with respect to economic issues and that citizens were apathetic with respect to educational issues. This was attributed to three structural deficiencies: an absence of channels for sustained communication between the board and the community, inadequate structural mechanisms providing for public involvement in issues and school board assessment of public opinion, and ineffective channels for the expression and mediation of dissent within the system. This situation, according to the author, is the result of depoliticization in school-community relations and professionalization in administration-parent relations. The study found that dissent was forced into outside channels which produced leadership changes in the system, resulting in a more responsive leadership.

Surkin, Marvin. "The Myth of Community Control: Rhetorical and Political Aspects of the Ocean Hill-Brownsville Controversy." *Race, Change, and Urban Society.* Edited by Peter Orleans and William Russell Ellis, Jr. Beverly Hills, California: Sage Publications, 1971, pp. 405-22.

The Ocean Hill-Brownsville controversy is used to illustrate "the general crisis of the established organizational structures in urban America to relate to the new demands and needs of the people." The author concludes that the symbolism of community control rhetoric was used to conceal and perpetuate the established and vested interests of the participants.

Sussman, Leila, with Gayle Speck. "Community Participation in the Schools: The Boston Case." *Urban Education* 7:4 (January 1973): 341–55. ERIC ED047–424.

This study describes groups in Boston which attempt to have an impact on decision making in local schools. About fourteen groups in Boston were studied and three were chosen for case studies. Leaders were interviewed and the groups were observed. Several common problems were identified: (1) the problem of legitimacy, i.e., who is the community? (2) the challenge these groups present to professional authority; (3) community apathy; and (4) the mutual isolation of community school groups. It was found that such groups can serve as channels for a few upwardly mobile minority individuals, but that they had little impact on education. The study also found that most groups were formed with federal impetus and that they were small and weak. The author concluded that community control is only illusionary, that the struggle for local control is basically a class struggle, and that educational issues will continue to be decided at the national rather than the local level.

Swanson, Bert W.; Edith Cortin; and Eleanor Main. "Parents in Search of Community Influence in the Public Schools." *Education and Urban Society* 1:4 (August 1969): 383–403.

This article reports the results of a survey of parental attitudes toward schools in New York City's three community control school districts. Six hundred parents from the three districts were interviewed in May 1968. Two-thirds of the parents favored more community influence in the schools. The parents favoring more community influence were more optimistic about improvement of the schools, were more critical of educational professionals, participated more often in community affairs, and were more active. Those parents favoring less influence were more trusting, accepting, satisfied, less articulate, and less involved.

Thomas, Michael P., Jr. *Community Governance and the School Board: A Case Study.* Austin: Institute of Public Affairs, University of Texas, 1966.

Thompson, Robert. *Factors Resulting in Variations in Citizen Interest, Involvement, and Support of Their Local Schools.* Eugene: Institute for Comparative Experimental Research on Behavioral Systems, University of Oregon, September 1970. ERIC ED054–531.

The author examines the role of income, family structure, home ownership, membership in organizations, and race in influencing citizen interest in local government. The investigation looks at four areas: (1) the relationship of participation in local government with participation in local schools; (2) the effect of the size and economic base of the community on the amount of citizen participation; (3) the relationship between race and participation; and (4) socioeconomic class as a factor in participation. Data were gathered in five Oregon cities of varying size and characteristics. It was found that there was little relationship between the variables mentioned above and participation.

Torge, Herman. *Guidelines for Lay Participation at School Board Meetings in Ohio.* Middletown, Ohio: Southwestern Ohio Educational Research Council, June 1971. ERIC ED056–402.

The objectives of this study were to identify items for school board consideration in both encouraging and controlling lay participation and to determine the extent to which such items have been included in school manuals and used in school board meetings. The study proceeded in five phases. First, statements on lay participation were elicited from administrators, school board members, professors of education, and graduate students in educational administration. The items were then generalized, synthesized, and validated in the field. Third, checklists of items were constructed for manuals and board meetings. Then the checklists were applied to manuals and board meeting procedures. Fifth, data from the checklists application were analyzed. The study found that there were significant differences in the theory espoused by respondents and the practice of boards. The respondents felt that more participation than what was written in the manuals and procedures was needed. The study then outlines "guidelines for participation."

Usdan, Michael D. "Strengthening Citizen Participation: An Analysis of the New York City Experiments." Paper presented at the Annual Meeting of the American Educational Research Association, Los Angeles, California, February 8, 1969. ERIC ED028–512.

Usdan discusses the New York City teachers strikes of 1968. The author feels that, although New York has received most of the publicity, the same problems exist in other cities. Community members, especially in the ghettos, have become disenchanted with bureaucratic organization and want to have a voice in policy decisions. Teachers feel that decentralization poses a threat to newly acquired power. The result in New York was the crisis at Ocean Hill.

The author feels that there are four lessons to be gleaned from the New York situation: first, the civil rights movement and other developments have triggered an irreversible response in the ghettos; second, since school systems are a prime stimulus of social mobility, they will continue to receive attention; third, there was a lack of communication between the board of education and the community governing board; and fourth, no attempts were made to hammer out compromises collectively.

Washington, R. O. "The Politicalization of School Decentralization in New York City." *Urban Education* 8:3 (October 1973): 223–30.

The author of this article describes the New York School Decentralization Act of 1969 and contends that its implementation has resulted in a "politicalization" of the school system and the increasing use of political patronage in the system. While admitting that it is still too early to "pass judgement on school decentralization," the author points out several features which the author interprets as negative impacts of the decentralization program.

Wiles, David K. "Community Participation Demands and Local School Response in the Urban Environment." *Education and Urban Society* 6:4 (August 1974): 451–68.

This article presents an analysis of the decision-making behavior of school principals in two large urban school districts in the late 1960s and early 1970s. It looks at the extent to which principals relied on traditional institutional assumptions in situations of decision conflict with some degree of perceived uncertainty of administrative authority.

One hundred eighty-seven schools were studied. Possible decision behaviors of principals were classified by type and frequency of behavior. Ninety-six principals were found to exhibit a pattern of institutional authority for decision making. They were generally located in suburban schools. Eighty-four principals relied on alliances with other groups (e.g., students, teachers, community groups) and seven had laissez-faire policies. These were usually located in change environments. In only eleven of these instances did the principals side with a local community-based group against the central system.

The implications and conclusions were as follows. Local schools are closed systems of professional decision making. The concept of local school "community participation" has three operational forms: participation to legitimize existing professional policy, participation as "outside" attacks to be guarded against, and participation as a viable political alliance for the principal to counteract the central authority. A true balance between institutional demands and the needs of a community in conflict is impossible.

Zimet, Melvin. *Decentralization and School Effectiveness: A Case Study of the 1969 Decentralization Law in New York City.* New York: Teachers College Press, 1973.

Zimet describes the decentralization law and the events leading to its enactment. The study, conducted during the first years of school decentralization in New York, focuses on District 7, which includes most of the South Bronx. The author describes the roles of community groups, teachers unions, and other actors and groups involved in school decision making under the decentralization plan. The author then assesses the impacts of decentralization upon school administration and governance and upon educational programs and achievement. Quantifiable criteria of effectiveness "do not indicate that great change has taken place during the early years of decentralization," but the author does find that there was a "substantial realignment of power" in school governance. He concludes that "the community should be given the opportunity to develop techniques and procedures necessary to make [community control] work."

ENVIRONMENT AND NATURAL RESOURCES

Bishop, A. Bruce. *Public Participation in Water Resources Planning: A Report by the U.S. Army Engineer Institute for Water Resources.* Springfield, Virginia: National Technical Information Service, 1970.

This report attempts to help the water resources planner in organizing participatory planning by: providing a framework for planning by relating water resources planning to concepts of planned social change, providing a guide to different kinds of citizen participation, and examining ways to organize public participation in planning studies. Planning is presented as a process of social change and three components of the planning process are identified: the hierarchical structure of decisions, the sequential structure of planning activities, and the institutional structure and participants in the process. The report goes on to list the objectives of the citizen participation process, how to achieve those objectives, and the implications of participatory planning for the Army Corps of Engineers.

Bolle, Arnold, W. "Public Participation and Environmental Quality." *Natural Resources Journal* 11:3 (July 1971): 497–505.

The author is an advocate of citizen involvement in natural resources agencies. He believes that administrators do not understand the participation process. He cites the case of the Bitterroot National Forest in Montana, where a dispute over cutting timber developed between citizens and the National Forest Service. The author says that accommodation of the public is not reflected in bureaucratic reward systems. He believes that citizen involvement will lead to proper identification of problems and mutual education for citizens and administrators, and will ensure that policy will not be made through litigation, challenged administrative fiat, and public conflict.

Borton, Thomas E., and Katherine P. Warner. "Involving Citizens in Water Resources Planning: The Communication-Participation Experiment in the Susquehanna River Basin." *Environment and Behavior* 3:3 (September 1971): 284–306.

This article discusses the Susquehanna Communication-Participation Study done by a research team from the University of Michigan in 1968–69. This pilot project centered on establishing communication between agency planners and local residents. Two categories of procedures were used: procedures to improve two-way communication and citizen involvement, including mailed information, workshops, and forums; and procedures to evaluate the impact of the communication-participation techniques, using interviews and questionnaires, and workshops for the staff. The authors conclude that the pilot project showed the need for a more effective communication-participation program in water resources planning.

Brown, Carl, et al. *Decision-Making in Water Resource Allocation.* Studies in Transportation and Regional Science. Lexington, Massachusetts: D. C. Heath, 1973.

This book presents a study of the decision-making process in the allocation of water resources. The subject of the study was the Lower Amazon and Flat Creek Watershed (or Junction City) Project in Oregon. The study, funded mostly by the Department of Agriculture, had eight objectives: (1) to identify and classify the sources of the demands for water resource development; (2) to analyze the process through which demands are transformed into political and economic concerns; (3) to delineate the decision-making network within the legal framework of the Water Resources Development Administration; (4) to determine the decision makers' perception of relative values and legal constraints; (5) to evaluate the extent to which various network decisions influence the final decision; (6) to examine the impact of decision making on public and private demands; (7) to evaluate the legal safeguards protecting the rights of persons traditionally "owning" water resources; and (8) to study the equity of the decision-making process with respect to the rights of the public and special interest groups.

Data were gathered through interviews with persons living in or associated with the water control district and with local, state, and federal agency personnel.

The author's conclusions were: (1) very few people actually participated in decision making, even though they had the right to do so; (2) the flow of information did not permit opposition to develop until it was too late to be effective; (3) the legal channels of communication were inadequate despite news stories and public hearings; (4) residents perceived that a specific category of people would benefit most from the project; (5) decision-making criteria changed at local, state, and federal levels; (6) understanding the nature of a public good and identifying advocates were fruitful approaches to this study; (7) the project was initiated as a flood control project, but when the concept of irrigation was introduced, it became paramount to some people; (8) the local administrative unit was composed of residents who did not necessarily see themselves as government officials; and (9) the name, Junction City Project, was misleading, as many thought the project would benefit only the city.

Brown, Kenneth F. "Involving the Public in Environmental Decision-Making." *Ford Foundation Experiments in Regional Environment Management.* A Symposium of the American Association for the Advancement of Science. New York: Ford Foundation, 1974, pp. 15–23.

The author describes the Hawaii Environmental Simulation Laboratory (a privately funded organization) and discusses its attempts to facilitate the interaction of governmental decision makers and community groups.

"The City: 'A Little Green Space'." *Time* 83:7 (February 14, 1964): 64.

This article describes the efforts of the citizens of Cambridge, Massachusetts, to preserve a "little green space." The Emergency Committee for the Preservation of Memorial Drive was formed when the residents of Cambridge discovered that Memorial Drive was to be widened at the expense of the land and trees on the Charles River side of the road.

Clark, Roger N.; George H. Stankey; and John C. Hendee. "An Introduction to CODINVOLVE: A System for Analyzing, Storing, and Retrieving Public Input to Resource Decisions." WSDA Forest Service Research Note, PNW–223. Portland, Oregon: Forest Service, U.S. Department of Agriculture, April 1974.

Dodson, Edward N. "Citizen Action in Environmental Management." *Public Management* 56:3 (March 1974): 22–23.

The author describes the Environmental Quality Advisory Board created by the city of Santa Barbara, California, after the massive offshore oil blowout in 1969. All of the members are professional people from the natural sciences; they recommend policy on all environmental matters.

Ebbin, Steven, and Raphael Kasper. *Citizen Groups and the Nuclear Power Controversy: Uses of Scientific and Technological Information.* Cambridge, Massachusetts: MIT Press, 1974.

Review:
Nelkin, Dorothy. *Administrative Science Quarterly* 20 (March 1975): 143.

Ebbin and Kasper describe three case studies which involved participant observation and more than one hundred interviews. One of the cases involved permit hearings for a proposed nuclear plant site, another involved operating license proceedings for a nuclear plant, and the third case focused on the rule-making hearings on criteria for emergency core cooling systems. The authors conclude that industry and government "have tended to become allied against small groups of concerned, even worried, citizens." They also point out that the weight of influence clearly lies with government and industry and that "citizen groups are usually restricted to raising questions about matters concerning which they possess little knowledge or expertise."

Frischnecht, Reed L. "The Democratization of Administration: The Farmer Committee System." *American Political Science Review* 47:3 (September 1953): 704–27.
This article describes the farmer committee system of agricultural price and income support programs begun by the Department of Agricul-

ture in 1933. The system was initiated to decentralize administration and put control of the program in the hands of those affected by it. State, county, and community level committees were formed. The author discusses the history of the system, its weaknesses and problems, and the politics involved. He concludes that participation was coopted and maneuvered by the national administrative agency.

Greer, Edward, and Paul Booth. "Pollution and Community Organization in Two Cities." *Social Policy* 4:1 (July/August 1973): 42–49.

The authors feel that large corporations are no longer predominant forces in the United States. They cite the case of U.S. Steel in the Gary-Chicago area. The corporation was once able to write its own "sweetheart" pollution agreements, but it must now yield to community pressures to cut down on pollution. The organization that brought U.S. Steel to the conference table was the Campaign Against Pollution, a middle and working class group. U.S. Steel was also being challenged with discrimination charges by the Equal Employment Opportunity Commission. The authors attribute much of the progress in the Gary-Chicago area to the new people who came into power with Mayor Hatcher. They contrast Hatcher with Chicago's Mayor Daley, who has not fought the corporation. The authors conclude that there is a need for a mass organization, encompassing many issues, to fight large corporations.

Hendee, John C. "Public Involvement in the United States Forest Service Roadless-Area Review: Lessons from a Case Study." Paper presented at a seminar on public participation at the School of the Built Environment and Center for Human Ecology, University of Edinburgh, Edinburgh, Scotland, July 1–3, 1974.

Hendee, John C.; Roger N. Clark; and George H. Stankey. "A Framework for Agency Use of Public Input in Resource Decision-Making." *Journal of Soil and Water Conservation* 29:2 (March/April 1974): 60–66.

Hendee, John C.; Robert C. Lucas; Robert H. Tracy; Tony Staed; Roger N. Clark; George H. Stankey; and Ronald A. Yarnell. *Public Involvement and the Forest Service: Experience, Effectiveness and Suggested Direction.* Report from the United States Forest Service Administrative Study of Public Involvement. Washington, D.C.: Forest Service, 1973.

This report grew out of a need to assess "the working relationship between the public and the Forest Service." The study team interviewed administrative officers in three forests in each of the nine administrative regions of the Forest Service; "sample case studies" were also conducted. The public involvement activities of each regional office were also examined.

The authors state that public involvement must be considered in five stages of decision-making processes: (1) issue definition, (2) collection, (3) analysis, (4) evaluation, and (5) decision implementation. The report recommends that for any specific issue, the objectives of public involvement be clearly articulated, that the responsibility for obtaining public input be decentralized, that the Forest Service obtain the views of all potentially affected interests, that the public be presented with an array of alternatives, that a number of public involvement techniques be employed, that public input be systematically analyzed, that the Forest Service develop "consistent procedures" for analyzing and evaluating public involvement, that feedback be given to the public, and that "all line and staff officers in the Forest Service" be exposed to a "broad program of training covering all stages of public involvement."

Irland, Lloyd C. "Citizens Participation—A Tool for Conflict Management on the Public Land." *Public Administration Review* 35:3 (May/June 1975): 263–69.

Lando, Barry. "Save-Our-Air." *New Republic* 161:15 (October 11, 1969): 12.

Lando describes the Delta County (Michigan) Citizens Committee to Save-Our-Air, formed to protest a proposed pulp plant that would bring pollution to an otherwise unpolluted area in Upper Michigan. The committee drew up clean air standards which were not accepted by the county board, but the board was considering submitting the standards to the electorate.

Mazmanian, Daniel A. "Citizens and the Assessment of Technology: An Examination of the Participation Thesis." Paper prepared for the American Political Science Association meeting, Chicago, Illinois, August 29–September 2, 1974. Mimeograph.

Public participation in Army Corps of Engineers' projects is examined in this paper. The "public participation thesis" and its modification and adoption by the corps are described. The author examines five corps projects and used mailed questionnaires to obtain data from citizens who had attended public meetings, seminars, workshops, and discussions. Approximately 450 respondents were included in the analysis. On the basis of these data, the author concludes that the "participation thesis" (bringing all interested parties together in the decision-making process results in the formulation of group goals) was not applicable in the decision-making processes studied. Thus, "favor cannot be won for old project ideas or even some innovative ones . . . simply by undertaking elaborate public participation programs," yet, "if the Corps views open planning as a longterm educational process for both itself and the public, it may strengthen support for the agency and its proposals."

Medalia, Nahum Z. "Citizen Participation and Environmental Health Action: The Case of Air Pollution Control." *American Journal of Public Health* 59:8 (August 1969): 1385–91.

The concepts of citizen involvement and community control are discussed. Examples of successful citizen action against air pollution in Cincinnati, St. Louis, Pittsburgh, and other cities are cited. The Air Pollution Control Association is described. It consists of mostly industry and trade representatives and encourages public acceptance of pollution prevention and helps cities adopt regulations. It emphasizes voluntary abatement. The author sees voluntary citizen efforts predominating in air pollution control at the present. He believes more responsible specialists at the national and state level will be needed in the future and envisions an expanded federal role in air quality control.

Morgan, Robert J. *Governing Soil Conservation: Thirty Years of the New Decentralization.* Baltimore, Maryland: John Hopkins Press, 1965.

Morgan reviews three decades of the Soil Conservation Service with its decentralized system of soil conservation districts. The book traces the origins and evolution of issues involved in the program and describes how the districts have functioned. Information was gathered from questionnaires sent to a sample of conservation districts and to all state conservation committees. The author found that the system had never been truly decentralized in that districts did not have exclusive responsibility in their areas. The participation of farmers was purely voluntary where it existed. The program, the author concludes, had been caught in the middle of political power struggles.

Olson, Laura Katz. "Power, Public Policy and the Environment: The Defeat of the 1976 Winter Olympics in Colorado." Paper prepared for the

American Political Science Association meeting, Chicago, Illinois, August 29–September 2, 1974. Mimeograph.

The author traces the events leading to the rejection of the 1976 Winter Olympics in Colorado through stages identified as "issue initiation, political decision-making, and policy impact." The activities and influence of a number of actors and groups are examined and the author focuses upon the strategies employed by business interests and an environmentalist citizen group, Citizens for Colorado's Future (CCF). CCF successfully initiated a proposal to cut off state funding for the games and encouraged the politicization of environmental issues in Colorado.

Warner, Katherine P. *Public Participation in Water Resources Planning: A State of the Arts Study of Public Participation in Water Resources Planning.* Ann Arbor: Environmental Simulation Laboratory, School of Natural Resources, University of Michigan, 1971.

After reviewing the role of public participation in governmental planning studies, the author presents a model for participation in the planning process and the results of a survey distributed to state, regional, and local planning agencies and to citizen groups concerned with environmental quality. A number of recommendations for more effective citizen participation in water resources planning are made by the author. These generally center around ways that agencies can encourage citizen participation through changes in programs and institutional arrangements. The report includes a number of examples of public participation program designs, applications, and experiences.

White, Gilbert F. *Strategies of American Water Management.* Ann Arbor: University of Michigan Press, 1969.

This book outlines a framework with which to examine decision making in water management. Six major strategies practiced in the United States are discussed: (1) single purpose construction by private managers (e.g., farm water supply); (2) single purpose construction by public managers (e.g., navigation); (3) multiple purpose construction by public managers; (4) single purpose action by public agencies using multiple means (e.g., flood loss reduction); (5) research as a conscious management tool (e.g., weather modification); and (6) a merging of multiple purposes and multiple means, including research.

Water management under each of these categories and the similarities and differences in decision making are discussed. Three questions are examined: Who makes what choices? What is the effect upon the public welfare? What is the effect upon the natural environment?

HEALTH

Abrams, Herbert K., and Robert A. Snyder. "Health Center Seeks to Bridge
the Gap Between Hospital and Neighborhood." *Modern Hospital* 110
(May 1968): 96–101, 112.

This is a description of the North Lawndale Neighborhood Health
Center sponsored by Mount Sinai Hospital in Chicago. The availability of
hospital facilities is seen as an advantage of hospital sponsorship. The goals
of the center are to provide high quality, comprehensive medical care to the
poor, to provide for participation of the poor, and to offer new patterns of
group medical practice. Plans for the center were made in consultation with
the community. The article describes the hospital and the community, the
community's reaction to the center, the organization of the center, the
approaches it offers to problems, and its activities.

Anderson, Donna M., and Markay Kerr. "Citizen Influence in Health
Services Programs." *American Journal of Public Health* 61:8 (August
1971): 1518–23.

Six citizens groups involved in health care were studied. Five were
associated with units providing health services to a defined population. One
was concerned with planning for quality health services for neighborhood
population. The study looked at the degree of involvement, the amount of
responsibility assumed, and the content of group meetings. Data were
collected through group observations, an opinion poll, and a formal
documents review.

Back, Edith B. "The Community in Community Mental Health." *Mental
Hygiene* 54:2 (April 1970): 316–20.

The author feels that the role of the community in community mental
health is unclear because of a lack of a clear definition of the community's
role, its purpose, and the relationship between professionals and consumers.
The author believes that a mental health community can be organized by
patients who share common problems. She also conceives of a council of
patients' relatives as another community through which the institution can
be forced to respond to patients' problems. The use of public money is seen
as the justification for involving the public in the operations of mental
health service delivery systems.

Bazell, Robert J. "Health Radicals: Crusade to Shift Medical Power to the
People." *Science* 173:3996 (August 6, 1971): 506–09.

The health radicals described in this article are a coalition of radical professionals, students, health workers, and community activists who have challenged the underlying assumptions of American medicine and want to give recipients a voice in health care delivery systems. The Medical Committee for Human Rights has begun to speak for some of these people. The committee was originally a politically neutral organization but later became involved in social protest. Some members have drafted their own health plan, which advocates nonprofit, tax-supported health care with emphasis on preventive medicine and consumer participation. They also offer community-based free clinics as an alternative model of health care delivery. Even liberals in the medical profession, the author believes, are resisting these ideas.

Beck, Bertram. "Neighborhood Organization in the Delivery of Services and Self-Help." *Social Welfare and Urban Problems.* Edited by Thomas D. Sherrard. New York: Columbia University Press, 1968, pp. 34–61.

The author presents a model neighborhood management system for more efficient delivery of health services at the neighborhood level. Twelve basic principles are presented: (1) roles for residents; (2) freedom of choice for residents; (3) lessening of distance between consumers and services; (4) relevant services in sufficient quantity and quality; (5) the relationship between the neighborhood system and outside health services; (6) realistic analysis of the diversities of the neighborhood; (7) channels for consumer grievances; (8) provisions for evaluation; (9) analysis of costs and services; (10) a system for keeping track of consumers; (11) opportunity for social innovation; and (12) the integration of the component parts of the system. The principles are then discussed in terms of implementation by the Mobilization for Youth Program on the Lower East Side in New York City.

Bellin, Lowell. "Can We Have 'Quality Control' in Health Care?" *Perspective* 6 (1971): 31–33.

This article considers the use of the concept of quality control in hospitals. The author feels that consumers cannot be responsible for quality control; only the government can reasonably do the job. He believes that auditors of health service must be accountable to the public.

Brieland, Donald. "Community Advisory Boards and Maximum Feasible Participation." *American Journal of Public Health* 61:2 (February 1971): 292–96.

Brieland discusses whether or not "maximum feasible participation" can be accomplished. The author identifies problems such as the danger of cooptation of militants, the selection process by which representatives are chosen, and the need for leadership development. Several principles involved in participation are listed: (1) advice on what? (2) necessary limits; (3) independence; (4) responsibility for financing; (5) rotation and leadership development; and (6) payment for services of participants. The author concludes that consumer boards should have definite policy-making functions so that they will be effective partners for the health professionals rather than window dressing.

Brooks, Wendy Goepel. "Health Care and Poor People." *Citizen Participation: Effecting Community Change.* Edited by Edgar S. Cahn and Barry A. Passett. New York: Praeger, 1971, pp. 110–28.

Reasons why poor people receive inferior medical care are enumerated in this article: (1) selectiveness of medical education which excludes the poor; (2) control of the AMA over policy making; (3) low expectations of the poor; and (4) the difficulty of organizing people around the issue of health. The author sees two kinds of roles for the poor as participants in health care: as employees of health care agencies and as consumers with a voice in the neighborhood health centers. Suggestions for encouraging participation are made: (1) neighborhood location of health centers; (2) training for the consumer participants; (3) delineation of the health care package with control over certain services provided for the poor; (4) maintenance of clear relationships between community people on the board of directors and those on the staff of the center; and (5) sponsoring groups must want community participation. The author believes that the primary issues in the coming years will be improvement of medical education, health benefits, and environmental health.

Campbell, John. "Working Relationships Between Providers and Consumers in a Neighborhood Health Center." *American Journal of Public Health* 61:1 (January 1971): 97–103.

This article describes the experiences of the Hough-Norwood Neighborhood Health Center in Cleveland, Ohio. There are three focuses of community input: two consumers serve on the twenty-four-member board, consumer participation in planning the neighborhood health center, and the Community Opportunity Board with annual review of all OEO-funded programs. The author describes conflicts between the consumer groups (between the neighborhood health center and the Community Opportunity

Board) and the relationship between consumers and providers. The author believes that advisory roles for consumers are not adequate and that they should be involved in policy making and in running the center. He also discusses the problems of representation and the need to involve less active segments of the community.

"Citizen Participation in Mental Health Programs." *Mental Health Digest* 2:5 (May 1970): 1–5.

Community Change, Inc., and Public Sector, Inc. *A Study of Consumer Participation in the Administrative Processes in Various Levels of HSMHA's Service Projects.* Report for the Health Services and Mental Health Administration, Contract HSM 110–71–135, Sausalito, California, 1972.

This report attempts to provide the Health Services and Mental Health Administration (HSMHA) with a description of consumer participation at the local project, regional, and administrative levels of eight health service programs: Indian Health, Comprehensive Health Centers, OEO-transferred Neighborhood Health Centers, Migrant Health, Maternal and Infant Care, Children and Youth, Community Mental Health Centers, and Family Planning. The descriptions and recommendations which follow are based on case studies of 18 projects and a mailed survey of 1,083 projects. A number of interviews with national and regional headquarters staff members were conducted, as well as an analysis of the appropriate legislative mandates and administrative policies and guidelines.

In general, the study concludes that "existing consumer participation policy for HSMHA service programs is inadequate," that the purposes of consumer participation were not uniform in HSMHA programs, and that the existing (1972) level of consumer participation in HSMHA programs was limited. Based on these and additional findings, the report details a number of recommendations for possible HSMHA implementation.

Community Participation for Equity and Excellence in Health Care. New York: Committee on Medicine and Society, New York Academy of Medicine, 1970. Reprinted from *Bulletin of the New York Academy of Medicine* 12 (December 1970).

This is a collection of papers and discussions from the 1970 Health Conference of the New York Academy of Medicine. The general theme of the conference was a call for a new health policy which would include consumer participation. Papers and discussions cover the following topics: (1) the role of the community in developing improved health care; (2) the role of the health professional in eliciting consumer participation; (3) specific cases of community participation in health care; and (4) the absence of a national health policy in the area of manpower training and utilitization, and in matters of financing.

Constantine, Anthony, and James E. Cassidy. "Community Concern, Hospital Interest: The Hospital Holds Itself Accountable to Community." *Modern Hospital* 113:2 (August 1969): 89–92.

The authors catalogue the efforts of the Metropolitan Hospital Center (New York) to improve its relationship to the ghetto community. The hospital brought in seven new administrators and initiated face-to-face contacts with members of the community. Administrators became involved with the community outside of their regular duties and began to listen to community complaints. Whereas the old community advisory board had been made up of more affluent people, the new board was more reflective of the entire community. The outpatient department became more responsive to community needs as the staff was reoriented to the philosophy that the patient is part of a total environment rather than a diseased entity.

Cornerly, Paul B. "Community Participation and Control: A Possible Answer to Racism in Health." *Milbank Memorial Fund Quarterly* 47:2 (April 1970): 347–62.

This article discusses three problems of racism in the health industry which can be partially solved through community participation and control. The first is racism in health investigation and research which always focuses on health problems of blacks rather than the assets which have enabled blacks to make progress under adverse circumstances. Second is racism in human service agencies which brutalize rather than serve the poor. Third is racism in the decision-making processes of health institutions which are, for the most part, run by whites.

Creditor, Morton C. "The Neighborhood Health Center. Where Does the Hospital Fit?" *American Journal of Public Health* 61:4 (April 1971): 807–13.

The author describes the experience of Michael Reese Hospital and Medical Center in Chicago in its attempt to develop a neighborhood health center. Michael Reese was originally founded as a community hospital, but the community changed and the hospital became an agent of the old community trying to serve the new community. The hospital's proposal was not funded, but a subsequent proposal of the Kenwood-Oakland Community Organization was funded. The hospital offered appointments for center physicians and back-up consultative and specialty services. The author feels that the community, rather than a hospital, should set up a health center, but he cautions against the isolation of centers and hopes that they will become a coequal component in health care systems.

Davis, James W. "Decentralization, Citizen Participation, and Ghetto Health Care." *American Behavioral Scientist* 15:1 (September/October 1971): 94–107.

The author is pessimistic about the chances for improvement of health care for the poor through decentralization and citizen participation in health care delivery systems. He cites a number of reasons why he feels such reforms will not work. He points out that doctors will probably not want to work under such conditions and will choose not to practice in the ghetto. He feels that decentralization would probably lead to inferior health services being located in ghettos. He believes that the solution is to improve the economic status of the poor, thus enabling them to afford adequate medical care.

Dumois, Ana. "Organizing a Community Around Health." *Social Policy* 1:5 (January/February 1971): 10–14.

Dumois was a community organizer for the North East Neighborhoods Association on New York's Lower East Side. The community became concerned with health because of an incident in 1966. A critically ill child received no medical treatment for several hours because the child's mother could not get transportation to a hospital. This stimulated demands for a community health center. The author describes the nucleus of interested women and a model of a neighborhood health center as visualized by this group. Community members wanted control over a center which would serve the entire community, not just the poor. The author discusses the problems encountered in dealing with medical people and public agencies in setting up the center.

Evaluation of Community Involvement in Community Mental Health Centers. New York: Health Policy Advisory Center, n. d.

Case studies of six community mental health centers conducted in 1970 and 1971 are presented. The purpose of the studies was to look for elements that the six centers might share vis-à-vis a community involvement. Data were gathered through site visits, background research, and interviews. The following conclusions were drawn: (1) peer group involvement was necessary to the functioning of a center; (2) advisory boards were the most important means of eliciting community participation, and paraprofessionals were not used enough for this purpose; (3) location of the centers was often a hindrance to clients; (4) the staffs and the communities were confused as to the role and mandate of the centers; and (5) there was a lack of experimentation with and discussion of therapeutic techniques.

Falkson, Joseph L. "Consumer Participation in Health: Control or Cooptation?" Paper presented at the Conference on Health Planning, Comprehensive Health Planning Program, School of Public Health, University of Hawaii, Honolulu, Hawaii, April 29–30, 1971. Mimeograph.

Feingold, Eugene. "A Political Scientist's View of the Neighborhood Health Center as a Social Institution." *Medical Care* 8:2 (March/April 1970): 108–15.

The author believes that neighborhood health centers can be characterized by power relationships. In this article he looks at power on several different levels: (1) the power of the individual in modern technological society; (2) the relationship between power and poverty; (3) the powerlessness of minority ethnic groups; (4) the relationship between the war on poverty and the distribution of power in the American government; (5) the relationship between the neighborhood health center and the constituents of its political community; (6) the relationship between the neighborhood health center and the black community; (7) the relationship between the community board, the center's sponsors, the local CAP, and OEO; and (8) the power relationships within the center.

Galiher, Claudia B.; Jack Needleman; and Anne J. Rolphe. "Consumer Participation." *HSMHA Health Reports* 86:2 (February 1971): 99–106.

This article describes the emergence of the consumer movement in health and its present status, the changes in the role of the consumer and in opportunities for participation, and factors involved in participation. A table of potential opportunities for consumer participation at local, state, and federal levels is included and illustrates a planned system of producing informed consumers. The needs for staff support, consumer training, and provider training are discussed. The authors call for a clear definition of roles for consumers and maintain that it is too early to measure the accomplishments of consumer participation.

Grant, Murray. "The Delivery of Health Services." *Medical Annals of the District of Columbia* 37:4 (April 1969): 179–82.

Grant discusses problems in health care delivery and innovative approaches toward solutions. The problems are seen as: (1) the high cost of medical care; (2) the inferior quality of health services offered to the poor; (3) the current organization of medical care where the poor usually utilize emergency room facilities in hospitals which are geared more to teaching needs than to patient needs; (4) the shortage of health manpower; and (5) the dichotomy between public health and medical care. Solutions discussed are neighborhood health centers, the group practice approach, and the group practice/prepayment insurance. All three have the common theme of citizen involvement in health services.

Graves, JoAnn. "Areawide Planning: Involvement of Consumers." *Hospitals* 44 (October 1, 1970): 46–50.

This is a description of the origins and functions of the Citizens Health Council for comprehensive health planning in the Baltimore area. The council acts as an advisor to the Regional Planning Council. The sixteen delegates and alternates were chosen by a process in which population characteristics were gathered and seats apportioned with the help of community organization leaders. Orientation sessions are described, as are the problems and activities of the council.

Greenblatt, Milton, and Frederick J. Hinman. "Citizen Participation in Community Mental Health and Retardation Programs." *The Practice of Community Mental Health.* Edited by Henry Greenbaum. Boston: Little, Brown, 1970, pp. 769–85.

Tracing the development of citizen participation in programs for mental illness and retardation in Massachusetts, the authors discuss the earlier contributions of informal groups and the later development of voluntary citizens organizations and government appointed citizens groups. Issues and problems in working with volunteers are discussed.

Hatch, John. "Community Shares in Policy Decisions for Rural Health Centers." *Hospitals* 43 (July 1, 1969): 109–12.

This article describes the Tufts Delta-Health Center in Mount Bayou, Mississippi, which serves 14,000 poor rural blacks. The center is committed to community participation and thus oriented to dealing with community-selected priorities even when they were not directly related to health care.

Health center personnel have helped the local people with problems related to housing and food. The North Bolivar County Farm Cooperative was organized with the help of the staff. The center has used local social patterns to organize a series of ad hoc local health associations which are represented in an areawide planning council.

Haynes, M. Alfred. "Professionals and the Community Confront Change." *American Journal of Public Health* 60:3 (March 1970): 519–23.

Changed relationships are envisioned by the author as poor people come to recognize the inferior quality of their health care and demand improvements. One possible solution is suggested here—a working relationship between organized medicine, the government, and the community, such as the National Medical Association Foundation's pilot program of health care for the inner city in Washington, D.C. The program received funding from the government, technical assistance from the government and the medical profession, and was mortgaged by an insurance company. Community participation is also part of the program. The purpose of the program is to provide health services in a comprehensive system of care which will preserve the dignity of the poor.

Health Policy Advisory Center, Inc. *Evaluation of Community Involvement in Community Mental Health Centers.* Report for the National Institute of Mental Health, Contract HSM–42–70–106, New York, New York, 1972.

This study reviews community involvement in six community mental health centers. The study concludes that providers of mental health care had more impact upon policy-making processes in the centers than did "current or potential consumers," that this results in limited community knowledge about a center and its activities and distorts the center's perception of the community's mental health needs.

Henry, Paul. "Pimps, Prostitutes, and Policemen: Education of Consumers for Participation in Health Planning." *American Journal of Public Health* 60:11 (November 1970): 2171–74.

Henry describes a ten-week course to train consumers for participation as change agents in community development. The course is offered by Community Human Resource Training (Cincinnati), sponsored by the Graduate Department of Community Planning of the University of Cincinnati and the Ecumenical Council for Continuous Education. The trainee can choose a specialty, but it must be interrelated with other systems of community development.

Herzog, Barry Allen. "Participation by the Poor in Federal Health Programs." *Wisconsin Law Review* 3 (1970): 682-725.

This article describes the regulations, statutes, and guidelines which govern consumer participation in health services. The programs discussed are the Hill-Burton Hospital Construction Act, the Regional Medical Program, Comprehensive Health Planning, the OEO Comprehensive Neighborhood Health Centers, and the Model Cities Health Programs. For each of these, there is discussion of the federal framework and the implementation of representative programs in California. The discussion indicates that, in general, consumers have very limited power in planning or governing health services. The conclusion of the article cites legal precedents by which the poor may protect their interests in public health care and urges poverty lawyers to make use of legal tools to protect the poor.

Hochbaum, G. M. "Consumer Participation in Health Planning: Toward Conceptual Clarification." *American Journal of Public Health* 59:9 (September 1969): 1698-1705.

The problems in implementing citizen participation in health programs are discussed in this article. The first problem is the differing attitudes of professionals and consumers on the question of sharing in decision-making processes. The second problem is the overlap of the decisional territories of consumers and professionals. The third problem is a lack of agreement on the meaning of participation. The author believes that the question of why consumer participation is necessary should be answered.

Howard, Lawrence C. "Decentralization and Citizen Participation in Health Service." *Public Administration Review* 32, special issue (October 1972): 701-17.

This article discusses the relevance of decentralization and participation in health services. The author describes consumer participation in medical services and discusses health in terms of what consumer participation can add to professional medical care and in terms of comprehensive neighborhood health centers.

Ishiyama, Toaru. "The Mental Hospital Patient-Consumer as a Determinant of Services." *Mental Hygiene* 54:2 (April 1970): 221-30.

The author argues that while changes have occurred in the field of mental health, they have been slight and will remain so as long as present basic circumstances exist. He feels that everything done for patients is based on staff benevolence and not on consumer demands. Because mental health institutions are not competitive, the patient does not have the power of consumer sovereignty. The public has power, but chooses to side with the institutions rather than the patients. The author believes that the nature of the "power system" must be changed. The patient should be given the option of selecting from whom he will receive services. This would create demands for competence among, and service from, staff members. An advocacy system should be set up for patients who cannot negotiate.

Jonas, Stephen. "A Theoretical Approach to the Question of 'Community Control' of Health Services Facilities." *American Journal of Public Health* 61:5 (May 1971): 916–21.

Jonas asserts that health personnel themselves do not control capital budget, expense budget, and size of staff; thus if community forces did make inroads into the health service system, the result would be community administration rather than community control. Community forces could produce only minor changes. The author believes that the struggle of the poor and powerless against powerless administrators is diversionary and retrogressive. He believes that professionals should become engaged in a struggle to increase the budget outlay and staff and to increase their control over such matters vis-à-vis the governmental apparatus.

Kane, Robert L. "Determination of Health Care Priorities Among Rural Consumers." *Health Services Research* 4:2 (Summer 1969): 142–51.

This study examined the expectations of a rural Kentucky population regarding location and type of medical services for their area and the relationship of their ideas to those of professional planners. Interviews were completed with 157 people over a five-week period in June and July 1968. The findings were: community travel and trade patterns differed from the pattern of medical services planned by the experts; people were satisfied with the old facility; priorities emerged as consumers stated their willingness to travel farther for more specialized services. The author concludes that consumers were more interested in the human aspects of health services delivery than in the technical quality of services and that early identification of consumer desires may thwart future problems.

Kane, Thomas J. "Citizen Participation in Decision Making: Myth and Strategy." *Administration in Mental Health* (Spring 1975): 29–34.

Kunnes, Richard. "Community Control of Community Health." *The.New Physician* 19:1 (January 1970): 28–33.

Kunnes discusses the health demands which the East Harlem community has made on the city of New York: (1) self-determination through an incorporated staff-community governing board; (2) the removal of all city hall-appointed administrators and staff in East Harlem health facilities with replacements chosen by the community; (3) an immediate end to health construction until the community board inspects and approves new plans; (4) free publicly supported health care for treatment and prevention; (5) total decentralization of services; (6) more health workers; (7) door-to-door preventive health services; (8) health education for all the people; (9) community board control over budget allocations, policy, hiring, firing, salaries, construction, and health code enforcement; and (10) all community, union, or workers organizations must support and work for these demands or they will be considered enemies of the community.

Lesparre, Michael. "Hospitals and the Ghetto: A Try for Rapport: Report on a Workshop to Improve Hospital Relations with the Urban Ghetto." *Hospitals* 43 (July 1, 1969): 55–62.

This workshop was held at Mount Zion Hospital and Medical Center in San Francisco to explore ways in which hospitals can improve communication with the urban poor. Hospital representatives and community people from fourteen cities attended. Points of discussion were: (1) patterns of manpower recruitment and training in the area; (2) misunderstandings between hospitals, patients, and visitors and how to solve them; (3) the shifting racial makeup of patient and visitor populations, boards of trustees, and hospital staff; (4) impact of civil disturbances on the hospital; (5) community desire for participation in policy making and in programs sponsored by the hospital; and (6) patterns of the hospital-community interface.

Levy, Richard C., and William B. Applegate. "Student-Community Health Projects: How to Win Friends Without Influencing People." *Journal of the American Medical Association* 220:8 (May 22, 1972): 1113–15.

The authors describe the Greater Louisville (Kentucky) Organization for Health, a project in which health science students involved themselves in community health projects. Three cases of attempts to set up screening clinics in poor neighborhoods are presented, and the problems of consumer participation in such settings are discussed. Instances of failure are attributed to unrealistic expectations. Success is attributed to the articulation of specific proposals. Specific proposals, according to the author, are necessary because the poor will not automatically trust professionals and yet do not have enough information for effective participation in the initial stages of a project.

Millis, John S. "The Future of Medicine: The Role of the Consumer." *Journal of the American Medical Association* 210:3 (October 20, 1969): 498–501.

The author sees a shift from the consumer as user or patient to the consumer as buyer of health services. This is being brought about by changes in society and in the medical profession. Health care has come to be regarded as a right rather than a privilege, and there are now legal guarantees for health care. The American people are becoming increasingly more sophisticated and have greater purchasing power. At the same time, the health profession has become more specialized, institutionalized, and organized and is also putting more emphasis on preventive medicine. Because of these conditions, the author sees consumers becoming more concerned with the quality, cost, and availability of health services. Consumers also want to know who is responsible for providing health care. In the future consumers will serve as trustees, provide expertise in the organization and management of delivery systems, develop new forms of health delivery, attempt to control costs, and support medical education and research. The author believes that the medical profession should regard increased consumer participation as an opportunity to improve the quality of the health care delivery system.

Moore, Mary L. "The Role of Hostility and Militancy in Indigenous Community Health Advisory Groups." *American Journal of Public Health* 61:5 (May 1971): 927–30. Also presented to the Public Health Education Section, American Public Health Association meeting, Houston, Texas, October 29, 1970. Mimeograph.

Participant observation was employed in examining five neighborhood health care clinics' policy advisory groups. Four were composed of mostly poor persons; one was composed of mostly professionals. The study found that in the groups made up of the poor, the participants tended to be leaderless and hostile and the few professionals in the groups tried to

function as leaders. The more hostile groups were more effective representatives of the poor and tended to identify goals and make decisions. Where
professionals were in control, this was not the case.

Moseley, Vince. "Who Is, and What Is the Role of the Consumer in Health
    Service Planning?" *Journal of the South Carolina Medical Association*
    66:6 (June 1970): 237–41.

The author feels that advocates of consumer participation in health
services have erred in comparing health services with commercial enterprises. He points out that the doctor-patient relationship is a one-to-one
relationship and that only the doctor can decide what that relationship
should be. The author believes that health care problems should be solved at
the local level and delineates what he sees as appropriate roles for
consumers: (1) identification and discussion of health needs from personal
experience and observation; (2) the establishment of priorities; (3) the
voicing of fears and frustrations to reduce hostility and produce cooperation; (4) providing expertise on nonmedical matters; (5) developing political
support when needed; and (6) education in health matters.

National Commission on Community Health Services. *Health is a Commu-
    nity Affair.* Cambridge, Massachusetts: Harvard University Press,
    1967.

    Reviews:
    Choice 4 (July 1967): 552.
    Library Journal 91 (November 1966): 5637.

This is a final report based on the findings and recommendations of six
task forces and twenty-one community self-studies for the National Commission on Community Health Services. It makes the following recommendations: (1) revision of outmoded, overlapping, and ambiguous jurisdictions;
(2) provision of quality comprehensive personal health services; (3) every
individual should have a personal physician; (4) prospective planning and
management of comprehensive environmental health services; (5) family
planning; (6) accident prevention; (7) citizen action to stop pollution; (8)
planning for a healthy urban environment; (9) health education; (10)
effective use of health personnel and continuous evaluation of health
manpower needs; (11) action to control costs of hospital care; (12) better
organization of health agencies with more coordination between them; (13)
extension of voluntary citizen participation in processes and services
delivery; and (14) a broader approach to planning and action.

New, Peter Kong-ming; Richard M. Hessler; Phyllis Y. Bagwell; and Seymour S. Bellin. "Consumer Control and Public Accountability: The Case of the Neighborhood Health Center." Paper presented at the 97th Annual Forum of the National Conference on Social Welfare, Dallas, Texas, May 17, 1971. Mimeograph.

New, Peter Kong-ming; Wilfred E. Holton; and Richard M. Hessler. *Citizen-Participation and Interagency Relations: Issues and Program Implications for Community Mental Health Centers.* Boston: Department of Community Health and Social Medicine, Tufts University School of Medicine, January 1972.

This report presents case studies of six community mental health centers in poverty areas. Data were gathered on issues related to citizen participation and interagency relations in the centers. In each case, fifteen to twenty-five people connected with the center, the community, and related agencies were interviewed. Three middle-class patterns of citizen participation were identified: elitist governing board, narrowly advisory governing board, and mixed governing board. Three other patterns found were: activist-adversary governing board, consumer control, and participation through staff. Patterns of interagency relations were identified as: isolationist independent, informally interdependent, and totally interdependent. Guidelines for dealing with the impacts of citizen participation and interagency relations, stressing responsible involvement of consumers, are presented.

Notkin, Herbert, and Marilyn S. Notkin. "Community Participation in the Health Services: A Review." *Medical Care Review* 27:11 (December 1970): 1178–1201.

The background of consumer participation is discussed. The current status of participation in health services is characterized as spotty and limited, but the authors see rising consumer demands. Some cases of consumer participation are described. Current organizational patterns are listed: (1) community advisory committees; (2) community health councils; (3) community-selected boards of directors; (4) boards of directors composed of consumers and providers; and (5) small, unaffiliated clinics in poor and ethnic-minority neighborhoods. The authors identify unsolved current issues as (1) power, (2) group psychology, (3) role relations, (4) community representativeness, (5) career ladders, (6) militancy and radicalization, and (7) community-staff relations. They feel that consumer participation will increase in the future.

Parker, Alberta W. "The Consumer as Policy-Maker—Issues of Training." *American Journal of Public Health* 60:11 (November 1970): 2139–53.

Parker describes the Berkeley Consumer Health Project, which trained consumer members of neighborhood health center policy-making boards. Three San Francisco Bay Area boards were chosen to enter the program—one black urban ghetto, one suburban ghetto, and one semirural, nonfarm, Spanish-speaking group. The phases of the training project are described—organizational, planning, workshops, and action. The project defined six basic types of relationships a board must establish: (1) internal; (2) between the board and the organization and its staff; (3) between the board and the community; (4) between the board and the outside health system; (5) between the board and the funding agent; and (6) internal commitments by individual board members to the board, the institution, and the community. The following conclusions were drawn from the experience: such a program should be continuous over many months; the organizational base of the program should not be a barrier, and the program should be relevant and flexible; skits and role playing are good tools for training; tasks of the groups involved in the program should be similar, and the groups should be trained together when possible; attention should be paid to narrowing the gap between the professional and the consumer.

Rogatz, Peter, and Marge Rogatz. "Role for the Consumer." *Social Policy* 1:5 (January/February 1971): 52–56.

The authors advocate consumer participation in three areas of health care: planning and policy making, medical education, and programs and services. A reasonable balance of power between providers and consumers should be maintained to best serve the community. The authors suggest the use of a "health ombudsman" until programs can successfully integrate consumers into policy-making processes.

Roman, Mel, and Aaron Schmais. "Consumer Participation and Control: A Conceptual Overview." *Progress in Community Mental Health.* Edited by Harvey H. Barten and Leopold Bellak. New York: Grune and Stratton, 1972, pp. 63–84.

The historical background of volunteer participation in mental health and the federal push for citizen participation in programs affecting low income people are discussed. Earlier forms of participation involved mostly middle class people, while later forms focused on accountability to users. The experiences and lessons of the neighborhood and community action programs of the 1960s are discussed.

Rooney, Herbert L. "Roles and Functions of the Advisory Board." *North Carolina Journal of Mental Health* 3 (Winter 1968): 33–43.

Rosenberger, Donald M. "Community Concern, Hospital Interest: Riots Taught Hospital to Build Community Links." *Modern Hospital* 112:2 (August 1969): 81–84.

This article deals with efforts of the health institutions in Newark, New Jersey, to relate to the community in the wake of the riots of 1967. Hospitals are now in more frequent communication with the community and hold meetings to discuss problems. Other efforts include patients clubs, a parents' advisory council for parents of pediatric patients, health education efforts, and the development of community clinics.

Rosenblum, Gershen. "Citizen Participation and Influence in Comprehensive Mental Health/Retardation Programs: Real or Apparent?" Paper presented at the American Orthopsychiatric Association Convention, San Francisco, California, March 23–26, 1970. ERIC ED041–297.

Rosenblum discusses the citizens area boards set up across the state of Massachusetts under the reorganization of the State Department of Mental Health. The purpose of the reorganization was to provide more effective mental health and retardation services in the state. The composition of the boards and their powers and duties are described. The boards generally advise, review, recommend, and consult. They do not have authority to spend money for program development or for the provision of services. A study of the Department of Mental Health found that most of the boards had involved themselves in at least one action-oriented project. Most board members defined their goals in terms of expanding services, but many members were beginning to wonder if their hopes would be realized. The activities of many boards were stimulated by professional leadership. The author feels that the survey poses the question whether lay citizens can take over control of mental health programs and whether professionals will give up such control.

Salber, Eva J. "Community Participation in Neighborhood Health Centers." *New England Journal of Medicine* 283:10 (September 3, 1970): 515–18.

Three possible models of community participation in health centers are presented: token community involvement, community control, and partnership of informed residents and professionals. A discussion of the problems of community participation follows. The author feels that problems arise from poor communication and unrealistic expectations among both consumers and professionals. She points to the advantages of hiring community residents to make the center an integral part of the community, the need for training to bridge the lay-professional gap, and the need for long-range educational efforts aimed at the institutions, their staffs, and community residents.

Schiff, Sheldon K. "Community Accountability and Mental Health Services." *Mental Hygiene* 54:2 (April 1970): 205–14.

This article describes two urban community health centers—Woodlawn Mental Health Center in Chicago and Lincoln Hospital in the Bronx—and the problems faced by white professionals in their relationships with these black communities. The centers are compared in terms of three characteristics: the nature of the professional-community contract; the nature of the professional's primary organizational base and its effect on the community contract; and the effects of the contract on the roles of the professionals and nonprofessionals. The author feels that in the case of both centers, most of the people advocating community control were not community residents. He feels that community control, far from being a solution in itself, can actually threaten professional accountability if the community takes control over bankrupt enterprises with complex problems.

Schorr, Lisabeth Bamberger, and Joseph T. English. "Background, Context, and Significant Issues in Neighborhood Health Center Programs." *Milbank Memorial Fund Quarterly* 46:3 (July 1968): 289–96.

The origins of health as an issue in the war on poverty are discussed. Issues to which neighborhood health centers must respond are presented: (1) development of new relationships and new roles for consumers and providers; (2) the extent to which organization for health can lead to other community action; (3) the possibility of health institutions serving other needs; and (4) changes in institutional arrangements to provide more personalized quality care. The authors feel that neighborhood health centers are good examples of federal action providing flexible responses to complex problems.

Schwartz, Jerome L. "Early Histories of Selected Neighborhood Health Centers." *Inquiry* 7:4 (December 1970): 3–16.

Schwartz describes the successes and problems of the neighborhood health center movement and presents case histories of a few such centers. The cases describe the initiation of the centers; relationships with OEO, the sponsoring agency, and the community; and the major issues and innovations of the centers. The centers described are the Tufts Health Center, the Montefiore Neighborhood Health Center, the Rural Health Project of King City, California, and the East Palo Alto-East Menlo Park Neighborhood Health Center. In each case, there is a lack of citizen participation in the initial stages of the center's development and a later recognition of its value. The author calls for efforts to close the communication gap between professionals and consumers.

Sellers, Rudolph V. "The Black Health Worker and the Black Health Consumer—New Roles for Both." *American Journal of Public Health* 50:11 (November 1970): 2154–70.

The Hill Health Center of New Haven, Connecticut, is located in a largely poor, black and Spanish-speaking area. This article describes the center, its relationship with the community, and its staff. The center was planned by Yale University and the local community. Community residents serve on the personnel committee and on the Hill Health Board, the community's advocate. The article describes the facilities and staff of the center, the services provided, and the team approach to health care delivery. The author asserts that black health workers must be in tune with the community and that they should ally themselves in support of the community.

Silver, George A. "Community Participation and Health Resource Allocation." *International Journal of Health Services* 3:2 (Spring 1973): 117–31.

The author describes the historical trend toward professionalism in social decision making and the need for consumer participation. He describes the Urban Coalition Health Task Force, which created pilot community health programs in several cities. The Urban Coalition set up the health task force to give the poor a voice in program design and then used the power of this community structure to influence health decision making.

Sparer, Gerald; George B. Dines; and Daniel Smith. "Consumer Participation in OEO-assisted Neighborhood Health Centers." *American Journal of Public Health* 60:6 (June 1970): 1091–1102.

The authors criticize the use of technology to evaluate neighborhood health centers and their socially desirable benefits, and then analyze factors relating to the degree of consumer participation. Data was gathered from contacts with neighborhood health centers and consumer groups during project reviews. A team of specialists reviewed twenty-seven centers during a site appraisal project and had two days of contact with each center. Of the twenty-seven centers, the team rated seven as having a high degree of participation, ten as moderate, and ten as low. The study found that better organized consumer groups function better and that the key organization elements are elections, bylaws, strong leadership, and consumer orientation of the staff. Strong staff personalities were also found to be important. Whether the community group was a board or an advisory group was found to be unimportant. Conflict between professionals and consumers was not a factor in most centers.

Stephanos, Robert C. "Citizen's Corporations as True Community Mental Retardation and Mental Health Centers." *Mental Hygiene* 55:3 (July 1971): 410–12.

This article describes Intercommunity Action, Inc. (Interact), in which a group of Philadelphia citizens attempted to set up a community health and mental retardation center in their community. The article describes the efforts of the group and the difficulties which doomed the center to failure. The group eventually became an advisory community organization for an existing institution.

"The Surge of Community Involvement: Partnership or Provocation?" *Medical World News* 13:20 (May 19, 1972): 51–63.

This article reviews the status of consumer involvement in health services and describes the Temple University Health Sciences Center in Philadelphia, Chicago's Cook County Hospital, Boston's "consumer's health council," the patient-advocate at the Yale-New Haven Hospital in Connecticut, and a pamphlet on consumer rights compiled by the Dr. Martin Luther King Health Center in the Bronx. Consumer participation is working in some places; in other places it seems only to increase conflict. Many doctors are wary of consumer involvement because of the medical inexperience of laymen and because of the danger of injecting politics into health care. The article points out that there is still insufficient evidence on which to judge the success or failure of consumer participation.

Task Force on Organization of Community Health Services of the National Commission on Community Health Services. *Health Administration*

and Organization in the Decade Ahead. Washington, D.C.: Public
Affairs Press, 1967.

This report reviews the issues involved in health needs and resources.
It looks at the health needs of local communities as they relate to state and
national agencies. Guidelines for better administration, organization, and
management of community health services are presented. An increase in
health planning is suggested. Also recommended are a single strong state
health agency and greater citizen participation in support of voluntary
efforts.

Tischler, Gary L. "The Effects of Consumer Control on the Delivery of
    Services." *American Journal of Orthopsychiatry* 41:3 (April 1971):
    501–09.

This is a case study of the Hill-West Haven Division of the Connecticut Mental Health Center and its initiation of provisions for consumer
participation. The author outlines the service model and describes the
transition from informal to formal consumer participation over a three-year
period. The author feels that the structural effects of the change were
minimal and that the functional effects consisted of the modification of staff
performance tasks. He identifies and discusses four patterns of staff response
to the change: (1) fear and disorganization, (2) retrenchment and denial, (3)
romance and surrender, and (4) collaborative engagement.

United States Department of Health, Education and Welfare. "Citizen
    Participation in Mental Health Programs." *Mental Health Digest* 2:5
    (May 1970): 1–5.

The work of the Citizen Participation Branch of the National Institute
of Mental Health (NIMH) is described in this article. It has brought together
national citizen organizations to advise NIMH on methods of working with
consumers and has encouraged the development of coordination among
national citizens groups involved in the advancement of mental health
programs. The branch has brought together volunteer agencies for advice
on program development and sought to stimulate interest in volunteerism in
community mental health. It organized Round tables for Central and
Regional Office Staff in which citizens and professionals present views and
talk with staff members, convened a national swapshop of twenty-one
mental health centers on the topic of citizen participation, and called a task
force meeting on the role of the religious community in national mental
health programs. The branch is also developing models of the role of citizens
in evaluating mental health centers.

Wells, Benjamin B. "Role of the Consumer in Regional Medical Programs." *American Journal of Public Health* 60:11 (November 1970): 2133–38.

Nine potential roles for consumers in regional medical programs are presented: (1) identification and articulation of needs; (2) adding perspectives to questions of priority; (3) improving communication between professionals and patients; (4) developing more realistic expectations on the part of both professionals and consumers; (5) providing expertise on nonmedical matters; (6) translating between medical specialties; (7) maintaining pressure for decentralized decision making; (8) providing a larger pool of skills and knowledge to increase chances for change; and (9) providing a community power base for health care. Elements of consumer concern are delineated: (1) the role of the consumer in the health care industry; (2) health insurance; (3) complete and continuous service; (4) consultation and ancillary services; (5) assurance of quality; (6) convenience and the amenities of health care; and (7) communication and education.

Wolfe, Samuel. "Consumerism and Health Care." *Public Administration Review* 31:5 (September/October 1971): 528–36.

The origins of consumer participation in health are traced from their beginnings in eighteenth-century Britain. Some of the reasons for its revival today are presented: (1) health care as a right; (2) high costs and low insurance coverage; (3) less accessible and less available care; (4) inferior hospital care in the inner city; (5) the revolt against authority; (6) the bureaucratization of institutions; and (7) the civil rights movement. Three areas in which consumers can become actively involved are in fiscal policy, communication with the staff, and creating interest in achievement of program goals. The origins and development of OEO Neighborhood Health Centers are discussed. The author believes that the impact of consumer involvement will be seen in new perspectives of professionals and in changes that will come about through conflict. He cites some examples of good provider-consumer partnerships in health programs, advocates structured roles for consumers and consumer training for participation, and calls for public administrators in the health field to provide leadership in effecting consumer participation.

HOUSING

Blonsky, Laurence E. "Formation of a Senior Citizen Tenants' Council." *Social Work* 18:5 (September 1973): 76–83.

Blonsky describes a tenants council in a private residential building for senior citizens, Parkview Towers in University City, Missouri. The tenants council was organized by a private organization, Older Adult Community Action Program. Organizational development and problems are described. The council had not yet participated in the management of the building to the degree that was expected and did not show much interest in doing so.

Eisemon, Thomas. "Simulations and Requirements for Citizen Participation in Public Housing: The Traux Technique." *Environment and Behavior* 7:1 (March 1975): 99–123.

The Traux Technique described in this article is a device for eliciting citizen participation in public housing. It was created for use at the Traux public housing project in Madison, Wisconsin, in the summer of 1971. The residents of the housing project simulate the construction of a housing unit that is both desirable and financially feasible.

The author claims that this technique could be used to fill the gap caused by the absence of a well-defined strategy for citizen participation in federally mandated programs. He feels that the Traux Technique can provide citizens with enough confidence and expertise to interact with planners and public officials on a more equal basis. This could facilitate fundamental changes in decision making in public housing.

Flaum, Thea K., and Elizabeth C. Salzman. *Urban Research Corporation Report: The Tenants' Rights Movement.* Chicago: Urban Research Corporation, 1969.

The authors identified eighty-nine tenants associations and examined major tenant grievances and various types of tenant activity. The major grievances were poor maintenance, rent, lack of tenant control, and inadequate security. Common activities were organizing legal action, withholding rent, and mass protest. Fifty-six percent of all activity was among low income people in private housing; 26 percent was among middle and upper income groups; and 18 percent was among people in public housing.

Hellman, Louis. "Housing and Participation." *Built Environment* 2:6 (June 1973): 328–32.

Knox, Michael D.; Marilyn S. Kalton; and Louis Dwarshuis. "Community Development in Housing: Increasing Tenant Participation." *Public Welfare* 32:3 (Summer 1974): 48–53.

In July 1972, thirteen local housing authorities received $25 million in contracts under the Housing Management Improvement Program. This article examines some of the ways those authorities are providing new opportunities for residents to participate in management.

Four major categories of tenant participation included in the programs were identified: (1) providing information about needs and concerns; (2) providing services and goods; (3) decision making, policy formulation, and planning; and (4) home ownership. Mechanisms for facilitating participation under each category are discussed.

Kramer, Bernard M. "Tenant Participation in Public Housing." *Community Mental Health Journal* 3:3 (Fall 1967): 211–15.

The author believes that tenant participation in public housing will help to develop and maintain viable communities and prevent slum formation. He explains the concept of a tenants' health council through which the tenants work out an agreement with a medical care agency to provide them with health services. The objectives of such a council are to make tenants' needs known, to provide an incentive for the organization of tenants, and to enable tenants to gain political sophistication. The same concept could be used with respect to other services.

Meyerson, Martin, and Edward C. Banfield. *Politics, Planning, and the Public Interest: The Case of Public Housing in Chicago.* Glencoe, Illinois: Free Press, 1955.

Reviews:
Booklist 51 (June 1, 1955): 403.
Grundstein, N. D. *Annals of the American Academy of Political and Social Science* 320 (November 1955): 172.
U.S. Quarterly Book Review 2 (September 1955): 386.

This book is a case study of the political decision-making process surrounding the issue of site locations for public housing in Chicago. It is a chronological account of the maneuvering between the prohousing forces described as "liberal-left" and the antihousing forces described as "conservative-reactionary." The most important issue seemed to be the question of race. There was a great deal of opposition to the location of public housing projects containing large numbers of black residents in white areas where the majority of vacant land was available. The Chicago Housing Authority wanted to build on the vacant land tracts but was politically outgunned and thus had to compromise. The authority lost its battle through lack of political acumen and inability to communicate with politicians. It simply did not have the powerful political support it needed.

Ward, A. Dudley. "Creative Venture in Housing." *Christian Century* 83:16
(April 20, 1966): 491–93.

This is a description of Community Organizations for the Improvement of Neighborhoods, Inc., an interdenominational and interagency
group in Washington, D.C., which attempts to involve the poor in solving
their own problems. The organization concentrated on the Cardoza area of
the city and planned to buy and rehabilitate a large number of apartment
buildings which they would then rent to area residents on a nonprofit basis.
The possibility of ownership would be available to building residents.

SOCIAL WELFARE

Ad Hoc Committee on Advocacy, National Association of Social Workers.
"The Social Worker as Advocate: Champion of Social Victims."
Social Work 14:2 (April 1969): 16–22.

This article presents the definitions of, and requirements for, social
work advocacy. The advocate may be a partisan defender of his client or a
defender of an entire class. The committee urges the National Association of
Social Workers to stand behind social worker advocates and proposes a
project to coordinate the program planning efforts of individual social
workers, policy makers, administrators, and community leaders at the local,
regional, and national levels.

Bailis, Lawrence Neil. *Bread or Justice: Grassroots Organizing in the
Welfare Rights Movement.* Lexington, Massachusetts: D. C. Heath,
1974.

Brager, George A., and Harry Specht. *Community Organizing.* New York:
Columbia University Press, 1973.

This book is a text on community organization practice; most of the
examples used are especially pertinent to organizing the poor. The book
focuses on organizing a constituency, institutional relationships and tactics,
and strategies used in effecting community change.

Brown, H. Frederick, and S. Lorraine Seifert. "Client Participation in
Service Delivery." *The Social Welfare Forum, 1972.* Official Proceedings, 99th Annual Forum, National Conference on Social Welfare,
Chicago, Illinois, May 28–June 2, 1972. New York: Columbia University Press, 1972, pp. 176–85.

The author first examines the major criticisms of citizen participation in federal programs. Most critics charged that citizen participation simply did not work. Some of the major criticisms were that participation is a process not a program, that participation of the poor became dysfunctional, that it provided a loophole in administrative accountability, that client-professional communication was lacking, and that the poor have no well-developed organizations to serve as a constituency for citizen representatives. Some elements of a new approach are presented: (1) retention of accountability for programs with program administrators; (2) reduction of conflict through objectivity in the selection of client representation; (3) restriction of participation to clients of agencies or consumers of services; (4) stressing articulation of client opinion on efficacy of services, problems, and solutions; (5) provision of feedback from clients for planning and administrative purposes; and (6) reporting back to clients on actions taken in response to their feedback. The authors also describe the Tri-County Project of the Illinois Institute for Social Policy (Peoria), which focuses on coordination of state services through centralized intake and follow-up using a computerized information system.

Cloward, Richard A., and Richard M. Elman. "Poverty, Injustice, and the Welfare State; Part 1: An Ombudsman for the Poor?" *Nation* 202 (February 21, 1966): 230–35.

The authors cite abuses in the welfare system and violations of the rights of the poor. They discuss ombudsmen's activities in other countries and literature advocating an ombudsman for the United States. They believe that an ombudsman for the poor cannot be of much use until there is basic reform of the welfare system.

Gelb, Joyce, and Alice Sardell. "Strategies for the Powerless: The Welfare Rights Movement in New York City." *American Behavioral Scientist* 17:4 (March/April 1974): 507–30.

The focus of this article is the welfare rights movement in New York City which launched a "minimum standards" campaign in 1968 and achieved some measure of success. The strategy of the campaign was to submit large numbers of applications for special grants to the welfare department. The purpose was to cause a crisis in the welfare system with the ultimate goal of replacing the welfare system with a national income maintenance system. The priority, however, seemed to be recruiting people for the movement rather than for the welfare rolls. There was a disagreement within the movement over whether they should concentrate on fiscal disruption or building the movement.

The campaign was a short-term success. The city responded by ending the special grants system and replacing it with the "cyclical grant," an across the board grant of $100 per person. However, this effectively ended the minimum standards campaign.

The authors present three reasons for the end of the movement: the movement was not the key to the rewards, nonmembers could benefit; incentives came from the system, not from the movement; and welfare clients became more likely to assert themselves. The authors suggest that neither community organization nor protest is likely to give the poor access to the policy-making process.

Grosser, Charles F. "Community Organization and the Grass Roots." *Social Work* 12:4 (October 1967): 61–66.

Grosser describes a new type of social welfare service developed in the 1960s. It consists of large-scale, diversified, social change-oriented welfare programs under public auspices, with public money, based in the neighborhoods. Such programs provide new and expanded services for the poor. The author points out that private welfare work is now supported by public monies and, thus, must include mechanisms which facilitate citizen participation.

Grosser, Charles F. "Organizing in the White Community." *Social Work* 16:3 (July 1971): 25–31.

This article discusses the special problems of the community worker who works with working-class whites. Grosser believes that working-class whites hold misconceptions that prevent them from seeing their problems in the proper perspective. They see poor minorities as their enemies, rather than recognizing deficiencies in the system. They also mistakenly believe that the welfare poor benefit from welfare. The author believes that community organizers in white working-class areas must recognize these attitudes and try to change them. Working-class whites will have to join forces with the welfare poor in order to work toward common solutions to their problems.

Jackson, Larry R., and William A. Johnson. *Protest by the Poor: The Welfare Rights Movement in New York City.* New York: Rand Institute, 1973.

Kahn, Alfred J. "The Citizen's Role in Social Welfare Policy." *Children* 10:5 (September/October 1963): 185–88.

The author calls for citizen participation at the policy-making level in social welfare programs. He feels that this is needed as a response to social change, to decide on policy in the face of new social realities, to prevent social breakdown, and to support sound development.

Lloyd, Gary A., and John Michael Daley, Jr. "Community Control of Health and Welfare Programs." *The Social Welfare Forum, 1971.* Official Proceedings, 98th Annual Forum, National Conference on Social Welfare, Dallas, Texas, May 16–21, 1971. New York: Columbia University Press, 1971, pp. 168–81.

The authors believe in community control of health and welfare programs but think that the odds are against its implementation. They present several issues on which the success of community control depends: (1) resource distribution; (2) the role of professionals and bureaucracies in community control; (3) the effects of pluralism; (4) efficiency and effectiveness; and (5) the problem of defining the public interest.

National Conference of Social Work. *Group Work and Community Organization, 1955.* Papers presented at the 82d Annual Forum of the National Conference of Social Work. New York: Columbia University Press, 1955.

A collection of eleven papers in the areas of community welfare planning and social group work, this book contains papers which cover the following topics: (1) recent developments within communities, especially citizen participation; (2) the place of professionals and citizens in community welfare planning; (3) an analysis of the effectiveness of citizen participation; (4) efforts of citizens in two major cities to improve decaying neighborhoods; and (5) community welfare planning in rural areas. The papers on social group work discuss theory, tools, and techniques.

O'Donnell, Edward J., and Catherine S. Chilman. "Poor People on Public Boards and Committees—Participation in Policy-Making?" *Welfare in Review* 7:3 (May/June 1969): 1–10ff.

This article discusses the involvement of low income persons in decision making in public welfare programs. The background of the participation movement is described, and its objectives are identified. The movement hopes to end alienation of the poor, give them an opportunity to make decisions that affect them, improve communication between the poor and the nonpoor, and to "socialize" the poor. The authors suggest a number of questions for further research on the effectiveness of participation. They conclude that the poor will be limited to restricted participation on welfare boards, serving as advisors rather than decision makers. The upwardly mobile poor will participate, more often, and participation will tend to be conservative and of limited effectiveness.

Paull, Joseph E. "Recipients Aroused: The New Welfare Rights Movement." *Social Work* 12:2 (April 1967): 101–06.

This analysis of the welfare rights movement asserts that the influence of the civil rights movement and community action programs has been important in the movement's development. The aim of the welfare rights movement is to protect the civil rights of public assistance recipients. It had its origins in the casual meetings of recipients and was encouraged by ideas of mass protest, the influence of poverty workers and poverty lawyers, and the public debates over public welfare. The goals of the movement are fairly traditional. It is oriented toward reform rather than toward revolution. It is seeking a more liberalized assistance program with more client participation. The author feels that this is a protest movement which lacks cohesive goals and theory. He urges an alliance between the social work profession and such groups.

Payne, James W. "Ombudsman Roles for Social Workers." *Social Work* 17:1 (January 1972): 94–100.

Payne discusses ombudsmen as used in Scandinavia and the use of ombudsman roles by social workers in the United States. Five role characteristics of ombudsmen are presented: (1) he is external to the system he investigates; (2) he is impartial in his investigation; (3) his only real power is prestige and public opinion; (4) he is not responsible for solving all problems between citizens and government; and (5) he can and does make policy recommendations as well as case recommendations. The author then points out the differences between the social worker as ombudsman and the social worker as advocate. He believes that for social workers to serve as ombudsmen, more specialized knowledge in various fields would be necessary.

Rothman, Jack. *Planning and Organizing for Social Change.* New York: Columbia University Press, 1975.

Review:
Kirscht, John P. *Administrative Science Quarterly* 20 (June 1975): 301.

This book, designed to provide "basic social-science research knowledge to social planners and community workers," contains one chapter on voluntary associations and one chapter on "social-action movements" and client participation in service delivery systems. The purpose of these chapters is to translate research in these areas into usable information which practitioners may apply in attempting to organize communities and client groups.

Schiffman, Bernard M. "Involvement of Low-Income People in Planning Community Change." *Social Work Practice, 1965*. New York: Columbia University Press, 1965, pp. 188–205.

Schwartz, Jerome L., and Milton Cherrin. "Participation of Recipients in Public Welfare Planning and Administration." *Social Service Review* 41:1 (March 1967): 10–22.

In the 1962 survey described in this article, questionnaires about client participation in welfare programs were submitted to sixty selected individuals who were familiar with public assistance programs and administration. Some of the findings were: (1) public welfare agencies had little experience with client participation other than at the level of case worker-client relations; (2) generally, respondents favored recipient participation; (3) generally, respondents were against appointment of clients to state and local boards but favored their participation on state and local advisory committees; and (4) they felt that the best type of committee would include recipients, directors, staff members, and board members. The authors call for experimentation with more client participation in public welfare planning.

Sherrard, Thomas D., ed. *Social Welfare and Urban Problems*. New York: Columbia University Press, 1968.

> Reviews:
> Madden, J. F. *Library Journal* 93 (April 1968): 1494.
> Wilbern, York. *American Political Science Review* 62 (December 1968): 1348.

This book contains papers presented at the 94th Annual Forum of the National Conference on Social Welfare, which explored social welfare's role in urban development and the goal of "social growth." The following topics are covered by the papers: (1) presentation of a model neighborhood management system; (2) the slum dweller and social mobility; (3) positive experiences of earlier ethnic ghetto groups as a resource for Negroes; (4) an ombudsman for welfare clients; (5) a comparison of two black ghettos and implications for welfare programs; (6) relationship of social and physical planning in the ghetto; and (7) bureaucracy and public welfare.

Van Til, Jon. "Becoming Participants: Dynamics of Access Among the Welfare Poor." *Social Science Quarterly* 54:2 (September 1973): 345–58.

Van Til examines criteria related to the participation of individuals in the social processes: ease of access of new groups to the pluralistic system, ease of access of individuals to groups, and active participation of individuals in group life. The research focuses on three groups of welfare recipients. Seven barriers to participation are identified and examined: (1) subcultural barriers, (2) problems in goal setting, (3) adaptation, (4) group integration, (5) ideology, (6) institutional nondecisions, and (7) overt defeat. The three groups were observed for over one and a half years. The study tested the impact of each barrier to access in individual relation to all other barriers as they retarded the efforts of the three groups. The importance of each barrier in limiting the access of each group was evaluated and ranked within three categories. The three most serious barriers were found to be community and institutional nondecisions, adaptation, and integration. The other four were secondary. The author concludes that the study illustrates the failure of American pluralism among the welfare poor.

Vattano, Anthony J. "Power to the People: Self-Help Groups." *Social Work* 17:4 (July 1972): 7–15.

TRANSPORTATION

Bleiker, Hans. *Community Interaction as an Integral Part of the Highway Decision-Making Process.* Cambridge, Massachusetts: MIT Press, 1971.

Citizen Participation in Transportation Planning. Highway Research Special Report, no. 142. Washington, D.C.: Transportation Research Board, 1973.

Fellman, Gordon. "Research Report: Neighborhood Protest of an Urban Highway." *Journal of the American Institute of Planners* 35:2 (March 1969): 118–22.

This is a case study of resistance to the Boston Inner Belt Highway. Resistance first developed in a low and lower middle income working-class area of Cambridge where protest was not expected. Professional groups later joined with the neighborhood groups to form Save Our Cities (SOC), which pressured the city council to call for a restudy. The author found that while most of the area residents were against the highway, only 27 percent joined in the protest. Most were politically "ignorant" and did not know what action to take. The neighborhood people needed professional allies to confront the bureaucracy on an equal footing. Even though the middle-class professionals did most of the work, the working-class contingent continued to meet. The author attributes this to a need for a cathartic release of anger. He concludes that groups like this one can accomplish little, relative to city agencies and prestigious citizens committees.

Fellman, Gordon, with Barbara Brandt. *The Decisional Majority: Politics and Protest in Middle America.* New Brunswick, New Jersey: Transaction Books, 1973.

> Reviews:
> *Choice* 10 (February 1974): 1934.
> Scarich, Kathryn. *Library Journal* 98 (October 1973): 3008.

Fellman and Brandt describe the protest of working-class residents of the Brookline-Elm area of Cambridge, Massachusetts, against the building of the Boston Inner Belt Highway. Data was gathered through participant observation and a survey of 10 percent of the population affected by the highway. The authors found that although most of the residents of the area were against the highway, two-thirds of them took no action other than signing one or more petitions.

The larger focus of the book is on social class oppression and limitations of freedom. A four-part typology of social classes is offered: (1) the rich and powerful class which rules; (2) the organizational class which serves the rulers; (3) middle America; and (4) the poor and powerless class. The last two classes are seen as being at a distinct disadvantage in looking out for their own interests. The authors believe that middle Americans have been tricked into blaming their problems on chance misfortune or on outside agitators when they are caused by the way American institutions function.

Milch, Jerome E. "Feasible and Prudent Alternatives: Airport Development in the Age of Public Protest." Paper prepared for the American Political Science Association meeting, Chicago, Illinois, August 29– September 2, 1974. Mimeograph.

The author argues that the efforts of environmentalists and neighborhood associations have virtually halted the development of major airports in the United States. It is further argued that citizens have been given the opportunity to react to airport proposals but that they have been given "neither incentives nor authority to develop positive solutions." Thus, protective reaction results and this contributes to a decision-making impasse.

Milch discusses three possible courses of action. He rejects leaving the system unchanged and relying upon "enlightened" experts, and argues for "establishing a viable participatory process in which citizens are expected to play a positive role in decision making . . . because an active role in decision making develops the social and political capacities of citizens and strengthens the democratic system."

Nelkin, Dorothy. *Jetport: The Boston Airport Controversy.* New Brunswick, New Jersey: Transaction Books, 1974.

An effort to expand Logan airport which aroused the opposition of community organizations is used to analyze the political and organizational relationships which affect technological policy. The positions of different actors in the controversy and the "distribution of influence on decision-making and how this operates as various parties negotiate to affect airport polity" are examined.

Sloan, Allan K. *Citizen Participation in Transportation Planning: The Boston Experience.* Cambridge, Massachusetts: Ballinger, 1974.

In 1970, in reaction to increasing public controversy, the governor of Massachusetts stopped construction of all interstate highways in Boston and Cambridge and ordered a restudy of transportation needs in the Boston area. The process through which the restudy was accomplished involved the participation of groups within the metropolitan community that had been urging changes in basic transportation policies. Sloan discusses the conditions that led to the governor's moratorium, the restudy process, and the resultant revised transportation plan.

Steger, Wilbur A. "Reflections on Citizen Involvement in Urban Transportation Planning: Towards a Positive Approach." *Transportation* 3:2 (July 1974): 127–46.

Steger discusses different interpretations of the role of community participation in transportation planning. The perspectives of different academic disciplines are reviewed and the author concludes that an "eclectic approach" is needed and that citizen participation can help provide "better transportation services for all people."

Taebel, Delbert A. "Citizen Groups, Public Policy, and Urban Transportation." *Traffic Quarterly* 27:4 (October 1973): 503–15.

This article describes the emergence of citizen group activities focusing on transportation policy-making processes. The author concludes that citizen groups currently have little input in such processes but that there are indications that the "balance of power" may be changing. The author points out that citizen groups can have negative effects upon transportation systems. They can merely impede or halt construction efforts rather than offer constructive input that might result in viable transportation policies benefiting "the entire community."

Wofford, John G. "Participatory Planning for Boston Metro-Area Transportation." *Civil Engineering* 43:4 (April 1973): 78–81.

The author describes attempts to achieve a balanced transportation system in Boston in terms of "balanced politics" (more input from non-technocrats), balanced policy, and a balanced process of decision making (more public debate). Private citizens, organized groups, and local officials, the author believes, should be involved.

Dissertations

Akponwei, Patricia Sapele. "Citizen Participation in the Health Care Delivery Aspects of the Indianapolis Model Cities Program." H.S.D., Indiana University, 1973. (Order no. 73–19,004) 137 pp.

Anderson, Floydelh. "The Function of Social Process in Recruiting, Training, and Upgrading Volunteer Indigenous Leadership." Ed.D., New York University, 1955. (Publication no. 13,643; Mic 56–625) 184 pp.

Au-Yeung, Benjamin. "A Study of Citizen Participation in a Community Mental Health Center." Ph.D., University of Pittsburgh, 1973. (Order no. 73–21,339) 141 pp.

Berner, William Frederick. "A Study of Citizens Committees for Reorganized School Districts in Indiana." Ed.D., Indiana University, 1964. (Order no. 65–2359) 120 pp.

Bernero, James Anthony. "A Critical Study of the Attitudes of a Select Group of Urban Elementary Teachers to the Concept of Community Control With a Comparison of Their Reactions to Those of Administrators and Community Residents." Ed.D., Loyola University, Chicago, 1973. (Order no. 73–19,854) 164 pp.

Blankenship, Ralph Leland. "The Emerging Organization of a Community Mental Health Center." Ph.D., University of Illinois, Champaign-Urbana, 1971. (Order no. 72–12,091) 285 pp.

Bostwick, Jay Dean. "Public Opinion Related to Citizen Participation in a Social Welfare Program." Ph.D., New York University, 1965. (Order no. 66–9550) 241 pp.

Brengarth, Joyce A. "Consumer Participation in the Administrative Processes of the Health Services and Mental Health Administration: A Case Study." Ph.D., University of Pittsburgh, 1972. (Order no. 73–12,358) 298 pp.

Cary, Lee James. "A Study of Participation in a Voluntary Association: The Case History of a Tenant Council in Public Housing." D.S.S., Syracuse University, 1962. (Order no. 63–3621) 219 pp.

Chestnut, Erma Ruth. "The Involvement and Influence of Voluntary Community Organizations in the Development of a Community College: The Schenectady Community College." Ed.D., State University of New York at Albany, 1973. (Order no. 73–24,352) 402 pp.

Chommie, Peter William. "A Study of Differential Participation in an Indigenous Welfare Rights Organization as Related to Value Orientation and Patterns of Alienation." Ph.D., University of Minnesota, 1969. (Order no. 70–1781) 153 pp.

Cline, David L. "An Analysis of Public School Citizens Committees." Ed.D., Temple University, 1956. (Publication no. 16,372; Mic 56–1716) 338 pp.

Collier, Ervin Keith. "Informed Citizens' Opinions Regarding the Citizens' Lay Committee in Central Valley School District." Ed.D., Washington State University, 1963. (Order no. 64–5783) 101 pp.

Cunningham, Luvern L. "A Community Develops Educational Policy: A Case Study." Ed.D., University of Oregon, 1958. (L.C. Card no. Mic 58–2342) 442 pp.

Daley, John Michael, Jr. "Participation in Comprehensive Health Planning: The New Orleans Experience, 1967–71." D.S.W., Tulane University School of Social Work, 1971. (Order no. 72–20,503) 203 pp.

DeVeau, Burton William. "A Study of the Ways in Which Educational Personnel, Parents, Pupils and Other Citizens Participate in Secondary School Curriculum Development in Ohio." Ph.D., University of Minnesota, 1957. (Publication no. 21,240; Mic 57–2009) 289 pp.

Farrah, George. "The Roles of Citizens Advisory Committees in Curriculum Development: A Special Case in Farmington, Michigan." Ed.D., Wayne State University, 1962. (Order no. 62–3916) 336 pp.

Fauri, David P. "Consumer Participation in the Planning and Administration of Public School Programs." D.P.A., Syracuse University, 1972. (Order no. 73–9517) 300 pp.

Ferreira, Joseph Lewis. "A Participant Observation Study of a Parent Group and its Relationships with School Personnel and Community

Forces in a Racially Mixed Urban Elementary School." Ph.D., Syracuse University, 1971. (Order no. 75–6650) 316 pp.

Goff, John McLaurin. "Recommendations for Inclusion of Citizen's Advisory Committees into a Total Program of School-Community Relations." Ed.D., Auburn University, 1972. (Order no. 72–31,358) 118 pp.

Golemon, Clarence E. "A Suggested Handbook for the Organization and Use of Lay Citizens Advisory Committees in Public Elementary and Secondary Schools in Louisiana." Ph.D., Louisiana State University, 1958. (L.C. Card no. 58–7330) 332 pp.

Grimes, Joseph, Jr. "Organized Citizen Groups Working on Curriculum: A Study of Lay Participation at the Local Level in Planning Educational Programs in Public Schools in 15 States Between 1945 and 1952." Ed.D., New York University, 1954. (Publication no. 10,665; Mic 55–287) 166 pp.

Hall, Howard Bruce. "Community Participation in the Management of Facilities Serving the Mentally Retarded." D.S.W., University of Southern California, 1972. (Order no. 72–23,129) 312 pp.

Harris, George Dewey, Jr. "A Study of Citizen Participation in the Educational Decision-Making Process as Perceived by Parents from a Lower Socio-Economic Neighborhood." Ph.D., Michigan State University, 1970. (Order no. 71–2081) 212 pp.

Hollister, Robert Maxwell. "From Consumer Participation to Community Control of Neighborhood Health Centers." Ph.D., Massachusetts Institute of Technology, 1971. (Order no. not available) 335 pp.

Holmes, Emory Hestus. "Community Representation in Educational Decision-Making: An Exploratory Case Study of School-Community Advisory Councils." Ed.D., University of California, Los Angeles, 1972. (Order no. 72–25,782) 219 pp.

Howrey, Gary Loren. "Citizen Participation in the Urbana, Illinois Public Schools 1948–49 and 1960–71." Ed.D., University of Illinois, Champaign-Urbana, 1973. (Order no. 72–17,565) 258 pp.

Kenny, Donald Francis. "A Functional Analysis of Citizens' Committees During School Financial Elections." Ed.D., Stanford University, 1962. (Order no. 62–5444) 159 pp.

Larson, James Roderick. "Community Involvement and Educational Decision-Making: The Development of a Mexican-American Curriculum Office in the Toledo Public Schools." Ph.D., University of Toledo, 1972. (Order no. 73–19,533) 202 pp.

MacKenzie, Donald Gordon. "The Development of a Community School Council Model From Responses of Selected Operating Community

School Councils." Ed.D., Wayne State University, 1971. (Order no. 72–14,593) 68 pp.

McGraw, Arthur Garfield, Jr. "Extent, Nature, Purposes, Structure, and Operational Practices of Citizens Committees in Education in Wisconsin." Ph.D., University of Wisconsin, 1958. (L.C. Card no. Mic 58–2567) 362 pp.

McKay, Robert Bruce. "The History of Citizens Committees in the Development of Connecticut Community Colleges: 1960–1970." Ph.D., University of Connecticut, 1972. (Order no. 72–32,235) 180 pp.

Meyers, Alfred Victor. "The Financial Crisis in Urban Schools: Patterns of Support and Non-support Among Organized Groups in an Urban Community." Ed.D., Wayne State University, 1964. (Order no. 65–1840) 111 pp.

Moler, James Milton. "A Study of Good Parent Participation in Elementary Schools." Ed.D., University of Virginia, 1958. (L.C. Card no. Mic 58–5554) 291 pp.

Nelson, Dale L. "The Extent of Citizen Participation in Educational Policy Making in Idaho School Districts." Ed.D., Brigham Young University, 1970. (Order no. 70–22,900) 240 pp.

Norris, Roy Edwin. "An Examination of Community Councils and Their Communicative Relationships with Municipal Government in New York City, 1960–1970: Implications for Adult Education." Ed.D., Columbia University, 1971. (Order no. 72–17,219) 378 pp.

O'Neal, John Furnifold. "The Status, Structure, and Functions of Citizens Advisory Committees for Public Schools in New York State." Ph.D., Cornell University, 1961. (Order no. 61–5166) 265 pp.

Peddicord, Paul Wallace. "Citizens' Committees in the Public School System of North Carolina." Ed.D., Duke University, 1965. (Order no. 65–7278) 243 pp.

Porter, Robert A. "Community Mental Health Planning Ideology of Organizational Participants in the Model Cities Program." Ph.D., The Florence Heller Graduate School for Advanced Studies in Social Welfare, Brandeis University, 1970. (Order no. 71–3241) 281 pp.

Purdom, Paul Walton. "Organizational Decentralization in a Governmental Executive Agency as Measured by Communications: A Study of the Community Health Services of the Philadelphia Department of Public Health." Ph.D., University of Pennsylvania, 1963. (Order no. 64–7393) 611 pp.

Randolph, Andrew Benton. "Participation Dynamics in a Neighborhood Health Center." Ph.D., Case Western Reserve University, 1969. (Order no. 70–25,991) 244 pp.

Rhodes, Harry Clement. "Citizen Participation in the Formulation and Administration of the School Budget in Selected Communities in Maryland." Ed.D., University of Maryland, 1960. (L.C. Card no. Mic 61–891) 232 pp.

Rosenfeld, Raymond Alan. "Points of Coalescence of Voluntary Organizations: Desegregation in Atlanta." Ph.D., Emory University, 1973. (Order no. 73–25,408) 279 pp.

Salmon, Kimball, Jr. "The California Citizens Commission on the Public Education System and Six Metropolitan Daily Newspapers." Ed.D., University of California, Berkeley, 1966. (Order no. 65–13,427) 219 pp.

Saunders, Leonard Joseph. "A Study of the Effect of an Ad Hoc Citizens' Group Upon a Referendum in the Southwestern Regional High School District." Ed.D., New York University, 1968. (Order no. 69–11,781) 216 pp.

Schooling, Herbert Woodrow. "The Use of Lay Citizens Advisory Committees in Selected Missouri Public Schools." Ed.D., University of Missouri, 1954. (Publication no. 10,131; Mic 55–106) 213 pp.

Skeen, Elois Marie Adams. "The Effects of Attending a Community Controlled School on the Belief and Control of Reinforcements and Attitudes Toward School of Pupils." Ph.D., University of Michigan, 1973. (Order no. 73–24,685) 310 pp.

Skelly, Alvin George. "A Descriptive Study of Community Involvement in the School Construction Program in the City of Detroit Between 1958 and 1967." Ed.D., Wayne State University, 1968. (Order no. 69–14,684) 811 pp.

Smoley, Eugene Ralph, Jr. "Community Participation in Urban School Government." Ph.D., Johns Hopkins University, 1965. (Order no. 65–6885) 226 pp.

Stanley, William Oliver, Jr. "Educational Policy and Citizens' Organizations in an Age of Confusion." Ph.D., Columbia University, 1951. (Publication no. 3117) 679 pp.

Stuve, Gilbert Edmund. "The Use of the 'Citizen's Committee' as an Educational Policy Device in an Area of Public Controversy: A Study of Sex Education Advisory Committees in Selected Detroit Suburbs." Ph.D., Wayne State University, 1972. (Order no. 73–12,604) 174 pp.

Tave, Susan Dorothy. "An Evaluation of Alternative Models of Citizens Participation in Public, Private, and Parochial School Systems." Ph.D., University of Michigan, 1973. (Order no. 73–24,698) 243 pp.

Terwillinger, Joseph Elmer. "An Investigation of Certain Characteristics Associated with Advisory Committees of Lay Citizens in Local School Districts in Illinois." Ed.D., University of Illinois, 1966. (Order no. 67–6754) 123 pp.

Thomas, Charles Richard. "A Study of Lay Participation in the Elimination of Defacto Racial Segregation in a Northern School District." Ph.D., Northwestern University, 1970. (Order no. 71–1986) 145 pp.

Torge, Herman. "Lay Participation at School Board Meetings in Ohio: Theory, Policy, and Practice." Ph.D., Miami University, 1971. (Order no. 71–25,530) 129 pp.

Van Til, Jon. "Becoming Participants: Dynamics of Access Among the Welfare Poor." Ph.D., University of California, Berkeley, 1970. (Order no. 71–9947) 279 pp.

Weisberg, Alan Phil. "Community Participation in Decision-Making for a Federal Compensatory Education Program." Ph.D., Stanford University, 1972. (Order no. 73–4621) 287 pp.

Werle, Henry Daniel. "Lay Participation in Curriculum Improvement Programs." Ed.D., Columbia University, 1964. (Order no. 65–4754) 199 pp.

White, Jack Winn. "Administrative Problems Encountered in the Operation of Community Mental Health Facilities." D.B.A., George Washington University, 1969. (Order no. 69–17,472) 239 pp.

Williams, David Ivor. "Citizens' Advisory Committees in the Colorado Public School." Ed.D., University of Colorado, 1959. (L.C. Card no. Mic 60–1054) 326 pp.

Willmon, Betty Jean. "The Influence of Parent Participation and Involvement on the Achievement of Pupils Attending the Leon County Head Start Program as Measured by a Reading Readiness Test." Ph.D., Florida State University, 1967. (Order no. 67–14,464) 78 pp.

Woons, George Joseph. "The Community-School Council: Functions, Characteristics and Issues." Ph.D., Michigan State University, 1972. (Order no. 72–30,069) 143 pp.

Young, Carlene Herb. "An Analysis of the Influence on Educational Policy of Community Organizations in a Large Urban Center." Ed.D., Wayne State University, 1967. (Order no. 68–2117) 186 pp.

5

Voluntary Associations and
Local Politics

As national and local government programs have attempted to facilitate increased citizen access to policy and decision-making processes, voluntary associations or self-initiating citizen groups have become more politically active. Sociologists have, for many years, been interested in voluntary associations and there is a large body of literature on the topic. Many contributions to this body of literature are cited in this chapter. These citations are limited to only the most important efforts focusing on association membership, structure, and social activity, all of which affect, to some degree, the political activity of voluntary associations. An attempt has nevertheless been made to be as comprehensive as possible in referencing materials focusing directly upon the political activities, strategies, and impacts of voluntary associations. (For a more comprehensive review of the literature on the characteristics and social activities of voluntary associations, see Smith, Constance, and Anne Freedman, *Voluntary Associations: Perspectives from the Literature,* in "Related Bibliographies," Chapter 1.)

A large portion of the citations which deal, specifically, with the political activities of voluntary associations refer to descriptive case studies. As valuable as these studies may be, the quality and quantity of analytic materials on the politics of voluntary associations do not seem to reflect their growing importance in local politics. Comparative research on the political strategies and impacts of voluntary associations should rank among the priorities of political scientists, sociologists, and other social scientists seeking to clarify and explain the dynamics of local political systems.

Abrahamson, Julia. *A Neighborhood Finds Itself.* New York: Harper, 1959.

Reviews:
Booklist 56 (September 1, 1959): 14.
Buck, Thomas. *Chicago Sunday Tribune* (July 5, 1959): 7.

Glazer, Nathan. *American Sociological Review* 25 (February 1960): 127.

Goldhor, Herbert. *Library Journal* 84 (June 1959): 2073.

Healy, G. M. *Springfield Republican* (August 9, 1959): 4.

Jaffe, D. K. *Christian Science Monitor* (July 16, 1959): 5.

Noar, Gertrude. *Social Education* 24 (February 1960): 91.

Tax, Sol. *Annals of the American Academy of Political and Social Science* 327 (January 1960): 146.

Thelen, H. A. *School Review* 67 (Winter 1959): 469.

Abrahamson describes the Hyde Park-Kenwood Community Conference, formed by residents of a community on Chicago's South Side to try to maintain a stable middle-class integrated community in the face of encroaching urban deterioration and whites moving out. The book reviews the history of the community and its decline. It then describes how the citizens organized to fight real estate speculators and to pressure the city for action that would halt deterioration of the area. There is also a discussion of the area's urban renewal plan.

Alexander, Chauncey A., and Charles McCann. "The Concept of Representativeness in Community Organization." *Social Work* 1:1 (January 1956): 48–52.

The author delineates the ways in which the concept of representativeness is applied in practice. He gives two definitions of the term: authorized functioning or acting by one person in behalf of another or others and the quality of being typical or typifying a group or class. The author believes that the concept needs to be further examined and clarified.

Alinsky, Saul D. "Community Analysis and Organization." *American Journal of Sociology* 44:6 (May 1941): 797–808.

In this article, Alinsky describes the genesis of the Back of the Yards Neighborhood Council in Chicago. Alinsky, in organizing the council, made operational the maxim that local problems must be viewed within the context of the socioeconomic issues of the larger society. Also, the council is rooted in the institutions of the community, specifically the Chamber of Commerce, the Catholic Church, and organized labor. The council is organized into eight committees with elected officials who, in turn, compose the executive board. A community congress meets twice a year. After eighteen months of the council's existence, Alinsky could identify seventeen tangible achievements. He also pointed out that there were intangible achievements such as community people getting to know each other.

Alinsky, Saul. "The Professional Radical, 1970." A Conversation with Marion K. Sanders. *Harper's* 209:1436 (January 1970): 35–42.

In this interview Alinsky talks about community organization for the 1970s. He had become interested in organizing frustrated middle-class people. He believed that they could be organized around issues of concern to them, such as the Vietnam War. He also talked about the problems of organizing lower middle class people, especially the problem of the race issue.

Aylor, Kay. "Citizen Power: Harlem Teams on Top." *American Education* 6:4 (May 1970): 32.

This is a description of Harlem Teams for Self-Help, Inc., a nonprofit organization which generates activities to improve Harlem. Each activity reaches a different clientele. Two of the activities are a consumer protection union and a drug detection and prevention center. Volunteer services include programs entitled Youth Leadership Corps, Education Action Program, and Community Hands United Mutually.

Babchuk, Nicholas, and Alan Booth. "Voluntary Association Membership: A Longitudinal Analysis." *American Sociological Review* 34:1 (February 1969): 31–45.

This study examines the extent of involvement in voluntary groups over time. In 1961 and 1965, 402 persons in one midwestern state were questioned in detail about their organizational affiliations. The authors conclude: (1) a majority of adult Americans belong to voluntary associations; (2) membership remains stable over time and membership in more than one association is common; (3) a majority of people add and drop memberships but continue active membership in at least one association; (4) there is no difference between urban and rural membership patterns; (5) the structure and function of associations affect the rates and changes in affiliation; (6) men and women have different patterns of affiliation; and (7) affiliation and pattern of membership are linked to family status and life cycle.

Babchuk, Nicholas, and C. Wayne Gordon. *The Voluntary Association in the Slum.* University of Nebraska Studies, New Series, no. 27. Lincoln: University of Nebraska Press, 1962.

Babchuk and Gordon examine community organization in a slum in order to identify the ways in which people become affiliated with voluntary associations. The central hypothesis is that members are incorporated and maintained in voluntary formal groups through personal influence. The secondary hypothesis is that a person incorporated into a voluntary formal organization through personal influence will participate more regularly. Nine more hypotheses relating specific variables to participation are presented.

The study examines groups organized under the auspices of the Council of Social Agencies in a slum neighborhood of Rochester, New York. These organizations include the Savannah-Manhattan Improvement Council, six children's organizations, and a senior citizens club. A typology of voluntary associations is presented: expressive, instrumental, and instrumental-expressive. Neighborhood residents affiliated with other groups were examined for purposes of comparison. The central hypothesis of the study was supported; the secondary hypothesis was not. An appendix to the book details the methodology used in the analysis.

Babchuk, Nicholas, and Ralph V. Thompson. "The Voluntary Associations of Negroes." *American Sociological Review* 27:5 (October 1962): 647–55.

This study focuses on the extent of Negro participation in voluntary associations and attempts to identify the determinants of such participation. The first hypothesis is that Negroes are less likely than whites to be affiliated with voluntary associations because of the predominant lower socioeconomic status of Negroes. The second hypothesis is that situational determinants and correlates of membership would not be significantly different for Negroes and whites. Interviews were conducted with a sample of 120 Negroes twenty years of age or older in Lincoln, Nebraska, in 1960. The first hypothesis was not supported. Negroes were affiliated with more organizations than whites. Also, there were positive relationships between occupational rank, educational achievement, family income, and membership in voluntary associations. The data seemed to confirm the second hypothesis. Negro participation was found to be similar to that of whites and was related to marital status, residential mobility, home ownership, religious affiliation, friendships, and sex. However, Negroes were affiliated with formal religious organizations to a greater extent than were whites. The findings support Myrdal's thesis of widespread participation among Negroes and also support the thesis that participation patterns of whites and Negroes differ.

Bailey, Robert, Jr. "Protest in Urban Politics: The Alinsky Approach."
Paper presented at the Meeting of the Ohio Association of Economists
and Political Scientists, Ohio University, Athens, Ohio, April 7, 1972.
Mimeograph.

Bailey presents an analysis of protest as a political resource as used by
Alinsky organizations in gaining access to power. The use of various tactics
by such organizations is discussed. Lipsky's theory that protest is not a stable
political resource is criticized (see Lipsky, Michael, "Protest as a Political
Resource," Chapter 1). The author found that protest as used by Alinsky
organizations is a stable political resource. He feels that protest is not
inherently stable or unstable and that its stability is dependent on the type
of organization. He presents a competing model which focuses on the
relationship between community organization leaders and urban decision
makers.

Bailey, Robert, Jr. *Radicals in Urban Politics: The Alinsky Approach.*
Chicago: University of Chicago Press, 1974.

Using two years of participant observation and almost three hundred
interviews with community residents and organizational activists, the
author details the formation, structure, and activities of one Alinsky
organization, the Organization for a Better Austin, on Chicago's West Side.
The Organization for a Better Austin is then compared with three other
Alinsky groups.

Bailey concludes that Alinsky organizations are dependent upon the
involvement of middle class residents and upon the existence of social
problems which become the focus of the organizations' activities. The most
important activity of Alinsky organizations is found to be the "[d]efining
and articulating [of] issues which might otherwise be ignored or marginally
dealt with. . . ." The author then identifies four features of Alinsky
organizations that "explain why Alinsky organizations function so well":
financial independence, the use of professional outside organizers, grass
roots organizations, and the use of protest. The author concludes that
Alinsky organizations are less radical and more conventional than many
observers have thought and that the "future of this new form of urban
pressure-group appears bright in certain kinds of neighborhoods."

Bailey, Robert, Jr. "Urban Radicals: Activists in an Alinsky Community
Organization." Paper presented at the Annual Meeting of the American Political Science Association, Washington, D.C., September 5–9,
1972. Mimeograph.

The purpose of this study was to compare activists in an Alinsky organization with other residents of the same community in order to find areas in which they differ. The study was conducted in the South Austin community of Chicago, where 230 community residents and the 47 most active participants in the Organization for a Better Austin were interviewed. The activists were found to have stronger community attachments, to be more dissatisfied with the quality of government, and to be more politically active. The author also presents two opposing questions about Alinsky organization members, i.e., are they good citizens or wild-eyed radicals? He believes that the data support both. He concludes that Alinsky organizations have not organized the hard-core poor and that organization members have the same qualities as those who participate in more conventional civic activities, albeit with a different orientation.

Barber, Bernard. "Participation and Mass Apathy in Associations." *Studies in Leadership: Leadership and Democratic Action.* Edited by Alvin W. Gouldner. New York: Harper, 1950, pp. 477–504.

The author rejects the often stated idea that democracy can work only if everyone participates. He cites the case of voluntary associations in the United States which generally consist of active minorities and inactive majorities. He explores the functions of voluntary associations and concludes that inactivity on the part of the majority of members is due as much to structural factors as to psychological apathy and democratic despair. He relates mass apathy to two aspects of the social structure: job and family obligations are perceived to be of primary importance in American society, and any other associations are thus segregated and relegated to a lesser role; the needs of large-scale organizations call for specialized leadership which precludes the notion that anyone can participate in organizational leadership. Leadership thus tends to become a career for certain individuals who then let their professional skills atrophy and who would, in any case, be unable to return to their former jobs.

Bell, Wendell, and Maryanne T. Force. "Urban Neighborhood Types and Participation in Formal Associations." *American Sociological Review* 21:1 (February 1956): 25–34.

This article presents part of a study of social participation conducted in San Francisco in 1953. It examined the relationships between formal association participation and certain individual characteristics and neighborhood differences. The study found the following: (1) over three-fourths of the men held memberships; (2) men belonged to more associations than women, attended more often, and held office more often; (3) in the lower of the two high economic status neighborhoods, more men belonged to no associations, fewer attended meetings, and fewer held offices; (4) in each neighborhood, higher economic status persons participated more, however, with economic status constant, those in higher economic areas participated more; (5) individual family status characteristics within neighborhoods showed no relationship to formal association participation; and (6) the relationship between age and association participation depended on economic level.

Black, Jonathan. "Block Power—The Jane Street Story." *New York Times Magazine* (May 7, 1972): 36ff.

Black describes the Jane Street Block Association in New York City's West Village. It was initially formed by thirty residents to fight blight and deterioration, crime, loud traffic, and drunks in the neighborhood. It supports a private guard patrol to discourage crime on the block; a recycling project for paper, bottles, cans, and rags; beautification projects; and also sends out a newsletter and holds parties. The association has been able to put pressure on the city to clean up the block. The article then briefly describes some of the varied activities of other block associations in New York City.

"Block Power." *Newsweek* 75:5 (February 2, 1970): 47–48.

This article catalogues the revival of block associations in several large cities. Their activities range from attempting to improve social services to beautification projects.

Booth, Alan; Nicholas Babchuk; and Alan B. Knox. "Social Stratification and Membership in Instrumental-Expressive Voluntary Associations." *Sociological Quarterly* 9:4 (Autumn 1968): 427–39.

Voluntary associations are divided into two types: those with instrumental functions (social influence organizations) and those with expressive functions (personal fellowship organizations). Five hypotheses were presented: (1) that middle class persons would be affiliated with voluntary associations more often than working-class and lower class persons; (2) that more middle class persons would be affiliated with instrumental associations than working-class or lower class persons; (3) that middle class persons would be more actively involved in instrumental organizations than working-class or lower class persons; (4) that working-class and lower class persons would belong to fewer voluntary associations in general and would belong to expressive organizations when they did belong; and (5) that working-class and lower class persons would participate more actively in expressive organizations than middle class persons. Fifteen hundred interviews were conducted with adults in a midwestern plains state. The data generally confirmed the above hypotheses.

Bullock, Paul. "On Organizing the Poor: Problems of Morality and Tactics." *Dissent* 15:1 (January/February 1968): 65–70ff.

Community organization is discussed in terms of four groups—(1) Alinsky and the Industrial Areas Foundation, (2) civil rights organizations, (3) New Left organizations, and (4) certain labor unions, working independently or in conjunction with other groups—which have been involved in community organization. The author criticizes New Left groups as intellectual, elitist radicals who do not really understand the aspirations of poor ghetto residents.

Costain, Anne. "Women's Lobbying: Political Power in Voluntary Organizations." Paper presented at the Annual Meeting of the Southern Political Science Association, Nashville, Tennessee, November 6, 1975. Mimeograph.

Curtis, Richard T. "Occupational Mobility and Membership in Formal Voluntary Associations: A Note on Research." *American Sociological Review* 24:6 (December 1959): 846–48.

Membership rates of occupationally mobile and stable people in specific types of voluntary formal associations were compared using data gathered in surveys conducted in the Detroit area. Variables considered were sex, occupation, types of associations, and status of membership. The study found that there was no difference in the participation of mobile and nonmobile men. Upwardly mobile families of white-collar workers participated more in sports and hobby clubs. Otherwise, there were no differences.

Dodson, Dan W. *Power Conflict and Community Organizations.* New York: Council for American Unity, 1967.

This is a collection of four papers on the problems of community organization. "Power as a Dimension of Education" discusses the role of power in group relationships. Dodson believes that power is a necessary ingredient in social life and that community organizers must help the powerless find sources of power. In "The Creative Role of Conflict in Intergroup Relationships," Dodson asserts that conflict is one of the few ways in which group relations can be restructured. "The Community Organization Worker and the Urban Encounter" presents a synthesis of concepts of power and conflict which can be used by community organization workers in promoting constructive social change. "The Church, Power, and Saul Alinsky" is a critical evaluation of Alinsky. Dodson praises Alinsky for having proved that organizing the powerless to fight for their own rights is a way of starting the process that will break their cycle of dependency.

Dotson, Floyd. "Patterns of Voluntary Association Among Urban Working-Class Families." *American Sociological Review* 16:5 (October 1951): 687–93.

Dotson examines forms of social organization found among people who are not affiliated with formal associations. Fifty families were interviewed in a working-class district of New Haven. Previous studies showing a lack of working-class participation in voluntary associations were confirmed. It was found that working-class people have active social lives with kinship and friendship groups.

Edwards, John N., and Allan Booth, eds. *Social Participation in Urban Society.* Cambridge, Massachusetts: Schenkman Publishing Company, 1973.

This volume contains some of the major previously published works on voluntary associations. The articles are:

1. "Forms and Extent of Participation"
2. "Correlates and Conditions of Participation"
3. "The Structure of Associations"
4. "Leadership"
5. "The Consequences of Participation"

A final section, written by the editors, is a summary entitled "Implications for Research in Social Participation."

Evan, William M. "Dimensions of Participation in Voluntary Associations." *Social Forces* 36:2 (December 1957): 148–53.

This is an examination of the concept of participation as it is used in the study of voluntary associations and a proposal for an alternative perspective for further research. The author has isolated three dimensions of participation: decision making, activity, and value commitment. From these dimensions, the author develops a typology which profiles membership participation and can be used to determine whether an organization is democratic or authoritarian. This framework suggests that decision making and value commitment have a direct relationship to activity. As the rate of decision making increases, the rate of value commitment increases, and as the rate of value commitment increases, the rate of activity increases.

Fish, John Hall. *Black Power/White Control: The Struggle of the Woodlawn Organization in Chicago.* Princeton, New Jersey: Princeton University Press, 1973.

Fish presents an analysis of the "internal and external" struggles of the Woodlawn Organization (TWO) in Chicago. Concentrating on three programs in which TWO was involved (the Youth Project, the Woodlawn Experimental Schools Project, and the Model Cities Program), the author traces the organization's attempts to achieve community control. The organization is examined as an example of Saul Alinsky's approach to community organization: TWO was founded in 1961 with tactical advice from Alinsky. The author assesses TWO's successes and failures and attempts to explain them.

Freedman, Ronald, and Morris Axelrod. "Who Belongs to What in a Great Metropolis?" *Readings in General Sociology.* 2d ed. Edited by Robert W. O'Brien, Clarence C. Schrag, and Walter T. Martin. Boston: Houghton Mifflin, 1957, pp. 112–18.

The author presents information from the 1952 Detroit Area Study by the University of Michigan about formal group membership. Seven hundred forty-nine persons representing a cross section of the Detroit metropolitan area were interviewed. Participation was found to be relatively low. One-third had no membership outside of church. Certain characteristics were associated with participation: income, education, race, age, sex.

Freeman, Howard E.; Edwin Novak; and Leo G. Reeder. "Correlates of Membership in Voluntary Associations." *American Sociological Review* 22:5 (October 1957): 528–33.

This study attempts to identify variables, other than social class, that distinguish members of voluntary associations from people who do not join such associations. Two hundred ninety-nine families were interviewed in Spokane, Washington. The study found that (1) using a number of variables as measures of social class did not increase the power of class as a predictor of membership; (2) both mobility and community attitude are associated with membership; (3) community attitude and mobility and social class are relatively independent of each other; and (4) several dimensions of community attitude seem to be associated with membership.

Freiberg, Peter. "A Polish Neighborhood Fights Back." *Race Relations Reporter* 4:22 (November 19, 1973): 6–7.

This is a short description of a neighborhood organization in Brooklyn and its efforts opposing a zoning code change which prohibited new residential housing construction in the area. A portion of the affected area was rezoned to a residential category and the city made other concessions which the author attributes to the "movement for neighborhood power in New York City."

Freiberg, Peter. "Situation Ethnics." *Commonweal* 94:4 (April 2, 1971): 81–83.

Freiberg discusses the ethnic community organizations that have been organized in some cities. The author feels that the fact that the organizations are so strongly neighborhood-based might lead to demands for radical decentralization. Catholic, Protestant, and Jewish groups are involved in activities in such cities as Newark, Detroit, and Baltimore, and the Calumet region. Many people who once wrote off the white ethnics as hopelessly racist are now working with such groups and attempting to improve race relations. The philosophy of such people is the populist belief that when people are given the power to control their own affairs, they will make rational decisions for the common good.

Gilbert, Charles E. *Governing the Suburbs.* Bloomington: Indiana University Press, 1967.
    Reviews:
    Choice 4 (November 1967): 1049.
    Fox, J. J. *Library Journal* 92 (July 1967): 2586.

In this book, a study of suburban government development in three suburban Philadelphia areas, Chapter 22, "Participation," presents data on how participation relates to community size and social rank. Civic and political community leaders were interviewed and surveys were conducted in several communities. Education was found to be the socioeconomic factor most closely associated with participation. Occupation was less closely associated and income was not a factor. Social rank of the community made no difference. Citizens' perceptions of their municipal government seemed to be influenced by community size and social rank. More criticism was found in communities of rapid growth and lower social rank. The following characteristics of participation were identified: (1) the functions of participation varied with social rank; (2) recognition and acceptance of small group or party "rule" was more general among upper and upper middle class residents; (3) participants' views of their community varied with its social, economic, and political circumstances; (4) social rank, rather than municipal size, was the dominant influence on participation.

Goldberger, Paul. "Tony Imperiale Stands Vigilant for Law and Order." *New York Times Magazine* (September 29, 1968): 30–31ff.

Goldberger describes white militancy in Newark, New Jersey, in the wake of the Newark riots. Tony Imperiale, the organizer of the North Ward Citizen's Committee, became the symbol of white militancy in Newark. He developed a large following among the white ethnics (mostly Italian) on the strength of his law and order rhetoric and entered politics in Newark on an anticommunist, antiblack platform. The article describes the largely Italian north ward, where residents feel that blacks are forcing "their backs to the wall." The author presents biographical material on Imperiale and follows him on his politicking rounds in Newark and its suburbs.

Gordon, C. Wayne, and Nicholas Babchuk. "A Typology of Voluntary Associations." *American Sociological Review* 24:1 (February 1959): 22–29.

A typology of voluntary associations which uses three criteria is presented: accessibility of membership, status-defining capacity of the association, and the function of the organization for the participant (instrumental or expressive). Degree of accessibility is characterized as high or low. Status-conferring capacity (prestige) is measured as high or low. Functions are seen as instrumental (external gratification), expressive (internal gratification), and instrumental-expressive (in between). The typology describes the relationship between membership characteristics and the organization, and the authors suggest that the typology can be used in comparative studies of organizations.

Greer, Scott A. "Social-Political Structure of Suburbia." *American Sociological Review* 25:4 (August 1960): 514–27.

Harrison, Paul M. "Weber's Categories of Authority and Voluntary Associations." *American Sociological Review* 24:2 (April 1960): 232–37.

The author points out that there is a conflict between the anti-authoritarianism of most American voluntary associations and the need for organizational centralization and bureaucracy. Through his observation of the American Baptist Convention, the author found evidence for modes of legitimation of authority different from those Weber used to analyze authoritarian systems. The author modifies Weber's three categories of authority by adding three subcategories. Weber characterized bureaucracy as rational-legal authority. The author suggests rational-pragmatic as a subcategory. The legal bureaucracy is more rigid, hierarchical, and career-oriented. The pragmatic type found in voluntary associations is more open. People tend to see their involvement in such a bureaucracy as a calling rather than a career. Quasi-charismatic authority is presented as a subcategory of charismatic authority. In anti-authoritarian organizations, the leaders are continually suspect. The subtype, mimetic-traditional authority, is based on tradition and is an unstable form of authority. This comes about because anti-authoritarian organizations need bureaucracy yet are rooted in democracy.

Hausknecht, Murray. *The Joiners: A Sociological Description of Voluntary Association Membership in the United States.* New York: The Bedminster Press, 1962.

> Reviews:
> Montague, J. B. *American Sociological Review* 27 (August 1962) 562.
> Simon, S. L. *Library Journal* 87 (September 1972): 2908.
> Westoff, C. F. *Social Forces* 41 (October 1962): 109.
> Wright, C. T. *American Journal of Sociology* 68 (November 1962): 371.

Hausknecht provides a description of voluntary association membership based on statistics from two national surveys (1954 and 1955). Socioeconomic status and urbanization were both shown to affect membership. Age was found to be important, but sex was not. Religion, home ownership, and stability of residence within the city were found to be important. Total length of residence within a city was not important. Political party affiliation affected membership as did race, but nativity was unimportant. Working-class people tended to belong to social, athletic, and fraternal organizations, while white-collar people tended to belong to civic associations. Voluntary association membership was seen as a part of a "configuration of linkages" to the community.

Helper, Rose. "Neighborhood Association 'Diary'." *Journal of Housing* 22:2 (March 1965): 136–40.

This is a chronological account of the six-year history of a neighborhood improvement association in Chicago that was formed to deal with the movement of blacks into an all-white area. The Winneconna Lakes Area Improvement Association was formed in 1957, when the first black families began to move into the area. Its purpose was to maintain a stable integrated community, but it failed to keep whites from leaving. This was attributed to a disagreement between members and leaders on organizational goals (leaders were more liberal than the membership) and a lack of cooperation and interest in the community on the part of residents. The organization's one accomplishment was that it prevented violence in the area.

Hyman, Herbert, and Charles R. Wright. "Trends in Voluntary Association Memberships of American Adults: Replication Based on Secondary Analysis of the National Sample Surveys." *American Sociological Review* 36:2 (April 1971): 191–206.

This study is a follow-up on a similar study done by the same authors in 1958 (see Wright, Charles R., and Herbert Hyman, "Voluntary Association Membership of American Adults," below). Both studies examine data pertaining to the magnitude and correlates of voluntary association membership in America. Secondary analysis of national survey data from methodologically comparable studies and some supporting data from other surveys were used. Most of the findings from the previous study were reaffirmed. However, there was a small but noticeable increase in the percentage of people belonging to voluntary associations since the mid-1950s. There was a sharper growth in membership among lower status groups and blacks.

Komarovsky, Mirra. "The Voluntary Associations of Urban Dwellers." *American Sociological Review* 11:6 (December 1946): 686–98.

Data on organized group affiliations of 2,223 adults in New York City are presented in this article. Questionnaires were given to employed persons at their places of work in 1934 and 1935. The focus was on class differences. The study found that in the working class, which constitutes the largest segment of the city's population, the majority of the people were not members of organizations. Sixty percent of working-class men and 88 percent of working-class women were found to have no affiliations outside of the church. Fifty-three percent of white-collar men and 63 percent of white-collar women were found to be unaffiliated. Participation seemed to increase with increases in socioeconomic status; and, in the business class, a majority were affiliated with some organizations. The number of affiliations of individuals rose with higher status. Sex was found to be of greatest significance in the lower class, where more men than women were affiliated. The difference diminished with increases in occupational status. Single professional women were found to participate in more organizations than men. Religion was found to be of much less importance than economic status.

Kopkind, Andrew. "Of, By and For the Poor: The New Generation of Student Organizers." *New Republic* 152:15 (June 19, 1965): 15–19.

This article describes the community organization efforts of the Students for a Democratic Society's economic research and action projects. The two projects described here were in Cleveland and Newark. The student organizers followed a "bottom up" method of community organization. The background of the students, their relationships to the poor, and the attitudes of the Old Left are also discussed.

Krickus, Richard J. "White Ethnic Groups." *Public Administration Review* 32, special issue (October 1972): 651–54.

Arguing that ethnicity is once again being recognized as an important political variable, the author presents a cleavage model in which groups compete for political advantage and in which individuals take cues for political behavior from reference groups with which they identify. He gives three illustrations: the black mayor vs. the white council, as in Cleveland and Newark; the movement for community control of schools in which whites in black-dominated cities are demanding community control; and the party systems in which the "new ethnic politics" may cause changes as white ethnics desert the Democrats and join the Republicans.

Lawrence, Paul R. "Organization Development in the Black Ghetto." *Social Innovation in the City: New Enterprises for Community Development.* Edited by Richard S. Rosenbloom and Robin Marris. Cambridge, Massachusetts: Harvard University Press, 1969, pp. 109–19.

Attributing the failures of ghetto life to an imbalanced organizational mix, the author believes that attention should be focused on what is wrong with the organization of ghetto life rather than what is wrong with individuals who live in the ghetto. The author sees the exchange process of a community in terms of a mix of four different types of organizations essential to developed community life: economic, political and religious, educational, and government service. He feels that the main problem in the development of the ghetto is that the primary flow of resources is from outside and is controlled by outsiders. He discusses movements in the ghetto that are attempting to rectify the situation: black capitalism is an attempt to improve the economic situation, black power is an attempt to change the political situation, and new educational institutions such as store front academies are attempts to improve the educational situation. Developments in these three areas, the author believes, will then lead to more effective influence on the quality of government services.

Lipsky, Michael, and Margaret Levi. "Community Organization as a Political Resource." *People and Politics in Urban Society*. Edited by Harlan Hahn. Beverly Hills, California: Sage Publications, 1972, pp. 175–99.

This article analyzes community organization as a political strategy through which powerless groups can attain leverage. Problems of creating and maintaining an organization are discussed. The relationships between community organizations and outside agencies are described. The authors conclude that while community organization strategies are more likely than protest to provide stable political resources, such organizations must often make compromises in order to obtain resources and develop incentives.

Litwak, Eugene. "Voluntary Associations and Neighborhood Cohesion." *American Sociological Review* 26:2 (April 1961): 255–71.

Litwak presents two opposing hypotheses: mature industrial bureaucracies put pressure on their members to utilize voluntary association to *disaffiliate* from local community and neighborhood primary groups; mature industrial bureaucracies put pressure on members to utilize voluntary associations to *affiliate* with community and neighborhood primary groups. Arguments that industrial bureaucracies and local communities have little in common are analyzed. Counterviews which argue that voluntary associations might well act to integrate individuals into neighborhood primary groups are presented. Some studies are reexamined and evidence from a neighborhood survey is used as documentation. The data tended to confirm the second hypothesis. The author does not conclude that modern industrial bureaucracies will dominate local communities but rather that they will seek to do so.

London, Bruce. "Racial Differences in Social and Political Participation: It's Not Simply a Matter of Black and White." *Social Science Quarterly* 56:2 (September 1975): 274–86.

This article examines the relationships between race, voluntary association activity, and political participation. The author uses survey data from four Connecticut cities. He concludes that socioeconomic status must be considered in examining the above relationships and that the phenomenon is not "simply a matter of black and white." Therefore, the author then examines within-socioeconomic-group variations.

Maccoby, Herbert. "The Differential Political Activity of Participants in a Voluntary Association." *American Sociological Review* 23:5 (October 1958): 524–32.

The hypothesis tested in this study is that voluntary associations stimulate their members to greater involvement in political activities in the wider society. Conclusions are based on a case study of the Warren County-Front Royal Recreation Association, Inc. (Virginia). The information was collected from established records and voting statistics (1949–1951). The study found membership to be related to political activity. Members of the association were more likely than nonmembers to be voters, to remain voters, and to become voters.

Miller, Kenneth H. "Community Organizations in the Ghetto." *Social Innovation in the City: New Enterprises for Community Development.* Edited by Richard S. Rosenbloom and Robin Marris. Cambridge, Massachusetts: Harvard University Press, 1969, pp. 97–108.

The author believes that the ghetto will continue to exist as such for a long time and that we should not treat it as if it were a short-term problem. He sees the need for widespread participation of residents to transform the slums, for a coordinated approach, and for changes in the fundamental economics of the slums. The author presents some information on existing ghetto community organizations. He discusses the East Central Citizens Organization of Columbus, Ohio, and the West Side Organization in Chicago. He sees the West Side Organization as more successful because it is more flexible and innovative and more tied to the community it serves. He discusses the business projects of these two organizations and asserts that the future of community organizations is in their development of economic potential. He believes that the government should offer incentives for such development.

National Federation of Settlements and Neighborhood Centers. *Making Democracy Work: A Study of Neighborhood Organizations.* New York: National Federation of Settlements and Neighborhood Centers, 1968.

The information presented in this book is based on case studies of neighborhood agencies throughout the country. The study examined neighborhood characteristics, organizational goals, organizational structure, participants, the role of the staff, and the relationship of the agency to the neighborhood. Guidelines are suggested. Some of the findings were: community characteristics have an impact on neighborhood organization programs; the choice of strategies is related to the kinds of goals sought and both are affected by the policies of sponsoring agencies and the style and skill of the employed staff; and the role of the staff is as an interpreter between the agency and the neighborhood and between the local people and the institutions of the larger society. They are a central element, especially in low income areas with traditionally limited participation. Three points were seen as important for an effective neighborhood organization: relevance to physical, social, and economic problems of the community; clear statements of goals and directions; and the process of work should reflect the relationships between community problems, resources, and the goals of the organization.

National Federation of Settlements and Neighborhood Centers. *Neighborhood Organizations: Case Reports.* Chicago: National Federation of Settlements and Neighborhood Centers, 1968.

This is a sequel to *Making Democracy Work: A Study of Neighborhood Organizations* (above). These case reports are meant for use in staff development programs of agencies. They contain information on the community setting, general goals, agency relationships to neighborhood organizations, structures, tactics, and the role of the staff in each case. The field work was done through interviews, observations, attendance at meetings in twenty-three cities, questionnaires, and documentary materials.

O'Brien, David, Jr. "The Public Goals Dilemma and the 'Apathy' of the Poor toward Neighborhood Organization." *Social Service Review* 48:2 (June 1974): 229–44.

The author uses the analytical framework for explaining the success or failure of interest-group activities to elucidate the "apparent indifference of the poor toward neighborhood organization." Applying this analytical framework suggests "viable alternatives to traditional organizing approaches."

Olsen, Marvin E. "Social Participation and Voting Turnout: A Multivariate Analysis." *American Sociological Review* 37:3 (June 1972): 317–33.

Olsen examines the social participation hypothesis—that involvement by individuals in nonpolitical social organizations will in turn motivate them to become politically active. Data came from the 1968 Indianapolis Area Project of the Institute of Social Research at Indiana University. Interviews were conducted with 750 urban adults. Voting turnout in three different national elections was examined. The study concluded that participation in voluntary associations, the community, and the church did mobilize individuals to vote.

Orum, Anthony M. "A Reappraisal of the Social and Political Participation of Negroes." *American Journal of Sociology* 72:1 (July 1966): 32–46.

The author reexamines the involvement of Negroes in voluntary associations in the light of previously overlooked data. The conclusions are based on data gathered by the National Opinion Research Center. The effects of socioeconomic status on the membership of Negroes were found to be much less pronounced than for whites. Lower class Negroes were more likely to belong to voluntary associations than lower class whites. Upper class Negroes were less likely to join such associations than were upper class whites.

Perman, Dagmar Horna. *The Girard Street Project*. Washington, D.C.: All Souls Church Unitarian, 1962.

Perman describes the founding and development of a block project by the All Souls Church in Washington, D.C. The project was organized in the 1400 block of Girard Street where residents were 90 percent black and where poor people lived side by side with the nonpoor. The purpose of the project was to create a sense of community where none had existed and to organize the residents to help themselves. The director of the project, a social worker, began by forming a mother's club for the women. Eventually the Girard Street Association was formed. Its activities included a block party, a tutoring project, a girls' club, a rent strike, and obtaining a playground. The group was able to buy two dilapidated buildings with the help of the church and Better Homes, Inc. The author draws two conclusions from the experience of the church with the project. First, a community effort must select certain groups and gear its effort to them. This project chose the poor with middle class aspirations. Second, if people can be motivated, half the battle is won. Progress will then reinforce and lift morale. The author calls for a general strategy for decentralization and community control.

Porter, Bruce. "Politics and Government: Getting Together with the Neighbors." *Saturday Review of the Society* 1:2 (March 17, 1973): 68–69.

This is a description of a block association on the Upper West Side in Manhattan. It was formed when an elderly man was mugged. The first activity of the association was to hire a guard to patrol the area; this succeeded in stopping muggings. The association then moved on to other activities—beautification projects, a volunteer emergency service, consumer services. The association was able to form ties with city hall and city departments. The author outlines a process for starting such a group: oppose something, accomplish something, and have a democratic group.

Pruger, Robert, and Harry Specht. "Assessing Theoretical Models of Community Organization Practice: Alinsky as a Case in Point." *Social Service Review* 43:2 (June 1969): 123–35.

Richey, Elinor. "Kenwood Foils the Block-busters." *Harper's* 227:1359 (August 1963): 42–47.

This article explains how the women of the Kenwood community in Chicago fought to save their neighborhood from the block-busters. The women—black and white—got together and decided that they wanted to continue to live in the neighborhood and to see it remain a stable integrated area. They watched the housing market closely and worked to find family buyers for houses that would have otherwise been converted into multifamily dwellings by the block-busters.

Riessman, Frank. "Self-Help Among the Poor: New Styles of Social Action." *Trans-Action* 2:6 (September/October 1965): 32–37.

After a general discussion of Alinsky's approach to community organization and action, the author concludes that community organizations can be effective in low income communities and that community action does not have to depend upon federal funding.

Roselline, Lynn. "Reform in Jersey City." *Reader's Digest* 102:610 (February 1973): 85–88.

This article describes how the Citizens Committee of Hudson County (New Jersey) was organized in 1965 to fight a boulevard-widening project that would line the pockets of local politicians. The organization continued to fight political mismanagement by sitting in on city and county meetings and going through city records. They fought the sale of lands in the

Palisades, stopped an illegal land fill, and stopped demolition of an old county courthouse.

Ross, Murray G., with B. W. Lappin. *Community Organization: Theory, Principles, and Practice*. 2d ed. New York: Harper and Row, 1967.

Ross and Lappin outline principles of community organization and describe the nature of community organization. The book presents several approaches to community work and discusses their differences in terms of objectives, methods, and pace. It suggests a method of community organization in which the community determines the nature of the process. The book defines community organization; presents assumptions concerning values, problems, and methods; and presents a number of hypothesized influences on community life. Aspects of planning and principles of community organization are presented, but the author emphasize flexibility. Four roles of the professional worker are described as guide, enabler, expert, and social therapist. A final chapter presents three case studies in which the principles of community action are illustrated.

Scaff, Alvin H. "The Effect of Commuting on Participation in Community Organization." *American Sociological Review* 17:2 (April 1952): 215–20.

Scaff examined the effects of commuting on the community of Claremont outside of Los Angeles. Data came from personal interviews with small family groups. The findings indicated that (1) the suburban town was increasingly becoming a commuter town; (2) the commuters were divided between their places of residence and places of business; (3) commuters usually participated very little; (4) the presence of commuters balanced the age groups of the community but increased pressures for schools and parks; and (5) community organizations were highly selective vis-à-vis education and profession of members.

Scott, John C., Jr. "Membership and Participation in Voluntary Associations." *American Sociological Review* 22:3 (June 1957): 315–26.

The purpose of this study was to determine the relationship between variations in sex, age, education, religion, occupation, marital status, family status, friends, nativity, residence, home tenure, and social status and variations in the degree of individual participation in voluntary association. Five percent of the population of Bennington, Vermont, (pop. 7628) were interviewed by the author and his wife in 1947. They found that 35.8 percent had no affiliations outside the church (25 percent men and 44 percent women). The average duration of membership in voluntary associations was ten years and frequency of attendance was low.

More men than women were members, but more women attended meetings. Membership increased with educational level. Protestants had more affiliations than Catholics, and Catholics had more than those with no religious preference. Nonmanual workers had more affiliations than manual workers and students. More married than unmarried persons were members. Parents with one child belonged to fewer organizations than those with none or two children. People with many friends had more affiliations. Homeowners were more often members than renters.

Sherrard, Thomas D., and Richard C. Murray. "The Church and Neighborhood Community Organization." *Social Work* 10:3 (July 1965): 3–14.

This article describes the current increased involvement of churches in the community. The authors believe that this is because of the impact of the civil rights movement, a concern with the low influence of religion, the economic troubles of churches, and a search for a new meaning for the church in society. The authors describe the approach of Saul Alinsky and the Industrial Areas Foundation to community organization which seems to appeal to young urban clergymen. The authors are rather critical of Alinsky's method, which they feel displays too much hostility to outsiders with whom the community will later have to work. They urge a union of social workers and clergy.

Silberman, Charles E. "Up From Apathy, the Woodlawn Experiment: Excerpts from 'Crisis in Black and White.' " *Commentary* 37:5 (May 1964): 51–58.

Silberman points to the failure of the American social welfare system and asserts that the only way blacks can be helped is for them to gain the means to help themselves. He believes that the Woodlawn Organization (TWO) in Chicago proves that poor blacks can be mobilized effectively. TWO was created in 1961 and is a federation of eighty-five to ninety groups representing 30,000 people. It was organized by Saul Alinsky and the Industrial Areas Foundation.

TWO was organized around the grievances of the community. It first attacked questionable practices of local merchants and then went on to fight for better housing and improved schools. Its largest battles were against attempts by the University of Chicago to extend its South Campus into Woodlawn and against a 1962 urban renewal plan about which the community had not been consulted.

Simpson, Richard L., and William H. Gulley. "Goals, Environmental Pressures, and Organizational Characteristics." *American Sociological Review* 27:3 (June 1962): 344–50.

This study concerns the influence of goals and environment on the internal characteristics of voluntary associations. It presents a typology of voluntary associations and tests of three specific hypotheses. Associations were classified as *focused* or *diffused* depending on the number of goals. Additionally, they were classified as *internal* or *external* depending on whether they had to satisfy only their own members or the community as a whole. Hypothesis one projected that focused internal organizations would be characterized as centralized and action initiated; diffused external would be decentralized; focused external and diffused internal would fall between the other two. Hypothesis two stated that diffused external organizations would stress loyalty and active involvement; focused internal would not stress such things; focused external and diffused external would be in between the two. Hypothesis three predicted that diffused external organizations would emphasize internal communications; focused internal organizations would not; the others would be between those two positions. Data were collected from 485 respondents (representing 211 organizations) using mailed questionnaires. All three hypotheses were supported.

Smith, David Horton. "Voluntary Organization Activity and Poverty." *Urban and Social Change Review* 5 (Fall 1971): 2–7.

Sower, Christopher, et al. *Community Involvement: The Webs of Formal and Informal Ties That Make for Action.* Glencoe, Illinois: Free Press, 1957.

> Reviews:
> *Annals of the American Academy of Political and Social Science* 320 (November 1958): 170.
> Cumming, Elaine. *American Journal of Sociology* 63 (May 1958): 676.
> Sills, D. L. *American Sociological Review* 23 (August 1958): 469.

A study of the processes by which a few professional persons in a midwestern county organized community action, this book is based on a house-to-house health survey of 10,000 families in twenty-three communities. The objectives of the survey were to educate the public about public health, to discover problems to be dealt with in future health planning, and to strengthen the two health organizations within the county.

The book describes how the survey moved from an idea originating with a few people to an action project involving the entire community. It presents a typology of community involvement, analyzes local participants and local organizational developments, and presents a case study of one community. Of the objectives of the survey only the second one was achieved; however, the authors emphasize the nature of the self-survey rather than its results.

Tannenbaum, Arnold S. "Control and Effectiveness in a Voluntary Organization." *American Journal of Sociology* 67:1 (July 1961): 33–46.

Tannenbaum uses the "control graph" to characterize the pattern of formal organizations. Various levels of organization are shown on the horizontal axis. The vertical axis shows the amount of control exercised by people at each level; i.e., how much effect each level has on the organization's decision making. Two hypotheses were presented: organizational effectiveness will be related to the degree of the positive slope of the control curve; organizational effectiveness will be related directly to the average height of the control curve.

Data were gathered through a survey of 104 of the autonomous local leagues of the League of Women Voters. There were three sets of measures: local effectiveness was measured by rating forms filled out by twenty-nine persons assigned to the national headquarters; control in the leagues was measured by questionnaires to twenty-five randomly chosen members in each sample league (more in the larger ones); and there were supplementary measures of league effectiveness. The data supported hypothesis one and partially supported hypothesis two.

Turner, John B., ed. *Neighborhood Organization for Community Action.* New York: National Association of Social Workers, 1968.

This is a report on the National Association of Social Workers' conference, "Citizen Self-Help Organizations: Relevance and Problems," in Cleveland, Ohio, March 15–17, 1967. The major ideas of the conference are summarized under the following topics: (1) citizen self-help organizations; (2) neighborhood action and lower class life style; (3) building social movements among the poor; (4) influence of community action on neighborhood action; (5) goals and means for social change; and (6) staff role in neighborhood organization. Discussions among the conference participants are included. The appendices contain information on the workshop staff and conference participants, characteristics of the organizations represented, and the case records of the workshops.

Unger, Craig. "TPF: Driving the Snakes Out of Boston." *Ramparts* 11:8
     (February 1973): 20–24.

Unger describes The People First (TPF), a community organization in
Dorchester, an Italian and Irish working-class community in Boston. The
organization was initiated by young college-educated radicals who later
yielded much responsibility to local people because of conflicts with more
conservative community residents. The organization fought injustices by
the utilities, organized a food co-op, tried to improve housing, and worked
to increase sentiment for the antiwar movement and for women's rights.

Warner, Keith W. *Voluntary Associations and Individual Involvement in
     Public Policy Making and Administration.* Lexington, Massachusetts:
     D. C. Heath, 1973.

Warner, Keith W., and Sidney J. Miller. "Organizational Problems in Two
     Types of Voluntary Associations." *American Journal of Sociology* 69:6
     (May 1964): 654–57.

Warner and Miller examine how the nature of an organization relates
to the problems it faces. A typology of voluntary associations is presented.
The consummatory organization is one within which the primary ends of
the organization are found. It is characterized by immediate gratification of
interests, with the members as primary beneficiaries of the organization.
The second type is the instrumental organization in which the primary ends
are outside of the organization. Gratification is less immediate and nonmembers may be the primary beneficiaries. The authors then describe ten
problems that organizations can face. The hypothesis is that the number of
problems encountered in effectively serving the ends of the organization
depends upon whether an organization is predominantly an end in itself or a
means to some other end.
     Data were gathered in 1962 in a study of 191 voluntary organizations in
rural Wisconsin. The study found that instrumental organizations face more
problems than consummatory organizations. The same results were obtained when size, proportion of members as officers, intended primary
beneficiary of the organization's purpose, and age of the organization were
controlled.

Wright, Charles R., and Herbert H. Hyman. "Voluntary Association
     Membership of American Adults: Evidence from National Sample
     Surveys." *American Sociological Review* 23:2 (June 1958): 284–94.

In analyzing patterns of voluntary association membership, this study considers the following topics: patterns of membership in general and of specific subgroups in American society; correlates of membership which might be considered determinants; and correlates of membership which might be considered consequences of significance to theories of functions of membership. Data used are from information gathered by the National Opinion Research Center.

The data showed that a large number of Americans have no voluntary association affiliation. Only a minority are members. More whites than blacks were members of such organizations. Jews had the highest percentage of families affiliated; Catholics were second, Protestants third. In individual membership, Catholics and Protestants reversed place. Membership increased with increases in socioeconomic status. Participation among blue-collar workers was extremely low. Business and professional people participated more. More highly urbanized people belonged to more voluntary associations than those in nonurbanized areas. No residential factors could be related to incidence of membership; however, homeowners and marrieds seemed more likely to be members. The study also found that persons belonging to associations were more interested in public affairs, showed more support for charities, and voted more often.

Young, Ruth C., and Olaf F. Larson. "The Contribution of Voluntary Organizations to Community Structure." *American Journal of Sociology* 71:2 (September 1965): 178–86.

This study relates organizational prestige to structural attributes of an organization. Data were gathered through structured interviews with at least one major officer in each of forty-three organizations in a small New York community. Organizations were ranked by the reputational method and then placed on the "J" Curve of organizational prestige. It was found that the highest prestige organizations were those encompassing the main values of the community. They showed more formal structure, tended to be outer directed, and served as links between the community and the wider society. Moderately prestigious organizations were more specialized, more social, and made few efforts to be influential. Low prestige organizations were marginal; they generally represented small, transient subcultures.

Zimmer, Basil G., and Amos H. Hawley. "The Significance of Membership in Associations." *American Journal of Sociology* 65:2 (September 1959): 196–201.

Zimmer and Hawley ask if there is a difference between the frequency of membership in voluntary associations among fringe area residents and central city residents. They also ask if membership is related to participation in other activities. The data came from two surveys done in the central city and fringe areas of Flint, Michigan, in 1957.

The study found that of the central city population surveyed 43.1 percent belonged to voluntary associations, while only 24.7 percent of the fringe area residents belonged to such associations. Frequency of membership in both areas varied with demographic characteristics. The lower rate of membership in fringe areas was not due to demographic composition. Membership in associations was found to be of some consequence in the affairs of the community, especially those having to do with political unification.

Dissertations

Badran, Hoda. "The Community Organization Practitioner's Decision-Making Behavior in Conflict Situations." D.S.W., Case Western Reserve University, 1967. (Order no. 67–8834) 180 pp.

Bailey, Robert, Jr. "Protest in Urban Politics: A Study of an Alinsky Community Organization and its Participants." Ph.D., Northwestern University, 1972. (Order no. 72–32,373) 272 pp.

Barber, B. "Mass Apathy and Voluntary Social Participation in the United States." Ph.D., Harvard University, 1948.

Bohrnstedt, George William. "Processes of Seeking Membership in and Recruitment by Voluntary Social Organizations." Ph.D., University of Wisconsin, 1966. (Order no. 66–13,400) 339 pp.

Chamberlain, Robert Marvin. "Participation in Voluntary Associations and Heterogeneous Social Characteristics of Rural-Urban Fringe Residents." Ph.D., University of Missouri at Columbia, 1969. (Order no. 69–70,2968) 242 pp.

Dobash, Russell Paul. "Formal Voluntary Association Participation and Community Identification." Ph.D., Washington State University, 1972. (Order no. 73–40) 78 pp.

Ellsworth, Allen Simmons. "Role Analysis in a Voluntary Organization." Ph.D., New York University, 1962. (Order no. 63–5343) 190 pp.

Estes, Margaret Turner. "The Emergence and Legitimation of Community Organizations: A Study of Youth-initiated Drug-Abuse Programs." Ph. D., University of Kansas, 1972. (Order no. 73–11,880) 244 pp.

Haroldsen, Edwin Oliver. "The Relationship Between Attachment to a Voluntary Organization and Conforming Behavior." Ph.D., Iowa State University, 1967. (Order no. 67–12,965) 221 pp.

Hertel, Michael Matthew. "Community Associations and Their Politics: An Evaluation of 12 Community Associations on the Irvine Ranch." Ph.D., Claremont Graduate School, 1972. (Order no. 72–26,236) 213 pp.

Hills, Stuart Lee. "Voluntary Associations and Communicative Integration in a Suburban Community." Ph.D., Indiana University, 1964. (Order no. 64–12,038) 268 pp.

Hunt, Gerard J. "Participation and Anomia: A Study of the Involvement in Work, Informal Interactions, and Formal Associations of Migrants to a Standard Metropolitan Area." Ph.D., University of North Carolina at Chapel Hill, 1969. (Order no. 70–3257) 142 pp.

Klein, Henry Louis. "Community Organization Leaders in Philadelphia." Ed.D., Temple University, 1965. (Order no. 65–9489) 182 pp.

Lane, John Hart, Jr. "Voluntary Associations Among Mexican-Americans in San Antonio, Texas: Organizational and Leadership Characteristics." Ph.D., University of Texas, 1968. (Order no. 69–6173) 229 pp.

McMahon, Anne Meneve. "Voluntary Participation in Formal Groups." Ph.D., Michigan State University, 1970. (Order no. 71–18,252) 157 pp.

McNeil, Elaine Ogden. "White Members of a Biracial Voluntary Association in Arkansas." Ph.D., University of Kansas, 1967. (Order no. 68–6926) 237 pp.

Penergrass, Lee Forest. "Urban Reform and Voluntary Associations: A Case Study of the Seattle Municipal League, 1910–1929." Ph.D., University of Washington, 1972. (Order no. 72–3770) 149 pp.

Pugliese, Donato Joseph. "Citizen Group Activity in the Delaware River Basin." D.P.A., Syracuse University, 1960. (Order no. Mic 61–1499) 333 pp.

Renzi, Mario A. "Correlates of Instrumental and Expressive Voluntary Association Membership in a Black Community." Ph.D., University of Notre Dame, 1971. (Order no. 71–19,086) 189 pp.

Rothrock, Kenneth Martin. "A Study of Voluntary Association Membership." Ph.D., University of Kansas, 1968. (Order no. 68–17,447) 195 pp.

Schindler-Rainman, Eva. "Community Organization: Selected Aspects of Practice." D.S.W., University of Southern California, 1962. (Order no. 62–1330) 249 pp.

6

Local Government Reactions
to Demands for Citizen Participation

As levels of citizen group activity have risen, local governments have attempted to react to increased demands for opportunities for citizen participation. Various mechanisms designed to facilitate both group and individual participation have been created. Some local governments and agencies have established additional grievance procedures or ombudsman offices; others have established citizen councils, boards, or commissions. Many city governments have considered, and some have begun to implement, structural changes, such as little city halls, neighborhood governments, and other forms of political or administrative decentralization. And some local governments have experimented with techniques utilizing survey research or the mass media to facilitate citizen participation. The materials cited in this chapter describe many of these efforts and some assess the impacts of these changes.

Abraham, Henry J. "The Need for Ombudsmen in the U.S." *The Ombudsman.* 2d ed. Edited by Donald Rowat. London: George Allen and Unwin, 1968, pp. 234–40.

In documenting the need for ombudsmen in the United States, the author stresses that the tremendous size of the bureaucracy and the cumbersome process of redress of grievances in the U.S. necessitate an ombudsman similar to the Danish-Norwegian model. The author discusses proposals for national, state, and local ombudsman institutions.

Abraham, Henry J. "A People's Watchdog Against Abuse of Power." *Public Administration Review* 20:3 (Summer 1960): 152–57.

The author asserts the need for a citizens' protector and documents the success of Denmark's parliamentary commissioner. He believes that the same system could not work on the federal level in the United States but recommends its consideration for use by state and local governments.

Anderson, Stanley V. *Ombudsman Papers: American Experience and Proposals.* Berkeley: Institute of Governmental Studies, University of California, 1969.

Anderson defines the institution of the ombudsman and discusses its use in the international community. Various proposals for ombudsmen at the federal, state, and local levels are discussed and analyzed. There is also a discussion of the possible need for campus ombudsmen. Appendices contain more information on specific ombudsman institutions and proposals.

Anderson, Stanley V., and John W. Moore. *Establishing Ombudsman Offices: Recent Experiences in the United States: Transcript of the Ombudsman Workshop, Honolulu, Hawaii, May 5–7, 1971.* Berkeley: Institute of Governmental Studies, University of California, 1972.

This is a partial, verbatim transcript of a workshop which discussed ombudsman offices in the United States. The focus was on the state ombudsman office in Hawaii and local efforts in Nebraska and Washington State. Procedures for how to set up an ombudsman office and methods for evaluation of an ombudsman are also discussed.

Browne, Edmond, Jr., and John Rehfuss. "Policy Evaluation, Citizen Participation, and Revenue Sharing in Aurora, Illinois." *Public Administration Review* 35:2 (March/April 1975): 150–57.

The authors describe Aurora, the city's revenue sharing committee, and the committee's composition and functions. The impacts of the revenue sharing committee are then described.

Capozzola, John M. "An American Ombudsman: Problems and Prospects." *Western Political Quarterly* 21:2 (June 1968): 289–301.

Two proposals for the establishment of ombudsman offices are presented—Henry S. Reuss's Administrative Counsel of the Congress, which would review citizens' complaints submitted by senators and representatives, and Kenneth C. Davis' proposal for a permanent office of administrative procedure and organization located in the executive office of the president to make studies to improve administrative process and to act on citizens' complaints. Nassau County's (New York) de facto ombudsman, the commissioner of accounts, is also described. Ten criteria, suggested guidelines for establishing an ombudsman office, are included.

"Citizen Participation in the Executive Budget Process." *Urban Data Service Report, June 1974.* Washington, D.C.: International City Management Association, 1974.

Describing the Service Area Program in Washington, D.C., this report details how citizens reviewed and influenced the budgeting process in Washington, D.C.

"The City Tells Its Story: Answers East and West." *American City* 84:2 (February 1969): 130–33.

This article describes ombudsmen in Tucson, Arizona, and Trenton, New Jersey. Tucson's ombudsman answers citizens' questions in print. In Trenton, a city staff member arranges displays of information for citizens to view in the lobby of the city hall.

"The City Tells Its Story: Chattanooga Puts Its Citizens to Work." *American City* 79:4 (April 1964): 159ff.

The accomplishments of citizens committees in Chattanooga are described in this article. The eight committees and thirty-one subcommittees, each with a specific purpose, have provided the city with specialized advice and services which the city would not have been able to afford otherwise.

Costikyan, Edward N., and Maxwell Lehman. *Re-structuring the Government of New York City: Report of the Scott Commission Task Force on Jurisdiction and Structure.* New York: Praeger, 1972.

This report presents the Scott Commission's plan for a model government in New York City. The purpose of the plan is to "bring the government closer to the people," and it provides for a strong central-city government within which local communities exist and people participate. The plan proposes a number of elected local governmental units for delivery of local services, a central government (with a mayor) for the delivery of central services, and a central governmental authority with ultimate jurisdiction over both. The central governmental unit would consist of a city policy board headed by the mayor and a city council made up of representatives of local districts. An appendix on the effects of all this on federal programs in New York City is included. An extensive bibliography is also provided.

Cunningham, James V. "Drafting the Pittsburgh Charter: How Citizens Participated." *National Civic Review* 63:13 (September 1974): 410–15.

In 1972 citizens groups in Pennsylvania responded to the newly passed Pennsylvania charter act by initiating a petition to put the question of a charter commission and its selection on the ballot. The candidates for the commission were all community activists. Those elected were, for the most part, nonelites and nonprofessionals.

This article describes the citizen involvement process the commission went through in writing the charter. Three sets of public hearings were held—the first hearings were to decide whether or not to write a complete new home rule charter; the second were neighborhood hearings; the third set of hearings—in churches, settlement houses, and schools—was organized by a professional organizer.

Danzig, Richard, and Benjamin W. Heineman, Jr. "Decentralization in New York City: A Proposal." *Harvard Journal on Legislation* 8:3 (March 1971): 407–54.

The authors present a detailed model of decentralization for New York City which indicates how the central administration and neighborhoods could share power. Sixty-two neighborhood councils would have an active role in determining the mix of city services within their own communities. The system is described as "decisional" or "allocational" decentralization" whereby revenue raising and important agency functions are centralized but resource allocation decisions and some operational decisions are made by local community councils.

Doi, Herman. "The Hawaii Ombudsman Appraises His Office After the First Year." *State Government* 43:3 (Summer 1970): 138–46.

Hawaii's first state ombudsman discusses his job. He presents the statute under which he operates, the procedures for complaints, and some examples of cases handled.

Dolan, Paul. "Citizens' Complaints in Saint Louis: The Case for an Ombudsman?" *University of Missouri Business and Government Review* 10 (September/October 1969): 25–31.

Dolan, Paul. "Pseudo-Ombudsmen." *National Civic Review* 58:7 (July 1969): 297–301ff.

The author examined city complaint offices in nine urban areas. The following factors were presented as political conditions and traditions preventing full use of such offices: (1) lack of public support; (2) lack of independence of the office; (3) offices serving as information and general service agencies in addition to dealing with complaints; (4) reflection of conflicts between the mayor and the council; (5) lack of support from the city council; (6) political jealousies under the separation of powers; (7) tendency to proliferate functions of the office; (8) inadequate staff; and (9) lack of tenured and status salaries. Of the nine cities examined, only Buffalo, New York, was seen as having a well-functioning city complaint office.

Fantini, Marion, and Marilyn Gittell. *Decentralization: Achieving Reform.* New York: Praeger, 1973.

Farkas, Suzanne. "The Federal Role in Urban Decentralization." *American Behavioral Scientist* 15:1 (September/October 1971): 15–35.

Farkas feels that the federal government could provide the impetus for urban decentralization through the redistribution of resources and political influence. However, she criticizes federal programs for contributing to the fragmentation of urban government while promoting centralization at the federal level. Guidelines and fiscal controls of such programs have restricted chances for urban political decentralization. Further decentralization could mean more centralization at the federal level. Decentralization could also result in the concentration of power in the hands of even smaller numbers of people at lower levels of government. She suggests that the role of the federal government should be to counter narrow interests and to act as a redistributive agent.

Farr, Walter G., Jr.; Lance Liebman; and Jeffrey S. Wood. *Decentralizing City Government: A Practical Study of a Radi-Proposal for New York City.* New York: Praeger, 1972.

Sponsored by the Association of the Bar of the City of New York, this study considers a two-tier system of government in the city and the creation of new, geographically distinct, multipurpose units of decentralized political authority. Existing institutions are analyzed, and changes needed for decentralization are examined. Discussion centers on the size of the decentralized units, governmental services, finances, and the role of the civil service and municipal unions. An appendix discusses sanitation services for a decentralized city.

Gellhorn, Walter. *When Americans Complain: Governmental Grievance Procedures.* Cambridge, Massachusetts: Harvard University Press, 1966.

Reviews:
Abramson, M. L. *Library Journal* 91 (December 1966): 5981.
Chazen, Leonard. *Commentary* 44 (August 1967): 93.

Dorsen, Norman. *Political Science Quarterly* 82 (September 1967): 446.

Economist 223 (April 22, 1967): 358.

Kass, B. L. *American Political Science Review* 61 (Summer 1967): 810.

Long, E. V. *New York Times Book Review* (November 27, 1966): 54.

Robbins, Richard. *Commonweal* 86 (May 19, 1967): 267.

Wells, R. H. *Annals of the American Academy of Political and Social Science* 372 (July 1967): 162.

Gellhorn examines arrangements for dealing with citizen complaints. The first section discusses foreign experiences. The second section discusses how citizen complaints are handled in Washington, D.C.; the focus is on how congressmen act as complaint handlers for their constituents. The third section examines grievance mechanisms at the state and local levels. The author recommends experimentation with ombudsmanlike institutions in the United States. He feels that such a system will not be a panacea but, nonetheless, will be an improvement.

Gwyn, William. *Barriers to Establishing Urban Ombudsmen: The Case of Newark.* Berkeley: Institute of Governmental Studies, University of California, 1974.

Haider, Donald. "The Political Economy of Decentralization." *American Behavioral Scientist* 15:1 (September/October 1971): 108–29.

The author discusses the historical and political background of decentralization. Decentralization is seen as related to two trends: the tendency toward more powerful chief executives and the tendency toward greater participation by higher levels of government in municipal government and finance. Arguments concerning centralization and decentralization are reviewed. The relationship between older municipal reform movements and the present movement for decentralization is explored. The economic costs of decentralization and the variables involved are discussed. The author concludes that the decentralization now going on will not solve problems but that it may alleviate frustrations.

Hallman, Howard W. *Administrative Decentralization and Citizen Control.* Washington, D.C.: Center for Governmental Studies, 1971.

This pamphlet discusses the issues involved in the concepts of administrative decentralization and citizen control. The issues in administrative decentralization are seen as hierarchical organization, physical decentralization, substantial discretion of public employees, central head-quarters vs. field operations, and multiple programs. The issues discussed under citizen control are elections, indirect representation, nonelectoral control, and neighborhood influence and control. Possible impacts on public administration and representative government are also explored.

Hallman, Howard W. *Government by Neighborhoods.* Washington, D.C.: Center for Governmental Studies, 1973.

The author advocates the establishment of neighborhood govern-ments in large cities as subunits of city government. They would encompass both political and administrative decentralization. From his studies of suburban municipalities, two-tiered metropolitan arrangements, and cit-izen participation in federal programs, the author believes that such a proposal is practical. He explored the activities of various small munici-palities and found that those with populations of 10,000 handled police, fire, street maintenance, garbage collection, recreation, zoning, and general administration. Those with populations of 25,000 could also handle environ-mental sanitation, health centers, libraries, and fuller recreational pro-grams.

Hallman, Howard W. "Guidelines for Neighborhood Management." *Public Management* 53:1 (January 1971): 3–5.

Hallman describes the move toward governmental decentralization and presents some ideas on how administrative decentralization might work. He discusses the difference between decentralization and citizen participation. He urges public administrators to prepare constructive responses to demands for decentralization and citizen participation.

Hawley, Willis D., and David Rogers, eds. "Decentralization." *Improving the Quality of Urban Management.* Beverly Hills, California: Sage Publications, 1974, pp. 211–334.

Part Three of this collection of essays focuses on the decentralization of city services. In "Service Delivery and the Urban Political Order," Douglas Yates discusses the development of urban service delivery systems and decentralization as one structural approach to the solution of urban problems. Annmarie H. Walsh, in "Decentralization for Urban Manage-ment: Sorting the Wheat from the Chaff," discusses reorganization and decentralization. The fiscal issues in the decentralization controversy are discussed by Jonathan Sunshine in "Decentralization: Fiscal Chimera or

Budgetary Boon?" In "Community Control and Government Responsiveness: The Case of Police in Black Neighborhoods," by Elinor Ostrom and Gordon Whitaker, one big-city and two neighborhood-sized police departments are compared in terms of the services they provide to residents of similar areas. The authors conclude that community control enhances the "possibilities of citizen-police communication" and "police responsiveness to citizen preferences."

Herbert, Adam W. "Management Under Conditions of Decentralization and Citizen Participation." *Public Administration Review* 32, special issue (October 1972): 622–37.

This article discusses the expansion of citizen participation in public policy making from the perspective of public management. Sections of the article cover: (1) background of American society and bureaucracy vis-à-vis citizen participation; (2) the ideology of public administration; (3) a group within public administration known as the "New Public Administrators," which is challenging traditional values; (4) the challenges of decentralization and citizen participation in administration; (5) managerial skills necessary for administrators working within a decentralized setting; and (6) the implications for schools of public administration, which, the author believes, should be more oriented toward human interaction, action, values, and policy.

Hertz, David B., and Adam Walinsky. "Organizing the City: What Cities Do Is What Cities Think." *Agenda for a City: Issues Confronting New York.* Edited by Lyle C. Fitch and Annmarie Hauck Walsh. Beverly Hills, California: Sage Publications, 1970, pp. 451–501.

The authors present a detailed plan for a programmatic government for New York City which suggests changes in the structure of the top echelons of city government and proposes neighborhood governmental units. The recommendations fall into two categories: those that will strengthen leadership toward the achievement of program goals and those that will ensure citizen participation in government. The authors interpret the recommendations in light of the needs of two groups of citizens—the poor and the lower middle class.

Hutcheson, John D., Jr., and Tim C. Ryles. "Survey Research as a Citizen Participation Mechanism." Paper presented at the Southwestern Political Science Association meeting, Dallas, Texas, March 29, 1974.

Mimeograph. A revision appears as "The Use of Surveys as Citizen Participation Mechanisms." *Georgia Political Science Association Journal* 2:2 (Fall 1974): 3–16.

This paper argues that surveys can be used to increase citizen access to local governmental decision-making processes. After describing some of the weaknesses of some widely used participatory mechanisms, the authors suggest that surveys can be used to overcome some of these weaknesses. The authors conclude that surveys should be used to supplement other forms of participation. Several recent surveys, conducted by or for local governments, are used to illustrate methods that might be employed in increasing the utility of surveys as participatory mechanisms.

Jackson, John S. III, and William L. Shade. "Citizen Participation, Democratic Representation, and Survey Research." *Urban Affairs Quarterly* 9:1 (September 1973): 57–89. Presented earlier as "Survey Research and Citizen Participation" at the Southwestern Political Science Association meeting, Dallas, Texas, March 23, 1973. Mimeograph.

The authors of this article describe a survey conducted in conjunction with the "Goals for Carbondale" program and compare the resulting community survey data with data obtained from a citizen's advisory committee (the "city's officially designated CP unit"). A comparison of the demographic characteristics of the survey respondents and the advisory board members revealed that the latter were generally better educated and of higher socioeconomic status. A comparison and factor analytic treatment of the policy preferences of each group led the authors to conclude that the members of the advisory board see "the city more as an active agent of change than as a service producer, while the average citizen views the city primarily in terms of a service providing and control agent, virtually ignoring any role as an agent of community change and social development." On the basis of these data the authors suggest that citizen advisory boards may "introduce additional complications and distortions into the policy-making" process.

Jones, Victor. "New Local Strategies." *National Civic Review* 59:3 (March 1970): 127–34.

In this article, the author maintains that the challenge of the 1970s is how to provide government that is efficient, effective, and at the same time representative. He presents fourteen questions raised as assertions that deal with new trends in local-state-federal relations. Among other things, he asserts that along with the movement toward larger cities, there is a movement toward smaller areas (e.g., suburbs) where more political participation is possible. He sees linkages between municipal government and neighborhood "governments." He feels that a mixed system of representative government will give minorities more representation in government.

Kass, Benny L. *Ombudsman: A Proposal for Demonstration in Washington, D.C.* Washington, D.C.: Washington Center for Metropolitan Studies, 1968.

The author presents a proposal for an ombudsman in Washington, D.C. On the neighborhood level, there would be neighborhood offices as one-stop complaint units containing neighborhood legal services, citizen information services, and a neighborhood ombudsman. On the citywide level a traditional Swedish-type ombudsman would exist. Several appendices on complaints, citizen information services, and neighborhood legal services are included.

Kotler, Milton. "The Ethics of Neighborhood Government." Paper presented at the American Political Science Association meeting, Chicago, Illinois, August 29–September 2, 1974. Mimeograph.

Kotler reviews the arguments for community control: (1) political power and justice for disadvantaged groups; (2) decentralization; (3) participation; (4) liberty; (5) efficiency; and (6) ecology. However, Kotler stresses that yet another reason for neighborhood government exists—the "ethical value of neighborhood government." In essence, the author argues that "democratic, or assembly based neighborhood government is a political institution which promotes a special province of good action by the tendency of its laws and education and their effect on virtue."

Kotler, Milton. *Neighborhood Government: The Local Foundations of Political Life.* New York: Bobbs-Merrill, 1969.

Reviews:
Best Sellers 29 (October 1, 1969): 225.
Christian Century 86 (August 27, 1969): 1118.
Fox, J. J. *Library Journal* 94 (July 1969): 2621.

The author traces the process of city expansion and argues that cities have expanded at the expense of neighborhood autonomy. The author discusses theories of community control before describing his experiences with a neighborhood organization in Columbus, Ohio. He concludes that neighborhood government is the "best practical approach whereby Americans can regain liberty and the right to govern their own lives."

Kotler, Milton. "Neighborhood Self-Government." *Political Power and the Urban Crisis.* 2d ed. Edited by Alan Shank. Boston: Holbrook Press, 1971, pp. 180–86. Reprinted from *Federal Role in Urban Affairs.* Washington, D.C.: U.S. Government Printing Office, part 9, pp. 2054–57. Milton Kotler's statements before the Subcommittee on Executive Reorganization, Committee on Government Operations. U.S. Senate, 89th Cong., 2d Sess., December 6, 1966.

The author discusses neighborhood self-government as a solution to poverty and slum conditions. He describes his experiences with the East Central Citizens Organization (Columbus, Ohio), its formation, how it governs, and what it does.

Kotler, Milton. "The Road to Neighborhood Government." *New Generation* 51 (Summer 1969): 7–12.

Krislow, Samuel. "A Restrained View." *The Ombudsman.* 2d ed. Edited by Donald Rowat. London: George Allen and Unwin, 1968, pp. 246–55.

This article presents arguments against an ombudsman at the federal level. The author sees federalism and the vast size of the United States as deterrents to the establishment of a personalistic ombudsman and the separation of powers as a deterrent to a formalized ombudsman. He concludes that an ombudsman is more relevant to state and local government.

Kristol, Irving. "Decentralization for What?" *Public Interest* 11 (Spring 1968): 17–20.

Kristol questions the viability of decentralization as a goal in a democratic society. He points out that many people have equated decentralization with democracy and that the two are not the same. He also feels that many urban problems arise from the diffusion of power throughout the bureaucracy and that power needs to be more concentrated. He feels that decentralization will be a barrier to the creation of a racially integrated society and that it will not solve the problems of the ghetto. He points out that bureaucracies have played an important role in integrating middle class Negroes into American society.

Mann, Dean. *The Citizen and the Bureaucracy: Complaint-Handling Procedures of Three California Legislatures.* Berkeley: Institute of Governmental Studies, University of California, February 1968.

This is a report on complaint handling procedures in the offices of three state legislators in California. A student observer was placed in each office to record these procedures. The conclusions were: (1) legislators facilitated the flow of information; (2) legislators helped individuals rather than interest groups; (3) legislators seriously tried to solve problems; (4) additional staff (i.e., the students) expedited the handling of complaints; (5) pressure from legislators did not change the manner in which agencies dealt with cases; (6) legislators and their staffs did not have the time and information needed to challenge bureaucratic decisions; (7) executive agencies responded quickly and relevantly to complaints; (8) the subjects of the complaints covered a wide range of state policies and agencies; (9) complaints came from a wide cross section of citizens; (10) complaints were concerned with individual difficulties with state laws and policies; and (11) the complaints indicated citizen awareness of the realm of legislative influence.

Mayer, Albert. "A New Level of Local Government is Struggling to Be Born." *City* 5:2 (March/April 1971): 60–64.

The author cites examples of problems in local government and discusses the trials and errors of experiments in neighborhood control. He feels that it is time to propose structural, constitutional, and environmental changes as solutions to the problems. He proposes a two-tiered (federated) city government.

Moore, John E. "Evaluating American Ombudsman Offices in Theory and Practice." Paper prepared for the American Political Science Association meeting, Chicago, Illinois, August 29–September 2, 1974. Mimeograph.

Nader, Ralph. "Ombudsmen for State Governments." *The Ombudsman.* 2d ed. Edited by Donald Rowat. London: George Allen and Unwin, 1968, pp. 240–46.

The author describes the rise of vast state bureaucracies which have undermined the functioning of checks and balances and have restricted the roles of legislatures. He believes that this points to the need for an ombudsman at the state level. He indicates the problems an ombudsman may face vis-à-vis the established institutions of government.

National League of Cities and United States Conference of Mayors, Library and Information Services. *Little City Halls: Selected Readings and References.* Washington, D.C.: National League of Cities and United States Conference of Mayors, 1973.

This book is a collection of documents, most previously published, that are related to municipal decentralization, citizen participation, and little city halls. Carl W. Stenberg's examination of various aspects of citizen participation and municipal decentralization (for the Advisory Commission on Intergovernmental Relations and later published in the *Municipal Yearbook 1972)* is included. Other selections are taken from the *Report of the National Advisory Commission on Civil Disorders,* several different issues of *Nation's Cities,* and the proceedings of the 48th Congress of Cities, National League of Cities, 1971.

Nordlinger, Eric A. *Decentralizing the City: A Study of Boston's Little City Halls.* Cambridge, Massachusetts: MIT Press, 1972.

> Reviews:
> Bell, J. R. *Annals of the American Academy of Political and Social Science* 410 (November 1973): 220.
> *Choice* 10 (February 1974): 1096.

Four decentralization models are presented and evaluated: bureaucratic, representational, governmental, and little city halls. The author believes that little city halls provide the best possibilities for decentralization. The little city hall program in Boston is analyzed and evaluated in terms of its successes and failures in fulfilling the three purposes of decentralization—improving city services, increasing governmental responsiveness, and reducing citizen alienation.

"The Ombudsman or Citizen's Defender: A Modern Institution." *Annals of the American Academy of Political and Social Science* 367 (May 1968): entire issue.

This issue contains articles on ombudsmen institutions and proposals in countries throughout the world. Three articles, by Oke Sandler, Jesse M. Unruh, and Frank P. Zeidler, present proposals for ombudsmen in the United States.

"The Ombudsman—What He Can and Cannot Do." *American City* 83:5 (May 1968): 40ff.

This article describes the comments of Dr. Randy H. Hamilton, executive director of the Institute for Local Self-Government (Berkeley,

California), at a meeting of the National Municipal League. He defines the duties, powers, and limitations of an ombudsman.

Pederson, Mary C. "Neighborhood Organization in Portland, Oregon." Paper presented at the American Political Science Association meeting, Chicago, Illinois, August 29–September 2, 1974. Mimeograph.

The author describes the development of neighborhood organization in Portland and the origins of a city ordinance requiring "citizen participation in all projects and programs affecting neighborhood livability." A process through which citizens participate in neighborhood planning was developed and a bureau of neighborhood organizations was established by the city government. The participatory planning process and the functions of the bureau are described.

Pottoff, E. H. "An 'Ombudsman', U.S. Style." *American City* 83 (July 1968): 152–55.

This is a description of the Community Information Officer in Saginaw, Michigan, whose duty is to improve communication between the government and the people. He has duties of a public relations nature and also of an ombudsman nature. The article goes on to define his responsibilities and the resources at his disposal.

Ryles, Tim C. *Citizen Perspectives on Goals for Georgia.* Atlanta: School of Urban Life, Georgia State University, 1973.

The author describes the Goals for Georgia program's attempts to encourage citizen input into the goal-setting activities of the state. One of the activities of the Goals for Georgia program (sponsored by the Georgia Planning Association) was the conducting of a statewide citizen survey. Seven hundred twenty-three respondents were included in the survey. The purposes of the survey were (1) to identify citizens' perceptions of problems in their communities; (2) to measure public support for state programs; (3) to compare public support for the state's eight program areas; and (4) to predict citizen responses to tax increases to fund state programs.

Sanchez, Sam. "Two Years of Ombudsman in San Jose." *Western City* 49 (June 1973): 12–14.

Savitch, H. V., and Madeleine Adler. *Decentralization at the Grass Roots: Political Innovation in New York City and London.* Beverly Hills, California: Sage Publications, 1974.

Schmandt, Henry J. "Municipal Decentralization: An Overview." *Public Administration Review* 32, special issue (October 1972): 571–88.

Schmandt examines literature and other materials relevant to municipal decentralization. The following areas are covered: (1) theory underlying decentralization of power and functions; (2) arguments for and against decentralization; (3) different forms of decentralization; (4) organizational issues associated with each form; and (5) the future of decentralization. The author feels that decentralization will be more administrative than political but will facilitate more neighborhood input.

Schmandt, Henry J., with William H. Standing. *The Milwaukee Metropolitan Study Commission.* Bloomington: Indiana University Press, 1965.

This book describes the activities of the Metropolitan Study Commission, a citizen agency established in 1957 by the Wisconsin State Legislature to study the governmental problems of the Milwaukee area. Conflict between the commission and academic proponents of reforms unsupported by the "philosophical predispositions" of the commission contributed to the demise of the commission. The authors describe the interrelationships among the commission, the governmental bureaucracy, politicians, and various groups within the community and analyze the work of the commission within a general theoretical framework that allows the development of conclusions relevant to the "movement for metropolitan governmental reform" and the movement's future.

Scott, Stanley, ed. *Western American Assembly on the Ombudsman: Report.* Berkeley: Institute of Governmental Studies, University of California, October 1968.

This booklet includes the assembly program, two addresses, and the assembly report. The first address is by Mark A. Hogan and describes his experiences as lieutenant governor of Colorado and informal ombudsman for the people of the state. He discusses cases that he handled. The second address is by Jere Williams, who discusses the Administrative Conference of the United States, a permanent, independent agency of the federal government that reviews procedures and practices of federal agencies and departments in order to make recommendations for their improvement. The assembly report recommends the implementation of the ombudsman concept at the federal, state, and local levels.

Shalala, Donna E. *Neighborhood Governance: Issues and Proposals.* New

York: American Jewish Committee National Project on Ethnic America, 1971.

This is a review of neighborhood government proposals. The traditional debate on American federalism and the new debate over decentralization are described. Justifications for neighborhood government are presented. Several different proposals for neighborhood government and the issues they suggest are discussed. Neighborhood government is also discussed vis-à-vis a metropolitan-neighborhood combination, and state and federal roles are considered. Appendices contain the specifics of four neighborhood government plans.

Shalala, Donna E. "Neighborhood Government: Has the Time Come?" *National Civic Review* 61:4 (April 1972): 185–89.

The author discusses neighborhood government as a solution to the urban crisis. Three different generalizations are presented: technology and the interdependence of systems will mean greater centralization; the process moves like a pendulum from centralization to decentralization and back; and concepts of centralization and decentralization are not necessarily in conflict and a system could be designed to encompass both (as suggested by the Committee for Economic Development). The author believes that neighborhood government is not a solution by itself but that it can be one part of a solution; it will provide a mechanism for needed citizen participation.

Shalala, Donna E., and Astrid E. Merget. "The Decentralization Approach." *Organizing Public Services in Metropolitan America*. Edited by Thomas P. Murphy and Charles R. Warren. Lexington, Massachusetts: D. C. Health, 1974, pp. 139–87.

Part Four of the above collection of essays includes three essays on the decentralization of service delivery systems in metropolitan areas by Donna E. Shalala and Astrid E. Merget. The first two essays discuss the arguments for and against decentralization and how they have been employed in different situations. In the concluding essay in this part of the book, the authors discuss the problems likely to arise in the implementation of different decentralization plans and how these problems might be overcome.

Stephens, Jack H. "Hawaii's Ombudsmen." *National Civic Review* 59:2 (February 1970): 81–84ff.

The author compares the first year's experiences of two ombudsmen institutions in Hawaii—a state ombudsman and a three-man board of appeals in Maui County. The state ombudsman received a good deal of publicity and spent a very active year. The Maui County board ended the year with no appeals. The author concludes that for an ombudsman office to be successful, the public must be informed of its existence and how to use it.

Sterzer, Earl E. "Neighborhood Grant Program Lets Citizens Decide." *Public Management* 53:1 (January 1971): 10–11.

This article describes a city-funded neighborhood grant program in Dayton, Ohio, which lets neighborhood residents decide how city funds will be used. It is administered directly from the mayor's office by a staff assistant and is designed to encourage participation at the neighborhood level.

Tibbles, Lance, and John H. Hollands. *Buffalo Citizens Administrative Service: An Ombudsman Demonstration Project.* Berkeley: Institute of Governmental Studies, University of California, 1970.

Unger, Stephen H. *Technology to Facilitate Citizen Participation in Government.* New York: Center for Policy Research, 1972. ERIC ED066–896.

After a discussion of how modern communications technology can be used to promote citizen participation, this report proposes the use of a system of telephone and cable television to facilitate dialogue and polling among large groups of people. As an example of how media might be used, the author describes how groups of representatives could be shown discussing an issue on cable television several times a day. Citizens wishing to participate in the discussion could telephone in and be assigned to small groups using telephone conference facilities.

Walls, Frank. "Savannah's New Problem Solver . . . Georgia's First Ombudsman." *Georgia Municipal Journal* 18:2 (February 1968): 17–18. Reprinted as "Savannah's 'Ombudsman'." *American City* 83:6 (June 1968): 70.

This is a description of the Community Service Officer in Savannah, Georgia, who serves as an ombudsman and reports directly to the city manager. The article describes the present officer, how the idea developed, and the duties of the office.

Walsh, Annmarie H. "What Price Decentralization in New York?" *City Almanac* 7:1 (June 1972): 1–11.

Walsh presents two definitions of decentralization: a reduction in the scale of public services and a wider distribution of political power. Three dimensions crucial to evaluating decentralization are presented: jurisdiction and power, services and function, and governmental resources. Goals of reorganization for decentralization are broken down into seven categories: (1) participation, (2) equity, (3) adaptability, (4) community, (5) finance, (6) management, and (7) accountability. The author reviews current plans for decentralization for New York City and focuses on those of the Task Force on Jurisdiction and Structure of the State Study Commission for New York City (the Scott Commission). The author believes that the decentralization proposals of the Scott Commission are based on fallacies, but she does recognize a need for decentralization.

Walton, Leland M. "Ombudsman Experiment in Seattle." *Western City* 49 (June 1973): 10–11.

Washnis, George J. *Little City Halls.* Washington, D.C.: Center for Governmental Studies, 1971.

The information in this pamphlet comes from a larger work by the author entitled *Neighborhood Facilities and Municipal Decentralization* (see Washnis, George J., below). That study looked at the experiences of twelve cities in decentralization of certain city hall functions. Four principal patterns were identified: (1) traditional branch municipal services; (2) multiservice centers; (3) neighborhood city halls; and (4) mayor's office outreach.

Washnis, George J. *Neighborhood Facilities and Municipal Decentralization.* 2 Vols. Washington, D.C.: Center for Governmental Studies, 1971.

This study examined decentralization efforts in twelve American cities: Atlanta, Baltimore, Boston, Chicago, Columbus (Ohio), Houston, Kansas City (Missouri), Los Angeles, New York, Norfolk (Virginia), San Antonio, and San Francisco. The first volume compares and analyzes the cities and discusses important concepts in decentralization. Fifteen major ingredients in the programs are discussed: (1) location; (2) size of staff; (3) budget; (4) size of centers; (5) community action, model cities, and the city; (6) coordination; (7) responsible city concept; (8) mini-cabinets; (9) central office of complaints and information computerization; (10) common service districts; (11) ombudsmen; (12) independent investigative staff; (13) citizen participation; (14) mayor and city council; and (15) resources and commitment. The author feels that each city must finds its own way of decentralizing government. Volume Two contains the case studies of the twelve cities.

Watson, Walter B.; Earnest A. T. Barth; and Donald P. Hayes. "Metropolitan Decentralization Through Incorporation." *Western Political Quarterly* 18:1 (March 1965): 198–206.

Two case studies of suburban incorporation movements, one successful and the other unsuccessful, are presented in an attempt to understand metropolitan decentralization. The outcomes of the movements were seen as being related to differences in certain structural and organizational factors. Success was found to be related to (1) agreement on local values, (2) personal involvement with the area, (3) well-organized leadership, (4) a variety of social organizations, and (5) an effective campaign.

Webb, Kenneth, and Harry P. Hatry. *Obtaining Citizen Feedback: The Applications of Citizen Surveys to Local Governments.* Washington, D.C.: Urban Institute, 1973.

This book describes and advocates the use of survey research as a method by which local governments can "obtain citizen feedback." The uses of surveys and possible sources of error are described. Survey procedures and costs are outlined in detail. Several sample survey instruments are appended.

Weber, Paul J. "A Friend in City Hall." *America* 119:12 (October 19, 1968): 352–54.

The origins and workings of the ombudsman concept are explained. Existing complaint mechanisms in the United States and their shortcomings are described. The author advocates the establishment of independent ombudsmen at federal, state, and local levels.

Webster, William E. *Decentralization: An Evolving Process in Local Government.* Washington, D.C.: Washington Center for Metropolitan Studies, 1971.

Several decentralization plans of local governments are reviewed: Washington, D.C.'s Service Area Alignment System, New York City's plan for neighborhood government, Boston's Home Rule Commission (little city halls), and Arlington County, Virginia's, use of junior high school districts as local service units. The author sees complex government reorganization as needing clear-cut objectives, new budget techniques, effective citizen input mechanisms, preparation for creative conflict by all levels of government, and the participation of all levels of government. He points out that the reorganization of centralized bureaucracy cannot be effective unless the participation of lower level bureaucracy is solicited.

Wilson, Kenneth D. "Case Study/Los Angeles: Neighborhood Proposal Aimed at Citizen Participation." *Public Management* 53:1 (January 1971): 12–13.

This is a discussion of a proposed provision of the Los Angeles City Charter under which a "neighborhood" could form via initiative petition procedures. This procedure would create an authorized neighborhood government.

Wyner, Alan J., ed. *Executive Ombudsmen in the U.S.* Berkeley: Institute of Governmental Studies, University of California, 1973.

The roles and functions of executive ombudsmen in the United States, at various governmental levels (state, county, and municipal), are examined in the selections included in this book. Of particular interest to students of governmental complaint handling in urban areas are Alan J. Wyner's examination of the grievance mechanism in Chicago, Eric A. Nordlinger's discussion of Boston's little city halls, and a description of Honolulu's Office of Information and Complaint by John E. Moore.

Wyner, Alan J. "The Political and Administrative Constituencies of American Ombudsmen: Some Comments on the Premise of Independence." Paper prepared for the American Political Science Association meeting, Chicago, Illinois, August 29–September 2, 1974. Mimeograph.

The author describes limitations on the independence of ombudsmen using information from Nebraska, Hawaii, Iowa, and Seattle/King County. It is argued that the ombudsman has "constituents in the political and administrative parts of government that he cannot ignore." The author then suggests different ways of protecting the ombudsman's independence.

Yates, Douglas. "Making Decentralization Work: The View From City Hall." *Policy Sciences* 5:3 (September 1974): 363–73.

Yates discusses problems that arise when city administrators attempt to implement decentralization efforts without considering "street-level behavior." Successful decentralization, Yates argues, requires a cooperative effort between decision makers, public employees, and citizens.

Yates, Douglas. *Neighborhood Democracy: The Politics and Impacts of Decentralization.* Lexington, Massachusetts: D. C. Heath, 1973.

This study is an attempt to evaluate the experiences and explain the successes and failures of decentralization experiments. A comparative analysis including seven experiments in New York City and New Haven, Connecticut, is presented. Organization leaders, district-level public employees, and city officials were interviewed and other survey and interview data concerning neighborhood residents were obtained. Minutes of meetings, file documents, and newspapers were analyzed. Four hypotheses were tested: (1) decentralization will increase representation and accountability; (2) decentralization will make government more responsive; (3) decentralization will develop indigenous political leadership; and (4) decentralization will diminish feelings of political powerlessness and alienation. The first hypothesis was clearly supported. The development of indigenous leadership was seen to be dependent on whether or not the experiment achieved results. The testing of the other hypotheses was inconclusive.

Yates, Douglas. "Neighborhood Government." *Policy Sciences* 3:2 (July 1972): 209–17.

The author explores the background and definition of decentralization and neighborhood government. Seven continua along which decentralization can be defined are presented: (1) intelligence gathering; (2) consultation and advisory planning; (3) program administration; (4) administrative accountability; (5) political accountability; (6) authoritative decision making; and (7) political resources. Governments with 1–3 display administrative decentralization, whereas governments with 4–7 show shared center/local control. Arguments for and against decentralization are discussed. Obstacles to decentralization are seen as: (1) costs (in time and effort) for community organization; (2) community conflict; (3) city hall-neighborhood conflict; and (4) general political conflict. The author is pessimistic about the future of current proposals for decentralization. He feels that decentralization will be difficult to achieve and that there is a lack of knowledge on the subject.

Yin, Robert K., and Douglas Yates. *Street-Level Governments: Assessing Decentralization and Urban Services.* Santa Monica, California: The Rand Corporation, 1974.

Yin, Robert K.; Robert W. Hearn; and Paula Meinetez Shapiro. "Administrative Decentralization of Municipal Services: Assessing the New York City Experience." *Policy Sciences* 5:1 (March 1974): 57–70.

Examining administrative decentralization in five agencies under the auspices of New York City's Office of Neighborhood Government, the authors focus on the degree of autonomy of district officers before and after decentralization. The authors conclude that major changes in responsibility occurred only in one management function, interagency communication. The authors conclude that this result questions the feasibility of using administrative decentralization as a device for reorganizing municipal services to increase service responsiveness to neighborhoods.

Zimmerman, Joseph F. *The Federated City: Community Control in Large Cities.* New York: St. Martin's Press, 1972.

Zimmerman examines the movement for the creation of neighborhood governments. Origins, rationale, models, and problems of the movement are discussed. Neighborhood control of schools in New York City and Detroit is discussed, as are a number of other responses of large city governments to demands for neighborhood control. The problems of citizen alienation from government and the possibility of a more representative electoral system are discussed. The author recommends revitalization of city government through a federated system, an improvement in city hall-neighborhood communication, decentralized delivery of certain services, and the adoption of proportional representation.

Zimmerman, Joseph F. "Neighborhood Governments and Service Provision." Paper prepared for the American Political Science Association meeting, Chicago, Illinois, August 29–September 2, 1974. Mimeograph.

The author discusses the relationship between the division of powers in citywide governments and the decentralization of services. Methods of improving communications and coordination of activities are discussed. A survey of 2,375 municipalities reveals the breadth of services delivered and the types of agreements for the provision of services that municipalities use in obtaining services from other governmental units and private firms. The author then suggests ways a neighborhood government might contract for the provision of services and cooperate with other neighborhood governments in establishing service delivery systems. Also, the author suggests that if neighborhood governments are to provide a wide array of services, "the governments should range in population from 25,000 to 250,000."

Zimmerman, Joseph F. "Neighborhoods and Citizen Involvement." Paper presented at the National Conference on Public Administration, Denver, Colorado, April 20, 1971. Mimeograph.

After discussing the need for neighborhood government to improve present city political systems and strengthen democratic local government, the author describes the movement for neighborhood control and its rationale. He then discusses various aspects of federated city systems including community development corporations, optimum size for neighborhood government, finances, and community schools.

Zimmerman, Joseph F. "The Politics of Neighborhood Government." *Studies in Comparative Local Self-Government* 5:1 (Summer 1971): 28–39.

The author discusses the movement for neighborhood government. Kotler's suggestion for private nonprofit, state-chartered neighborhood corporations and his example of the East Central Citizens Organization of Columbus, Ohio, are presented. Hallman's observations about the problems of community corporations and neighborhood boards are considered. Objections to neighborhood government are: (1) it ignores citywide needs; (2) it may lead to corruption; (3) it lacks leaders in the ghettos; and (4) it encourages legal segregation. Possible accomplishments are: it may increase citizen participation by reducing the scale of government and providing new access points, and it could relieve the mayor and city officials of responsibility. The author concludes that neighborhood government is one solution to urban problems, and he advocates other structural and electoral reforms.

Dissertations

Besharat, Ali-Reza. "Political and Administrative Decentralization." D.P.A., University of Southern California, 1962. (Order no. 62–6038) 306 pp.

Garvelink, Roger H. "A Study of Citizens' Committees: The Relationship of the Positions in the Community Power Structure of the Citizens Serving as Members of Citizens Committees and the Citizens Advocating the Use of Citizens Committees." Ph.D., University of Michigan, 1970. (Order no. 71–15,157) 181 pp.

Keeney, Jerry Frederick. "A Study of Opinions Concerning the Role of Citizens Advisory Committees Established in Section 49 of Article 77 of the Annotated Code of Maryland, 1969." Ed.D., George Washington University, 1972. (Order no. 72–31,943) 155 pp.

Petosa, Anthony L., Jr. "The Role of Members of Permanent Citizens' Advisory Committees in the State of New Jersey." Ph.D., Fordham University, 1969. (Order no. 70–11,466) 330 pp.

Yates, Douglas Thomas, Jr. "Neighborhood Democracy: The Politics and Impacts of Decentralization." Ph.D., Yale University, 1972. (Order no. 73–16,414) 342 pp.

7

Guides and Handbooks
for Citizen Group Members and Leaders

Provided in this chapter are references to and descriptions of guides and handbooks that might be useful to members and leaders of citizen groups. Many of the items included here describe strategies for organizing and leading citizen groups, and some suggest activities and tactics that might be employed in efforts to influence public policy making. Information relevant to specific policy-issue areas which may be of concern to citizen groups is also provided by some of these materials.

Alinsky, Saul D. *Reveille for Radicals.* New York: Vintage Books, 1969.

> Reviews:
> Adams, Scott. *Library Journal* 71 (January 1946): 69.
> Bates, Ralph. *Nation* 162 (April 20, 1946): 481.
> Brown, R. A. *Social Education* 10 (May 1946): 238.
> Brunner, E. DeS. *New York Times* (January 13, 1946): 4.
> Clayton, H. R. *New Republic* 114 (January 21, 1946): 97.
> Fellman, David. *American Political Science Review* 40 (April 1946): 398.
> Fink, R. E. *Social Forces* 25 (October 1946): 107.
> Kincheloe, S. C. *Christian Century* 63 (June 5, 1946): 719.
> Lee, A. M. *American Sociological Review* 11 (June 1946): 370.
> Lynch, W. S. *Saturday Review of Literature* 29 (January 19, 1946): 10.
> McGinnis, H C. *Catholic World* 164 (October 1946): 89.
> O'Leary, J. J. *Yale Review* 35 (Spring 1946): 553.
> Seidman, Joel. *Survey Graphic* 35 (May 1946): 174.
> Shanas, Ethel. *American Journal of Sociology* 52 (September 1946): 163.
> Shiel, B. J. *Book Week* (January 13, 1946): 1.
> ——. *Booklist* 42 (February 1, 1946): 177.
> ——. *Bookmark* 7 (May 1946): 4.

Skillin, Edward. *Commonweal* 43 (January 18, 1946): 359.

——. *Current History* 10 (April 1946): 350.

Slotnick, Emanuel. *Springfield Republican* (December 27, 1945): 4.

Smith, T. V. *Ethics* 57 (October 1946): 69.

Time 47 (February 25, 1946): 98.

Walsh, J. R. *Weekly Book Review* (January 30, 1946): 8.

This book, first published in 1946, represents Alinsky's attempt to explain his activist philosophy and describe some of the tools and strategies available to community activists in "The Building of People's Organizations" (the title of Part Two of the book). The 1969 Vintage edition of this book is introduced by Alinsky asking and answering the question: "[W]hat would I change if I were writing *Reveille* today?" He suggests that the intervening decades of activism have taught him "to become in many ways the master rather than the servant of my tactics, and to develop far more effective tactics—economic, political, and social—than the simple, hot, angry, personalized denunciation." But he concludes the introduction by affirming, "I have been faithful to my youth."

Part One of the book, "Call Me Rebel," explains the philosophy which compelled Alinsky to become one of contemporary America's most influential community organizers. The second part of the book deals with organizational leadership and tactics and draws heavily from Alinsky's experiences in Chicago. Though largely anecdotal, Part Two offers some insight into the dynamics of community organizations and the problems of community organization leadership that could be useful to contemporary community groups and their leaders.

Alinsky, Saul D. *Rules for Radicals: A Practical Primer for Realistic Radicals*. New York: Random House, 1971.

Reviews:

Claiborne, Robert. *Book World* (December 19, 1971): 12.

Conlin, J. J. *Best Sellers* 31 (July 1, 1971): 153.

Coyne, J. R. *National Review* 23 (June 15, 1971): 659.

DuBois, H. J. *Library Journal* 96 (May 1971): 1717.

Gans, C. B. *New York Times Book Review* (November 7, 1971): 44.

——. *New Yorker* 47 (August 21, 1971): 92.

Gitlin, Todd. *Nation* 213 (October 18, 1971): 373.

Lasch, Christopher. *New York Times Book Review* 17 (October 21, 1971): 44.

Maddocks, Melvin. *Christian Science Monitor* (May 6, 1971): 7.

McWilliams, Carey. *Nation* 213 (August 16, 1971): 121.

New Republic 164 (June 5, 1971): 36.

This is Alinsky's personal philosophy of community organizing written for the younger generation of radicals whom, he felt, lacked a sense of purpose in their radicalism; i.e., how to foster revolutionary change within the system. The discussion includes Alinsky's philosophy, his ideas on organizers and organization, and suggestions on how to organize.

Alpern, Robert. *Pratt Guide: A Citizen's Handbook of Housing, Planning and Urban Renewal Procedures in New York City.* Brooklyn, New York: Pratt Institute Community Education Program, 1965.

A handbook to inform New York City citizens about how city government functions and who the responsible officials are, this book includes chapters covering the following areas: planning procedure and personnel in New York, long-range planning, budgeting, zoning, neighborhood character and appearance, schools, transportation, parks, and housing and urban renewal. Each chapter has an introduction, a section on New York City procedures, and facts for reference. The book also has a bibliography and appendices on housing terms.

American Institute of Architects, Committee on Urban Design. *Checklist for Cities: A Guide for Local Action in Improving the Design of Our Cities.* Washington, D.C.: American Institute of Architects, 1968.

Bell, Louise N. *The Commissioners' Handbook: An Introduction to Housing and Community Development for Commissioners of Local Housing Authorities and Urban Renewal Agencies.* Washington, D.C.: National Association of Housing and Redevelopment Officials, 1968.

This handbook is designed to introduce new commissioners to their responsibilities as policy makers and to the programs with which they are working. It is also for veterans not familiar with new federal policies and laws and for laymen wishing to become familiar with the field. The book investigates housing and renewal programs and the role of the commissioner. It also focuses on the history and evolution of housing and urban renewal, its impact, and the role of private citizens.

Biddle, William W. *The Cultivation of Community Leaders: Up From the Grass Roots.* New York: Harper, 1953.

Reviews:
Booklist 49 (March 1, 1953): 215.
Bookmart 12 (July 1953): 233.
G.E.A. *San Francisco Chronicle* (May 10, 1953): 26.

Hobbs, S. H. *Social Forces* 32 (October 1953): 102.
Kirkus 20 (December 1, 1952): 754.
Rooney, J. F. *Springfield Republican* (March 22, 1953): 8.
School and Society 77 (January 31, 1953): 79.
U. S. *Quarterly Book Review* 9 (June 1953): 208.
Wilson, E. K. *American Journal of Sociology* 59 (Summer 1953): 168.

Written for citizen-leaders and for college teachers and administrators who want to adapt their institutions to community needs, this book discusses campus involvement in the community and the Program of Community Dynamics at Earlham College. There are chapters on how to train local participant leaders, future citizens, and professionals who will be community educators. Other chapters discuss methods of influencing people, social conflict, participatory public relations, social research, and how to balance individual and group claims. The last chapter contains a handbook for practitioners of community development. An appendix lists a bibliography of helpful works.

Biddle, William W., and Loureide J. Biddle. *Encouraging Community Development: A Training Guide for Local Workers.* New York: Holt, Rinehart and Winston, 1968.

A community development training guide for local workers who will live with the people of a community for a while, this book is aimed at the problems of nonprofessional and preprofessional workers in the Peace Corps, Vista, civic associations, churches, and volunteer organizations. It is concerned with local and personal development in large-scale programs and the contribution volunteers can make. The book focuses on the role of the community development volunteer—what he should know and what he can do.

Brown, Lance Jay, and Dorothy E. Whiteman. *Planning and Design Workbook for Community Participation: An Evaluation Report.* Princeton, New Jersey: Research Center for Urban and Environmental Planning, School of Architecture and Urban Planning, Princeton University, 1973.

This publication reports the results of the first evaluation of the use of the *Planning and Design Workbook for Community Participation.* The purpose of the study was to determine the extent to which methods and materials were applied and the areas in which they were most useful. This was an attempt to determine the practicability of the method of emphasizing citizen group participation. It also identified necessary revisions and future directions for research. The report includes the evaluation survey, and appendices have further information on the project.

Caldwell, William W., ed. *How to Save Urban America: Regional Planning Association Choices for '76.* New York: New American Library, 1973.

This is an effort by the New York Regional Planning Association to inform the public about important urban issues with which citizens' groups should be concerned. It separates issues which necessitate citizens' expertise from those which necessitate technical expertise. The areas of focus are housing, transportation, environment, poverty, and cities and suburbs.

Chamber of Commerce of the United States. *Forward America: A Process for Mobilizing Total Community Resources.* Washington, D.C.: Chamber of Commerce of the United States, 1968.

Suggesting ways of mobilizing to solve community problems, this publication outlines the steps in the mobilization process: (1) defining the community; (2) identifying the leaders; (3) determining what is needed for total community participation; (4) involving people; (5) identifying goals and problems; (6) studying problems; (7) developing priorities; (8) assigning responsibility for action; and (9) reviewing, reporting, and advising.

Crosby, Alexander L. *Building a Citizen's Housing Association.* Washington, D.C.: National Housing Conference, 1954.

A Final Report and Model Curriculum of Health Training Conducted by the National Self-Help Corporation and the Public Health Service. Washington, D.C.: National Self-Help Corporation, n. d.

This is a report on a training project for consumer participants in health care projects which focuses on the health rights of low income people and welfare recipients. Materials on group meetings and site visits are presented. A model curriculum is included. Appendices contain documents on various aspects of the program.

Gannon, Thomas M., and Joseph R. Hacala. "Waking Up People Power." *America* 123:19 (December 12, 1970): 520–21.

The authors describe how Jesuits, using a grass roots organizing approach, helped people achieve building improvements in housing projects on Chicago's West Side. It suggests how a grass roots organizer should work and describes the pattern employed by Jesuit workers.

Haber, Ernest B., and Arthur Dunham, eds. *Community Organization in Action: Basic Literature and Critical Comments.* New York: Association Press, 1959.

This is a collection of readings designed primarily for graduate and undergraduate students in social work. It is also relevant to persons involved in community organizations. The book contains seventy-five selections on community organization by over fifty authors. The selections are mainly articles and papers written in the years 1900–1958. They are organized into six sections:

1. The Community and Social Welfare
2. The Process of Community Organization
3. Community Organization in Practice
4. Agencies and Programs
5. Personnel—Professionals and Laymen
6. Community Development in the United States and Elsewhere

There are introductions for each section and subsection. Most of the articles are edited excerpts. The authors have generally attempted to exclude case studies.

Haltrop, Donald G. *Changing Things: A Citizen's Guide.* East Lansing: Institute for Community Development and Services, Continuing Education Service, Michigan State University, 1973.

This short (19-page) guide focuses on "tools for achieving change," and could serve to help community groups assess their resources and actions in attempts to influence community decision making. The six "major tools" discussed by the author are: (1) Information; (2) Education and Persuasion; (3) The Law, Law Enforcement, and Court Action; (4) Public Exposure; (5) Economic Power; and (6) Political Power. Further, the author contends that "emotional factors" can also be used to the advantage of groups seeking change.

Hamberg, Jill, et al. *Where It's At: A Research Guide for Community Organizing.* Boston: New England Free Press, 1968.

Heydelker, Wayne D., and Philip Schatts. *Community Planning: A Manual of Practical Suggestions for Citizen Participation.* New York: Regional Planning Association, 1932.

Huenefeld, John. *The Community Activist's Handbook: A Guide to*

Organizing, Financing, and Publicizing Community Campaigns.
Boston: Beacon Press, 1970.

The author's purpose in writing this book is to encourage an "underground" of community activists and also to help people committed to less controversial kinds of change. The book presents ways of organizing complex volunteer activities. The first section explains how to run an organization. The second section tells how to organize and run a campaign. The third section deals with what to do when the campaign is over. Appendices contain the following: sample agenda notes for an organizational meeting; a sample publicity release; a sample project timetable; a sample organizational chart; a sample project budget; sample bylaws; and information pertaining to accountability for funds.

Jones, W. Ron. *Finding Community: A Guide to Community Action Research.* Palo Alto, California: James E. Freel and Associates, 1971.

This is a guide for students, community groups, and individuals concerned with community problems. The author believes that society has institutionalized rather than relieved conditions of poverty, social injustice, and exploitation and that we must reorder priorities. Each of the eleven chapters deals with a specific problem area: food, business, welfare, health care, housing, police, education, the draft, the warfare economy, corporations, and the environment. Every chapter includes a description of the particular problem, suggested readings, guidelines for community research and action, and alternative institutions as solutions to the problems.

King, Clarence. *Working With People in Community Action: An International Case Book for Trained Community Workers and Volunteers.* New York: Association Press, 1965.

A casebook, this book contains examples from the U.S. and around the world which illustrate selected problems facing community workers. The sixty-two cases, for the most part, come from the files of the United Nations International Cooperation Administration and the author's experience. The cases deal with getting acquainted with the community, the felt needs of the community, community workers as catalysts for action, the use of specialists, committees, community and neighborhood councils, and training for new community workers.

Lindbloom, Carl G., and Morton Farrah. *The Citizen's Guide to Urban Renewal.* West Trenton, New Jersey: Chandler-Davis Publishing Company, 1968.

This is a handbook designed to inform interested laymen and professionals about the requirements of a successful urban renewal project and how to fit an urban renewal project to the needs of a community. The book discusses the concept of urban renewal; it also explains how to implement a project and what the advantages and disadvantages of urban renewal might be for a community. There are chapters on project prerequisites, administration, selection, planning, execution, financing, implementation, and citizen participation. Some examples of how particular aspects of urban renewal have been handled in certain cities are included. The last chapter summarizes available federal assistance programs for community renewal. The appendices cover the following subjects: the history of urban renewal, the relationship between urban renewal and the courts, government agencies involved in urban renewal, noncash local grants-in-aid, and basic reference works on the subject.

Lurie, Ellen. *How to Change the Schools: A Parents' Action Handbook on How to Fight the System.* New York: Random House, 1970.

> Reviews:
> *Choice* 8 (July 1971): 714.
> *Commonweal* 94 (April 16, 1971): 150.
> Wasserman, Miriam. *Saturday Review* 54 (August 21, 1971): 5.
> Weiner, H. R. *Library Journal* 96 (January 1971): 73.

Written for parents who want to understand and have some impact on their local schools, this book identifies issues with which parents should be concerned—aspects of the school system which most directly affect children and parents. The author identifies the following areas: curriculum, staffing, the reporting system, cumulative records, and students' and parents' rights. Tactics for organizing to fight the "system" are then suggested.

Meisner, Lisbeth, et al. *A Training Program for Consumers in Policy-Making Roles in Health Care Projects.* Berkeley: Division of Public Health and Medical Administration, School of Public Health, University of California, n. d.

This report describes a one-year (1968–69) project funded by the U.S. Public Health Service. The project staff developed and implemented a training program with the help of consumers who had served in policy-making roles in health facilities. Trainees in the program were members of the policy-making boards of three federally funded neighborhood health centers and members of a model cities health planning committee. Prior to the training program, the consumer participants had experienced difficulty in effectively working with professional personnel. Thus, the purpose of the project was to develop and test a training program that would help consumers in participating effectively in the policy-making processes of health care organizations. The training techniques and contents of the training program were successful, but the authors note that full cooperation between consumer participants and professional personnel could not be accomplished unless training for professionals could also be provided.

Nader, Ralph, and Donald Ross. *Action for a Change: A Student's Manual for Public Interest Organizing.* Rev. ed. New York: Grossman Publishers, 1972.

> Reviews:
> *Choice* 9 (May 1972): 414.
> Malm, Harry. *Library Journal* 97 (March 1972): 1184.

This is a guide for college students who wish to form a Public Interest Research Group (PIRG). A PIRG is an alliance of students and professionals. Full-time professional organizers are recruited by the students to represent them in public interest advocacy. The book discusses the background of modern American student movements and the PIRGs. It then gives detailed instructions on how to form a PIRG and how to organize public interest campaigns. There is also a chapter on how to form a PIRG in a high school.

National Municipal League. *The Citizen Association: How to Organize and Run It.* New York: National Municipal League, 1953.

A guide for association leaders, this publication presents information on different aspects of running a citizens association. The first organizational steps are discussed. Structure, membership, the board, the staff, and the committees are described. It tells how to take action, the importance of education and publicity, what kinds of research are needed, how to appraise candidates, how to pick a slate, what types of publications are needed, and presents suggestions for a budget and for bylaws.

National Municipal League. *The Citizen Association: How to Win Civic Campaigns.* New York: National Municipal League, 1953.

This guide presents a formula for running a civic campaign and tells citizens how to organize to win a campaign, how to educate participants, how to answer the opposition, how to get out the vote, and how to handle finances. Specific cases of campaigns in thirteen cities are described.

The O. M. Collective. *The Organizer's Manual.* New York: Bantam Books, 1971.

A manual for students wishing to organize for social change, this book was a result of the student movement and the national student strike of May 1970. It is a practical "how to do it" manual which focuses on the organizing process itself. It tells how to run meetings, use a mimeograph machine, and organize a mass rally, among other things. It discusses mass education, communications, legal and medical self-defense, and strategies for organizing different groups. There is a list of essential books and organizations.

Oppenheimer, Martin, and George Lakey. *A Manual for Direct Action.* Chicago: Quadrangle Books, 1964.

> Reviews:
> Hentoff, Nat. *Book Week* (June 27, 1965): 20.
> ——. *Christian Century* 82 (April 7, 1965): 440.
> *Virginia Quarterly Review* 41 (Summer 1965): 106.
> Wheeler, R. S. *National Review* 17 (May 18, 1965): 426.

The authors provide "a practical training manual for non-violent direction action." It is intended for activists in civil rights and related groups, such as labor, peace, community and neighborhood organizations, and students. The book gives alternative courses of action and information to use in formulating plans. Points covered are: examination of the community, levers of change, organization for direct action, education of participants, choosing effective tactics and training, legal problems, and nonviolent defense. Appendices include reference material suggested for reading in jail.

Raymore, Henry B., and H. Stuart Ortloff. *It's Your Community: A Guide to Civic Development and Beautification.* New York: M. Barrows and Company, 1965.

Stressing the need for positive public action to enhance civic beautification, this guide is written to educate the lay public about the dangers of urban blight and neglect and to arouse interest in the efforts for an improved civic environment. The first chapter is a brief survey of urbanism, followed by a description of what the modern American community should be. The bulk of the text is concerned with practical solutions to what the authors consider to be the most pressing urban problems—traffic, parking, open spaces, landscaping, local planning and zoning, and urban renewal and rehabilitation. The last chapter gives suggestions on how a civic beautification project might be organized and suggests some specific projects that might be undertaken in any community.

Reilly, William K., ed. *The Use of Land: A Citizens' Policy Guide to Urban Growth.* New York: Thomas Y. Crowell, 1973.

This is the report of the Task Force on Land Use and Urban Government sponsored by the Rockefeller Brothers Fund. It stresses the problem of how to control urban growth and development to protect the environment. The report is intended for all levels of government, as well as for professionals and citizens. Its proposals are for immediate action, although the task force also sees the need for long-range action. The report favors the rearrangement of processes and the redesign of incentives in favor of quality land use. The recommendations cover the following areas: open space, historic sites, use of existing laws for new values, mechanisms to regulate development, use of incentives and opportunities to foster quality development, rural land use, and the role of the citizen in urban development.

Ross, Donald K. *A Public Citizen's Action Manual.* New York: Grossman Publishers, 1973.

Reviews:
Christianson, E. B. *Library Journal* 98 (June 1973): 1903.
McKenna, Stephen. *Best Sellers* 33 (July 15, 1973): 181.

This book is written to inform citizens about what they can do to make American institutions more responsive. The author has gathered together a number of projects which serve as models for citizen action. The projects are based on the work done by Ralph Nader and are designed to serve as practical guides for citizen action in the following areas: consumer protection, health care, discrimination, tax equity, government responsiveness, and citizen organizing.

Ross, Murray G. *Case Histories in Community Organization.* New York: Harper and Brothers, 1950.

This book is a text designed for community workers; one section deals with the community worker and community groups. Using case histories for illustrative purposes, the author stresses that the community worker must enhance group cohesiveness, consider group ethics, and try to enlist the support of influential people and groups.

Sanders, Irwin T. *Making Good Communities Better: A Handbook for Civic-Minded Men and Women.* Lexington: University of Kentucky Press, 1950.

Reviews:
Henry, N. B. *School Review* 59 (November 1951): 489.
Phillips, W. M. *Annals of the American Academy of Political and Social Science* 276 (July 1951): 142.
Poston, R. W. *Saturday Review of Literature* 34 (March 3, 1951): 16.

A handbook designed for people actively involved in efforts aimed at community improvement, this publication discusses basic principles of community organization and suggests possible problem-solving techniques. The first section discusses four elements that are part of a good community. The second section uses six communities to illustrate the different types of communities. Section Three suggests a five-step approach to promoting a program or project. The fourth and fifth sections discuss community organization and a "philosophy of community service." The last section contains suggested procedures by twenty-one experienced authorities in the field.

Smith, Herbert H. *The Citizen's Guide to Planning*. West Trenton, New Jersey: Chandler-Davis Publishing Company, 1961.

This is a book written to explain planning and the planning profession to newly appointed planning board members and newly interested private citizens. It is organized to cover issues in planning that will face such people and is therefore nontechnical. The book is based on the author's experience in 200 municipal planning programs. It covers the background of planning, some of the aspects involved in the planning process, different types of planning, and the relationship of the community to the planning process. Appendices include suggested bylaws for planning boards, sources of information, and suggested references.

Smith, Herbert H. *The Citizen's Guide to Zoning*. West Trenton, New Jersey: Chandler-Davis Publishing Company, 1965.

Swift, Henry, and Elizabeth Swift. *Community Groups and You: How to Manage and Participate Effectively in Boards, Clubs, Committees, Fund Drives, Charities, Etc.* New York: John Day Company, 1964.

Intended for members of voluntary associations, this book explains how to organize and run an effective organization. The authors have taken the techniques of management from the business world and applied them to running a volunteer organization.

The book opens with an explanation of how an individual can become involved in community organizations and why such involvement is important. It then goes into the "do's and don'ts" of specific aspects of organization—oral and written communication; how to plan, organize, and hold meetings; how to select people for certain tasks; and how to delegate authority and develop leadership within the organization. The emphasis is on efficiency and competence as the most important characteristics of a successful organization. There is a suggested reading list on management and organizations.

Thelen, Herbert A. *Dynamics of Groups at Work.* Chicago: University of Chicago Press, 1955.

Thelen deals with the problem of effective leadership. The goal of effective leadership should be to encourage behavior that will lead to the solution of problems. The book discusses organizational goals, organization, the utilization of resources, and the assimilation of the experiences of group members. The first section of the book analyzes successful practical approaches in the following areas: citizen participation, classroom teaching, inservice professional training, administration and management, human relations training, and public meetings. The chapter on citizen participation uses the Hyde Park-Kenwood Community Conference as a case study. Principles of the block program, development of leadership, and facilitation of services are included in the discussion. The second section presents concepts relevant to group activity. It covers the following areas: membership, integration, reality, control, leadership, and community. There is an annotated bibliography of selected readings at the end of the book.

Thelen, Herbert A., and Bettie B. Sarchet. *Neighbors in Action: A Manual for Community Leaders.* Chicago: Human Dynamics Laboratory, Department of Education, University of Chicago, 1954.

United States Citizens' Advisory Committee on Environmental Quality. *Community Action for Environmental Quality.* Washington, D.C.: U.S. Government Printing Office, 1970.

This is a guide for citizens who want to participate in action to improve their communities. It reviews various federal programs and explores recommendations on how they can be strengthened. Questions that need to be asked in getting action started are suggested. Recommendations are made for organizing action in the areas of open space and recreation, townscape and landscape, and clean air and clean water. There is a section on the importance of training youth and a section on how to follow through on the energies harnessed for action. An appendix provides a list of relevant public and private agencies and useful publications.

United States Department of Housing and Urban Development. *Technical Assistance Bulletin No. 3: Subject: Citizen Participation in Model Cities.* A HUD Guide. Washington, D.C.: U.S. Government Printing Office, 1968.

This bulletin is intended as a guide to help city governments and model cities citizen participants evaluate the strengths and weaknesses of their participation mechanisms. Areas of evaluation are: structure and process, representativeness, sufficient information, technical assistance, financial assistance, and employment of residents. There is also some description of how "first round" model cities projects have met the citizen participation requirements of HUD.

United States Department of Housing and Urban Development, Management Assistance Program. *Citizens Organizations.* Model Cities Management Series Bulletin, no. 6. Washington, D.C.: U.S. Government Printing Office, 1971.

This bulletin discusses alternatives for organizing citizen participation mechanisms in the Model Cities Program. It includes information on HUD's philosophy of citizen participation and HUD requirements for citizen participation. The bulk of the document is composed of appendices with examples of the following: procedures; contracts between the city and the nonprofit citizen corporation; agreements between citizens organizations and the city; organizations in operations years; specification for citizens organizations' staffs; organization bylaws; meeting-reimbursement policy; internal reporting system; procedures involving other agencies; and community action agency and citizen organization joint procedures. There is also a selected bibliography on citizen participation.

United States Environmental Protection Agency. *Don't Leave It All to the Experts: The Citizen's Role in Environmental Decision Making.* Washington, D.C.: U.S. Government Printing Office, 1972.

United States Farmers Home Administration. *Build Our American Communities: A Community Development Program for High School and Young Adult Groups.* Washington, D.C.: U.S. Government Printing Office, 1970.

A series of lesson plans on community development, this publication was written to encourage young adults to become active in their communities. The emphasis is definitely rural. There are three background units, one unit on community development projects, one on business corporations, and one on the press.

United States Housing and Home Finance Agency. *Urban Renewal: What It Is . . . Teamwork by Citizens and Government to End Community Slums and Blight.* Rev. ed. Washington, D.C.: U.S. Government Printing Office, February 1971.

This pamphlet informs citizens about the essential facts of Urban Renewal Assistance as authorized by the Housing Act of 1954. It explains programs for community improvement, what the citizen can do, the use of federal aid, and how to get federal help and information.

United States Office of Economic Opportunity. *How to Organize a Co-op: Moving Ahead Together.* Washington, D.C.: U.S. Government Printing Office, October 1969.

A pamphlet written to inform poor people of how to organize a cooperative, this work describes three kinds of co-ops—marketing, purchasing, and service. It discusses what a co-op is and what it does. It contains information on how to start a co-op; i.e., how to take a survey, how to do market research, and how to organize the co-op.

United States Office of Revenue Sharing. *Getting Involved: Your Guide to Revenue Sharing.* Washington, D.C.: U.S. Government Printing Office, 1972.

Providing the public with "an understandable presentation of General Revenue Sharing and its importance," this publication describes how citizens may become involved in reviewing and influencing local government's use of general revenue sharing funds. It describes the process through which fund allocations are planned and reported, mechanisms which facilitate citizen participation, and some examples of how citizen groups have influenced fund allocations in different locales.

United States Urban Renewal Administration, Urban Renewal Service. *Neighborhood Organization in Conservation Areas.* Washington, D.C.: U.S. Government Printing Office, March 1961.

A pamphlet written to provide citizens with the guiding principles on how to build a successful neighborhood organization, this publication discusses the purpose of a neighborhood organization and what it can do, the role of the local public agency vis-à-vis the organization, and the role of the block organization and neighborhood council.

Urban Land Institute. *The Homes Association Handbook.* Washington, D.C.: Urban Land Institute, 1964.

This publication is the result of a study which gathered data on existing homes associations. An automatic-membership homes association is an incorporated, nonprofit organization which operates under a recorded land agreement. Each lot owner in the prescribed area is automatically a member and is charged for a share of the maintenance of common property. This handbook contains guidelines for the development and conservation of residential neighborhoods where common open space and facilities are privately owned by such associations. It describes homes associations, presents information on existing associations, and makes recommendations for associations.

Wachtel, Dawn Day. "Structures of Community and Strategies for Organization." *Social Work* 13:1 (January 1968): 85–91.

This article discusses two different types of community power structures—elitist and pluralist—and shows how certain organizational strategies are relevant to each. It contains suggested guidelines for those working in community organizations who need to know how to work with the type of power structure existing in their communities.

Warren, Roland L. *Studying Your Community*. New York: Russell Sage Foundation, 1955.

> Reviews:
> Cook, L. A. *American Sociological Review* 20 (October 1955): 629.
> ——. *Booklist* 51 (July 15, 1955): 460.
> Porter, B. M. *Journal of Home Economics* 47 (October 1955): 636.

This is a manual aimed at nonprofessionals who wish to study their communities. The beginning chapters present information on how to gather general data on the community; i.e., background, economics, government, politics, and laws of the community. The main body of the text is devoted to chapters about specific aspects of the community: planning, housing, education, recreation, religion, social welfare, health care, communications, intergroup relations, associations, and community organizations. All of these chapters include lists of questions that should be asked in each area, suggest programs for community improvements, and provide references for further study. The remainder of the book deals with how to plan, organize, and conduct community survey work. These chapters also include references for further study.

Author Index

Author Index

Key:

d   = *dissertation* by the author is cited

r   = book *review* by the author is cited

t   = author is mentioned in the *text* of an annotation or in an introductory essay

If no letter follows the page number, the author's work is cited as a bibliographic entry.

C

D

Y

Z

Citizen Groups in Local Politics was copy edited by Paulette Wamego; proofing by Amanda Clark.

Text design: Paulette Wamego.

Cover design: Raymond Glass.

Composition: Computer generated for Harris TxT using Caledonia for text and display, set by Computer Typesetting Services, Inc., Glendale, California.

Offset by Edwards Brothers, Inc., Ann Arbor, Michigan, on 55-pound book natural stock, opacity 92, bulking at 390 PPI.

Binding, also by Edwards Brothers, uses Kivar 6 over .080 boards, with 80-pound plain white endsheets.